Working in T.V. News:
The Insider's Guide

*"I find television very educational.
Every time someone switches it on, I go into
another room and read a good book."*
—Groucho Marx (1890-1977)

WORKING IN T.V. NEWS

The Insider's Guide

Carl Filoreto

with Lynn Setzer

Mustang Publishing Co.
Memphis, TN

Distributed to the book trade in the U.S. by National Book Network, Lanham, Maryland. For information on other distributors, please contact Mustang Publishing.

Library of Congress Cataloging-in-Publication Data:

Filoreto, Carl, 1955-
    Working in T.V. news : the insider's guide / Carl Filoreto, Lynn Setzer.
        p. cm.
    ISBN 0-914457-50-0 (acid free) : $12.95
    1. Television broadcasting of news--Vocational guidance.
I. Setzer, Lynn, 1955- . II. Title III. Title: Working in TV news.
PN4784.T4F55   1992
070. 1 ' 95--dc20   92-50413
                                                                       CIP

Printed on acid-free paper. ∞

10 9 8 7 6 5 4 3 2 1

Dedicated to Peter Peelgrane,
who proves that the spirit is stronger than the body
and that every moment of life is worth fighting for.

Also dedicated to the memory of
Dr. Henry W. Setzer (1916-1992).

Acknowledgments

During any undertaking as comprehensive as writing a book, you discover that you need to rely on a lot of people. And when you finally get the damn thing done, you realize these people deserve a huge "thank you."

First, I must thank my brilliant and beautiful wife, Lynn. Not only did she write several chapters and edit my sometimes feeble copy, but also she understood what a time-consuming task creating a book can be. Without her support and encouragement, this never would have been completed.

I'd also like to thank my mom, Alice Sorlie, who addressed and licked many envelopes during the course of this project. Her help and support made writing this book much easier.

And, of course, I'd like to thank all the people who agreed to talk with me, and all who responded to my surveys, during the course of gathering material for this enterprise. The advice and information I received from News Directors, Assistant News Directors, and Managing Editors was invaluable.

Thanks also to Brian Olson, Cris Johnson, Don Fitzpatrick, and John Betancourt. And special kudos to Rollin Riggs, who brought this project to us and saw it through to the end.

In addition, I'd like to thank all the people who have given me a chance in T.V. news. Although we didn't always see eye to eye when it came to the news-gathering process, I appreciate their willingness to let me do my job. It's a job that has a lot of "moments."

I'd also like to mention Dave Minshall, Derek and Devin Reich, Scott Carrico, Jeff Winn, and Steve Dalton. They didn't directly contribute anything to this book. They are, however, friends of mine who, for no particular reason, are not mentioned anywhere else in these pages. I sort of promised them that I'd get them in this book, so here they are, prominently mentioned right at the beginning.

Finally, I'd like to note the role that our two golden retrievers, Gansett and Remington, had in this process. They spent countless hours with me in the den, alternately playing, sleeping, and fighting with each other. And they kept me constantly amused, though I'll never understand their fascination for shredding and eating paper. Go figure.

Carl Filoreto
Golden, Colorado

Contents

Introduction 10

Chapter 1: Diary of a Big Story 13

Chapter 2: Who Does What 33

Chapter 3: A Day in the Life 51

Chapter 4: A Tale of Two Stations 63

Chapter 5: The State of the Art 73

Chapter 6: Now That I'm Ready to Work, Where
Do I Look? What Do They Expect of Me?
What Should I Expect of Them? And What
Am I Getting Myself into, Anyway? 77

Chapter 7: The Right Stuff 94

Chapter 8: Cover Letters, Résumés, & Résumé Tapes 98

Chapter 9: So You Want to Be on the Air? 113

Chapter 10: Internships...121

Chapter 11: CNN...126

Chapter 12: That's the News... 134

Appendix:

    Television Markets Ranked by Size..........................141

    Addresses of U.S. Television Stations
      with News Programs..146

    Stations in Areas Not Covered by ADI Rankings........185

    U.S. Networks & Their Bureaus.............................186

    Canadian Stations with News Programs...................187

"There is much to be said in favour of modern journalism. By giving us the opinions of the uneducated, it keeps us in touch with the ignorance of the community. By carefully chronicling the current events of contemporary life, it shows us of what very little importance such events really are. By invariably discussing the unnecessary, it makes us understand what things are requisite for culture, and what are not."
—Oscar Wilde (1854-1900)

Introduction

So you've given the idea a lot of thought, and you've decided you want to work in the exciting field of television news. Well, there are worse ambitions. Like wanting to become a lawyer. (Now there's a cheap shot!)

Actually, there are plenty of similarities. Both professions usually demand a few years of "paying dues" before one can make a decent wage and assume some responsibility. Both professions have a few high-paid "stars" and a lot of poverty-wage grunts. Both professions have "ambulance chasers." Both professions require self-confidence and aggressiveness for success. And both professions are often portrayed as incredibly glamorous, with chauffeurs, chic restaurants, and big shots everywhere you turn—where the next big case or the next big story will just land in your lap, and you'll become instantly famous, bringing a flood of cash, fame, and movie offers.

Oh, if only that were true. In reality, both lawyers and television journalists will claim their work can be incredibly boring, pointless, and devoid of any redeeming social value. But, as with most things in life, the truth lies somewhere between these extremes.

There is, however, one constant in both professions: They

are extremely popular these days. In college, communications and pre-law courses are packed, and graduates fight to gain acceptance to the prestigious journalism and law schools. Everyone is going to be the next Sandra Day O'Connor/F. Lee Bailey, or the next Diane Sawyer/Peter Jennings.

But there's one problem—there just aren't enough jobs to go around. I can't address the situation in the legal profession, but I know that scores of broadcast journalism majors will never collect a paycheck from a television station. Thousands of Dan Rather and Barbara Walters wannabes will never realize their dream.

That's where this book comes in. Its sole purpose is to help you understand television journalism and get a job in T.V. news. And unless you've got an uncle who's a vice-president at the network, getting that first job is a very tough deal.

Now, you may be a top student in a top program at a top university. You may even have a summer internship at a local T.V. station under your belt. You think you know the drill. After all, how tough can it be?

Well, after talking with dozens of News Directors at stations big and small, I discovered many people make a lot of fundamental mistakes along the job trail. In this book, you'll hear from your future bosses. You'll find out what they are looking for, and how you can help them find it.

This book also provides insight into the world of local T.V. news, so you can get an idea of just what the heck you're getting yourself into. It will give a little of the flavor and ambiance of working in a newsroom and covering a story, warts and all—but it's not a kiss-and-tell, sex-and-scandal-under-the-anchor-desk book. I like working in T.V. news, I like my current job, and I'm not going to risk my career by telling lewd stories about my colleagues—though I have more than enough to fill a book. As you'll discover in this guide, T.V. journalism is a very small industry.

This book is **not** based on our personal ideas of the best way to land a job. The advice herein comes straight from the people who do the hiring. News Directors, "headhunters," and consultants all shared their tips and knowledge of what they look for when they hire someone. You'll also discover how to learn about job openings as they are posted. There's nothing more futile (or frustrating) than applying for a job that's already filled.

Despite occasional cynical ranting about the horrors of working in T.V. news, I must confess that I enjoy my job. I don't enjoy every minute of every day, but, overall, I've been pretty happy with a life in local television. If Lynn and I didn't think it is a worthwhile career, we could never have written this book. So please read the following carefully and consider thoughtfully whether television journalism is for you. If so, pursue your career with everything you've got. If not, there's always law school.

Chapter 1

Diary of a Big Story

"I feel like 50 billion dollars!"
—a jubilant Thomas Sutherland,
a hostage in Beirut for 2,354 days,
as he and his family prepared to leave
Wiesbaden, Germany for the U.S.

Monday—Denver, Colorado—5:15am: The phone is ringing. Again. The first call went unanswered. Whoever it was hung up before I could get to the phone and before the answering machine kicked in. This time, unfortunately, I'm ready.

Phone calls at 0-dark-thirty are always answered with some trepidation in our house. When you work in the news business, a late-night call usually means you'll be on your way to work a lot earlier than you'd planned. In fact, you'll probably be rushing out the door in a major hurry.

I pick up the receiver. "Is Lynn there?" It's the voice of the station's overnight photographer, Steve Kady. Lynn is my wife, and she's a reporter and the weekend anchor at KMGH-TV, the CBS-affiliate in Denver. I also collect paychecks from KMGH; I make my living as a news photographer (or, in the politically correct 90's, a "photojournalist").

Still groggy with sleep, I ask the quintessential news question: "Is this important?" It's a stupid question. Obviously it's important, or the poor guy wouldn't be waking me up at 5:15am.

But when you work in news for any length of time, you tend to get pretty cynical, and if somebody's going to wake you up from a deep sleep, he'd better have a good reason.

"They're going to release Tom Sutherland this morning, probably within the hour," Kady says.

Hey, this *is* big. "I'll wake up Lynn."

Tom Sutherland had been held captive for over six years by the Islamic Jihad. When he was abducted, he was the Dean of Agriculture at the American University in Beirut, Lebanon. He'd also been a faculty member at Colorado State University in Fort Collins for over 25 years. His daughter Kit still lived in Fort Collins, a sleepy college town in the foothills of the Rocky Mountains, about an hour's drive north of Denver.

Lynn and I had been covering the Sutherland story for several years, and we had seen his relatives endure the emotional roller-coaster that comes with being a "hostage family." They'd suffered through false starts, dashed hopes, and a prying media. But they stayed together with a steely resolve, and they never stopped working for Tom's release. They are also extremely likable people, and through the years Lynn and I had privately rooted for the end of their ordeal.

Finally, after 2,354 days, Tom Sutherland was going to be a free man again.

By 6:15am, Lynn was on her way to Fort Collins. The release was still a rumor, and everyone was waiting for official confirmation that Sutherland had indeed been set free. The station had established a live-shot from Kit's house, and I stayed home and started to pack. If Sutherland did get released, Lynn and I would be flying immediately to Lindsey Army Hospital in Wiesbaden, Germany—the first stop on the way home for freed American hostages.

After I finished packing, I also headed for Fort Collins. As I started to drive there, the champagne corks were popping, and video of Sutherland's arrival in Syria was being broadcast. It was true—Kit's father was free.

While charging up Interstate 25, I get turned around by the station's Assignment Desk. Head for the airport, they tell me. Kit Sutherland, her friends, and a media entourage had formed a high-speed caravan to Denver.

Things are now moving quickly. It's critical that Lynn and I get on the same plane as Kit—not an easy task at the last minute. To make matters worse, we're not even sure which flight she's taking. People back at the station are working feverishly to make the arrangements.

Meanwhile, I pack gear in the media parking lot at the airport, and people bring stuff out to me from the station: shipping cases, extra tapes, a spare deck. Probably $100,000 of electronics, and it's all sort of flung randomly around my car. Finally, about the same time the Sutherland's convoy arrives at the airport, one final and much-needed item arrives—cash.

As Lynn and I stand at United's international ticket counter, things start to deteriorate. There's confusion about our tickets. We're on the wrong flight, and we need the tickets rewritten. The clock is ticking. Finally, all the problems are solved, and we're all set to fly. It's 11:45am. The plane leaves at 11:53am.

"You'd better hurry," the woman at the ticket counter advises.

No shit.

More delays. We're on the plane but we're not moving, thanks to some mechanical problem. As we sit there, we see Kit Sutherland get escorted off the plane. The media types on board panic. We've got to stay with Kit! Several minutes later, the flight attendant tells all international passengers to disembark. There's another flight in several minutes. We trudge down to the gate and re-book our tickets.

The plane's packed, but we're finally in the air—with Kit—for the first leg of the trip. Midway through the flight, we arrange an impromptu press conference with her. This is not easy in the aisle of a 757, with half the Colorado media on board. But Kit had always tried her best to accommodate us, and she and her family would continue to do so in the coming days.

At O'Hare, the gate area is filled with T.V. cameras and reporters. When I get off the plane, I give my tape to a producer from WBBM, the CBS-affiliate in Chicago. They'll put Kit's interview on the satellite, so our station can run it on the early news. CBS will also be able to use it on their national news, if they need it.

We change planes in Chicago. I'm still having a difficult time grasping exactly what is happening. A few hours ago I was asleep in my bed in Denver, and I expected to wake up to another average day in the news business. Instead, I'm flying to Germany to cover a major international story. It's hard to fathom.

Actually, we can thank a well-timed ratings period as much as the weight of the story for ensuring our departure. The station was currently in a "ratings book" or "sweeps month," which is a four-week period when research companies measure a station's viewership around the clock. Since viewership levels determine advertising rates (i.e., the more viewers you have, the more money you can charge advertisers—and vice versa), local stations try desperately to pump-up the ratings for their news shows during a sweeps period. This explains why you see a flood of titillating series— "Transsexual Child Molesters," "Bathrooms of the Rich and Famous," "Bowling and Drugs: An Eye-Team Undercover Investigation," and so on—on your local news every few months. Plus, a local station cannot afford to be beaten on a major story while a "book" is in progress. Hence, without hestitation, we're off to Europe.

Lynn phones in a report from the plane for the evening news in Denver. The signal is weak and the connection is marginal, but it's a nice element to have for the show. The station is doing a half-hour special at 7:00pm on Sutherland's ordeal, and we're supposed to try a live phone interview with Kit on the plane. We decide to tape it in advance, just to ensure we'll have something. "Never take anything for granted" is the operative motto for journalists, especially those who depend on temperamental electronics. On this trip, we'll be tested by these words of advice several times.

By the time our early news is over and the audio booth is

available, the phones on the plane go dead. We can't even send them out a taped interview. Oh, well—sometimes even the best plans go down the tubes.

Tuesday—Wiesbaden, Germany—9:00am: We arrive at a soggy Frankfurt International Airport. It's threatening to rain, a condition that would remain for our entire stay.

We need to get our luggage, which is substantial. When you're a T.V. news photographer, you travel with lots of stuff. We also need to clear customs, get our rental car, and find Wiesbaden. No easy task when the only German you understand is *"gesundheit."*

The first pleasant surprise occurs at the rental counter. "We don't have any 5.35's left, so we'll give you a BMW 7.35i instead for the same rate," the Hertz person informs me. Yes! I look at Lynn, who's guarding the luggage, and throw up my hands in victory. She looks at me quizzically, thinking I'm acting a little goofy.

The day takes on a surreal character. We're in Germany, and we've had about two hours of sleep. We cruise down the Autobahn in our sleek silver Beemer and find our way into Wiesbaden and, eventually, to our hotel. We check in, but there's no time to rest.

We're starting to get our bearings. We find the U.S. Army base, the media room there, and the CBS work area in that order. CBS, located in a makeshift compound in the parking lot of a local sports center, is 200 yards from the Army hospital that now houses Tom Sutherland.

CBS has two small house trailers and a 14-foot truck that serves as their center of operations. From all appearances, we could have been in Duluth or Toledo. In fact, we could have been in any parking lot in any city that had a good reason for a bevy of T.V. trucks and apparatus. Television pack journalism always looks the same: a lot of trailers, giant portable generators, and satellite trucks scattered in the closest area large enough to accommodate them.

CBS has a satellite truck at its disposal, as well as two edit packs and a bunch of phones. A platform has been constructed in front of the hospital for live-shots. The same group of network people has covered all the hostage releases, so much of the encampment is set up in a semi-permanent fashion. Every major network, with the notable exception of ABC, is arrayed in a similar way.

CBS has tape of Sutherland's arrival in Damascus and Wiesbaden, and he appears to be in remarkable spirits and good physical condition. The tape will provide the bulk of our insert for our live-shot on the midday newscast back in Denver. Since there's an eight-hour difference between Denver and Wiesbaden, we must do our report for the midday show at 7:30pm in Wiesbaden. Then I realize: the live-shot for the 5:00pm news will be at 1:00am our time. And if they want a live-shot for the 10:00pm show, it's at. . . It's too ugly to contemplate, especially on two hours of sleep.

The CBS people are genuinely helpful. Peter Van Sant, the network's correspondent, offers Lynn a transcript of Sutherland's remarks at the airport. We scan some tapes, and Lynn writes the insert for the midday live-shot. When CBS finishes editing, I jump in and edit the insert. When you're sharing facilities, it's critical to get things done as quickly and efficiently as you can. Besides CBS and us, KCCI-TV from Des Moines, Iowa is there. Sutherland and his wife Jean lived in Ames, the home of Iowa State University. Jean's father died the night before Tom was released, a tragic twist of fate for the Sutherland family. The funeral is scheduled for Friday in Ames.

We learn that the Sutherlands have scheduled a "photo op" at 4:00pm on the balcony of the hospital. It's pouring rain as we gather up our stuff for the short walk to the hospital. Of course, neither of us remembered to pack an umbrella.

We get a momentary reprieve from the rain as I'm setting up my equipment in front of the hospital. The sky brightens slightly. Photographers and reporters are scattered all over the hospital grounds. Right on time, the Sutherlands emerge from the building. Tom, Jean, Kit, and Joan (another of their three daughters) are beaming as they stand on the balcony above us. They seem to glow with happiness. Standing there, you can't help but feel their incredible joy. It's an amazing moment.

The whole thing lasts just ten minutes, but the pictures are memorable. We head back to the workspace and add these shots to our previous taped insert.

At 5:00pm Wiesbaden time, we've got everything done for the midday show, so we've got several hours to kill before the live-shot. Because we haven't even had a chance to take a shower since we left Denver, we decide to return to the hotel. We figure we'll have enough time for Lynn to take a shower and freshen up before her live-shot. News Directors like their reporters to look "perky" when they're on the air, and, after all, it's not every day Lynn gets to report live from Germany.

Bad idea. It's dark, and we've got only a vague recollection of how to get back to the hotel. Sure enough, with just two wrong turns we become dreadfully lost. And, just to add another complication, it's rush hour. We finally get onto a familiar road and decide to head back to the workspace. We can't afford to jeopardize a live-shot by getting lost again. The shower will have to wait. Lynn resorts to using massive amounts of hair spray and assorted chemicals to revive her hair.

Considering our lack of sleep and general grungy feeling, the live-shot goes well. Now we've got to put together another insert for our live-shot for the 5:00pm show, as well as a package for the 10:00pm newscast. (In the Central and Mountain time zones, the primary local newscasts run at 5:00pm and 10:00pm. On the coasts, they're usually at 6:00pm and 11:00pm [though that's starting to change].) Luckily, we talked to the honchos at the station and convinced them that a live-shot for the 10:00pm show would just be too difficult and would probably ruin us for the rest of the trip, since it would pretty much dictate another night without sleep.

The rest of the evening goes well. By 2:00am, we're back at the hotel, armed with dinner from that famous German institution, Kentucky Fried Chicken. What could we do? It was the only restaurant open, and we could order in English. We'd traveled thousands of miles just to eat some Original Recipe drumsticks. It didn't seem fair.

Wednesday—Wiesbaden, Germany: Tom Sutherland has scheduled a press conference at 2:00pm. It's a merciful piece of scheduling, because it means we can actually get some sleep— over seven hours. What a deal!

It also means we can eat a legitimate meal. Since it's a German holiday, businesses are closed, so the hotel restaurant is offering a delectable buffet for lunch. We meet our counterparts from KUSA (the ABC-affiliate in Denver) and trade war stories over a long, delicious meal. (It was the only real meal we had in Germany.)

We linger too long. We realize we've committed a cardinal journalism sin: we don't know the exact location of the press conference. We hustle over to the CBS workspace, but it's empty, so we dash to the hospital, and I drag all my gear in—only to learn that I'm in the wrong place. The press conference is at the main base.

It's still a half-hour before Sutherland's arrival, but the room is packed. Fourteen cameras are lined up in front of a long table where the family will sit. Space is tight because there are two floor-to-ceiling columns in the front of the room. They severely limit the angles and make it difficult to get a shot of the entire table. The prime spots have already been taken.

I'm in a mild panic. I make it a rule to get to this type of thing early, but fatigue and hunger led me to make a mistake. I maneuver to a spot next to a crew from Des Moines. I'll have a good shot of Sutherland, but I don't have a view of the entire table. It's not great, but it could be worse. I can improvise later to get the shots I need.

In his best brogue, Tom Sutherland begins the press conference by quoting a passage from Scottish poet Robert Burns. Sutherland, a native Scotsman, stuns the media with his candor, charm, and unabashed enthusiasm. Most of the journalists there have seen a succession of hostages who, for the most part, looked much worse for their ordeal. But Sutherland exudes an infectious intensity as he recounts his years in captivity. He talks about his capture, a beating from his captors, the acquisition of a radio with which he and fellow hostage Terry Anderson could listen to the BBC and the Voice of America, his daily routine, and almost any other question put to him. The whole thing lasts well over an hour. Sutherland captured the total attention of a pack of seen-it-all journalists who usually tune out after the first ten minutes of any press conference.

Afterwards, Lynn and I race back to the workspace. CBS is pulling out and returning to their London bureau. They say there's not enough national significance in the story to warrant further coverage. However, they leave some editing equipment and enough people to let us continue our live-shots. But we must now arrange our editing time carefully, since we've got to split the system with the crew from Des Moines. This effectively cuts our time in half.

The rest of the day consists of more editing, more live-shots, and one surprise.

Late in the afternoon, Kit Sutherland passes word that her family, minus Tom, will meet with the Colorado media at the Pente, a downtown Wiesbaden hotel. This will give us something fresh for our evening newscasts.

At 8:00pm, Kit, her mother Jean, and her sister Joan arrive at the hotel. "We have to do this fast," Kit warns, "because Dad is in the car and the State Department isn't thrilled about this impromptu meeting."

As we gather our cameras, we hear a commotion from the lobby. Unbelievably, here comes Tom Sutherland! He apparently told the State Department that he didn't want to wait in the car and would rather join the rest of his family. So he comes bounding in, shaking hands and doling out hugs. He joins his family on the couch, and we do a festive ten-minute interview. Suddenly, covering this story has become a lot of fun.

More live shots, more editing. Finally, we're done. The Sutherlands are scheduled to board a United flight to the U.S. in the morning. They're heading for Ames, Iowa and a bittersweet reunion with their relatives.

Thursday—Frankfurt, Germany: We finish packing at 3:30am, and we need to be up by 6:00am and on the way to the airport by 7:00am. Once again, sleep is a scarce commodity. Exhausted, my body is beginning to rebel. I'm hungry, I'm tired, my back has a constant dull ache, and we've got to be on the move again in three hours.

We've again arranged to be on the same flight as the Sutherlands, and Tom has agreed to do interviews on the flight. We've also talked our boss into upgrading us to business class for the trip to Des Moines. It could be a great flight.

We'll have no time to dawdle in Des Moines. We're due to arrive at 4:00pm, and a parade has been arranged in Ames to greet the Sutherlands at 5:00pm. We need to get to Ames in time for Lynn to do a live-shot for the top of the news. Fortunately, a crew is coming from Denver to shoot the festivities, and a satellite truck is also driving up. But there will be no time to spare.

Less than an hour before our scheduled departure, we bump into the crew from Des Moines. They've got some interesting news: Sutherland isn't leaving Wiesbaden. In fact, he's still at the hospital, and apparently he's got a stomach ailment.

What should we do? We're convinced that the family will make every effort to get back to Iowa for the funeral. Sutherland had a tooth pulled the previous day, and we assume (wrongly, as it turns out) that he's had a reaction to the medication. Since he had passed a battery of medical tests and was cleared to return home, we figured he'd leave on the next flight. If we go ahead and board our flight, we'll get to Ames ahead of him and be ready for the family's arrival. It seemed like a plan. We knew the KUSA crew was leaving, along with the two crews from Des Moines. But we didn't see the crew from KCNC (the NBC-affiliate in Denver), and that made us worried.

As we approached the gate, a United representative confirmed that the Sutherlands were not going to be on the flight. And while we could cancel our tickets and re-book a later flight, we couldn't get our luggage off the plane. Another instant dilemma.

I had my camera and one crammed gear bag. I make it a practice to carry enough tapes, batteries, and microphones to do basic T.V. whenever I travel. If the luggage gets lost, I can still do my job, though in a more rudimentary form to be sure. If we stayed, I had enough supplies to work for two days. Of course, we'd have no clothes, no toiletries, and no margin for error with the equipment.

The flight was leaving in 15 minutes. That gave us time to make one more mistake: We didn't call the hospital. It was the one place that could have given us the information we needed. Of course, it's easier to think of these things when you've had a little more sleep. Instead, we called our station, but to no avail—no one's there. The decision is ours. We get on the plane.

As the plane becomes airborne, we begin to reconsider our decision. The KCNC crew is not on the plane. The only reason, we decide, is because something's up. And it's probably something major.

We went from the high that accompanies doing a great job on a demanding story to feeling like goats. The station management was thrilled with the job we had done so far. But we began to think we had just committed a fatal error on a major international story. And there was no way to correct it. We had just handed our competition an exclusive presence in Wiesbaden. I started feeling nauseous.

When we arrive in Chicago, we call the station. They tell us Sutherland has a stomach ulcer, and he'll be confined to the hospital for a few more days. For better or worse, we're heading home.

Friday—Denver, Colorado: I'm in my bed in a semi-stupor. My head is buzzing. A double-dose of jet lag has finally taken its toll. Sixteen time zones in four days. Whew.

I'm tense as I wait for KCNC's noon news to come on. Our bosses are still very happy with our performance, and they aren't second-guessing our decision to leave Wiesbaden. That's nice, but I still fear disaster. There are too many things that could happen and turn us into instant chumps.

KCNC's show starts. "And we now join Jim Hanchett, the

only Denver reporter still in Germany with the Sutherlands..."

My heart sinks. KCNC is a promotion-driven station. They've grabbed this gift that landed in their laps, and now they're going to make a huge deal about their exclusive in Germany. Great. At least there's nothing in Hanchett's report that could be considered real news. They covered a medical press conference, but that's about it. My panic ebbs for the moment.

Time for a commercial break. What's this? "The first station with a live report from Germany, and the only Denver reporter still on the scene!" Jeez, they've already got an ad trumpeting their coverage of the Sutherland story! But a lot of it is just hype. As for their claim they were "the first station with a live report from Germany" —big deal. We were all on the same plane. They just have an earlier newscast to go live in. But it sounds good. And they *are* still there. I have nightmares that they'll get all this great family stuff—you know, shopping in Wiesbaden, getting ready to go home, and so on—and finally have an exclusive on the flight home. The Sutherlands have always had a rule that they won't grant anyone an exclusive, but if Hanchett is the only reporter around. . .

Lynn is at the station preparing several stories for *Crossroads*, a *Nightline*-style public affairs show that the station airs weekly. She'll also do an on-set report and discussion during the program. It's another long day for Lynn. I marvel at her energy. I feel like I've been sacked by the defensive line of the Broncos, and Lynn is still doing TV.

Saturday—Vail, Colorado: The sky is blue, the sun is out, and fresh snow is everywhere. It's the best early season conditions in years, as a series of November storms have blanketed Colorado's Rockies with powder.

I'm still pretty tired, but I seize an opportunity to go skiing with our neighbor, Pete Zwolinski. I always feel skiing is like a mental enema—it has a way of cleaning out your head. It's one of the great things about working in Denver; Vail is just 80 miles from our house. As I ride the lift to the top of the mountain, I feel a million miles from work, from Germany, and from the worry that KCNC is going to scoop us.

Lynn doesn't get to share this little vacation. We are still in the middle of the November ratings period, and she has to anchor the evening newscast. It's her eighth consecutive day of work.

After a magnificent day at Vail, I get home and the phone rings. It's the station. A propane explosion has destroyed a house in Nederland, a mountain town about 45 minutes from our house, and a six-year-old girl is missing. They want me to relieve the photographer there, so he and the reporter can return to the station to get the story on the 10:00pm show. I've got to stop answering phones.

My mind is racing. I'm trying to figure out a good reason why I can't go. But the station has run out of options. With great regret, I agree to go. I really don't have a choice.

The phone rings again. I'm spared, sort of. The photographer is blocked in at the fire scene, so the reporter will hitch a ride to a corner market with a crew from another station. I merely have to play taxi and drive the reporter and the tapes back to Denver. To say the least, I'm relieved.

Sunday—Denver, Colorado: The Sutherlands probably will fly to San Francisco tomorrow morning. They have a daughter there, Anne, who is eight months pregnant, so she couldn't go to Germany to join the reunion. She's also got a husband and a four-year-old daughter whom Tom has never met. She's his only—at least for a month—grandchild.

It's a little after 9:00am, and I'm running late. I drive up to Fort Collins with a reporter (Lynn and I often work together, but not always) to do a story on the town's preparation for Sutherland's return. Over 10,000 people are expected to fill Moby Gym for a raucous homecoming. "Welcome Home!" signs dot the town streets, and yellow ribbons are wrapped around everything.

When we return to the station, Lynn, who is anchoring the newscast, tells me that the Sutherlands have confirmed their plans for San Francisco tomorrow. Lynn does her job at 5:00pm, and we head home to pack. Again.

Monday—San Francisco: We arrive in the Bay Area at 11:00am and immediately head to KPIX, the CBS-affiliate there. The Bay Bridge dominates the skyline as we wend our way down Market Street toward the Embarcadero. It's a gorgeous day.

KPIX is not gorgeous. The newsroom resembles a dungeon. Even though it's on the fourth floor and the San Francisco Bay shimmers a few blocks away, the newsroom has no windows. But T.V. stations are notorious for having rooms without windows. Of course, if I'm in a dimly lit, state-of-the-art editing suite, I find that environment, well, pretty cool. There's something to be said for being surrounded by flickering red LEDs and big bucks, high-end video toys. But if I'm in a large, crammed newsroom that doesn't have any natural light, then it's just depressing.

We get into an editing booth and scan some tape. KPIX did a brief interview with Anne at her house yesterday. CBS has also sent footage of Tom Sutherland leaving Wiesbaden and shopping at the airport with Jean for tiny *lederhosen* for their granddaughter.

We edit an insert for our 5:00pm live-shot, which we'll do from the airport prior to Sutherland's arrival. There's supposed to be a press conference immediately after he arrives.

We check into a hotel and then head for the airport. This time, we're plenty early, and I secure a prime spot. In an hour, the space in front of the podium will be jammed with cameras. Delta officials have given us an area next to the gate where Sutherland is arriving.

Lynn does her live report for the 5:00pm show. We wait.

More cameras appear, T.V. and newspaper both. By the time the plane lands, there are about 50 photographers vying for position near the podium. This has all the signs of becoming a media circus.

And it does. Big time.

Sutherland emerges from a private room, where he was reunited with his daughter and her family. No pictures allowed in there. As he comes out, he's holding his cherubic granddaughter and smiling. He walks over to the podium, and the circus begins. The newspaper photographers, who were crouching in front of the podium, suddenly stand up to get their shots of Sutherland. As a result, they block the T.V. cameras. Some of the T.V. crews start shouting at the newspaper guys to get down, and, of course, the newspaper guys are shouting back. The shouting match is so loud, we can't hear Sutherland. All we get on tape is photographers yelling at each other. Nice.

It was the press at its worst, an embarrassment for many of us there.

After the event, the San Francisco T.V. journalists congratulate each other on the fine job they did getting those jerks in front out of the way. I suggest that they try working together so everyone can get a good shot without the yelling and shoving. They look at me like I'm from Mars.

Lynn and I head back to KPIX (from now on known to us as "The Dungeon") and start working on our piece for the 10:00pm show. Lynn will do a live report from the KPIX newsroom, usually a simple thing to set up.

Our story is edited, and, ten minutes before the live-shot, we think everything is hunky-dory. One problem: the crack staff at "The Dungeon" can't find anyone to operate the newsroom camera. Nor can they seem to establish the IFB. (An IFB hookup lets the reporter hear the show's audio, plus the producer and director in the control room, back in Denver. This way, the anchor can ask a question, and the reporter can hear it. Usually, all it takes is a call to a dedicated phone line, and presto!, IFB.)

After some frantic conversations, it doesn't look good. So we resort to the basics. I get on the phone directly to the control room. Lynn will do the live-shot "blind" —she'll never hear anyone in Denver. (I guess we should say she'll do the live-shot "deaf," but "blind" is the proper lingo.) It's not the best way to do T.V., but sometimes you've just got to make do.

Ten seconds before the live-shot, the IFB link is established. Lynn's report goes perfectly. We all breathe a sigh of relief.

Lynn and I are doubly relieved. We never saw any sign of our rival, KCNC. They chose to have a reporter from KRON, the NBC-affiliate in San Francisco, report their live-shot for their 5:00pm show. Later, we learn that they pulled their crew from Germany on Saturday and decided not to send them to San Francisco.

We're feeling like front-runners again.

Tuesday—San Francisco: We get a good night's sleep and wake up early to walk around Fisherman's Wharf. Lynn has never been to San Francisco, so we want to see as much as time will allow.

The sea lions are making a racket on the docks, and we play tourists, oohing and ahhing over the plump, whiskered creatures. I keep thanking the heavens that Sutherland's daughter lives in San Francisco and not on some dirt-farm in east Arkansas.

Kit Sutherland calls and says the family doesn't want to deal with the media today. Tomorrow, she says, they'll have a news conference outside Anne's home in Berkeley. But she wants the number of cameras limited and asks us to handle the arrangements. Great—now we've got to negotiate with the animals we saw at the airport yesterday.

However, it turns out to be easy. We get three stations to represent the three networks and CNN, and we call the Associated Press to take care of the newspapers and magazines. Four cameras, four reporters, no circus. We will represent CBS, and we call our friends from KUSA to handle ABC. KRON in San Francisco will cover it for NBC.

That chore completed, we hop in the rental car and take the rest of the day off—the first break for Lynn in ten days. We head down Route 1 along the coast for Monterey. As we drive through the coastal fog, we both silently re-live this exhilarating story. And we both keep returning to the same image: Tom Sutherland standing on the hospital balcony in Wiesbaden, radiating absolute joy. We both smile at the memory. Sometimes, this can be a great job.

Wednesday—San Francisco: After a leisurely morning, we drive across the Bay Bridge to Berkeley. The family "photo-op" is scheduled for 1:00pm. We know we'll have to shoot quickly and get back to "The Dungeon" fast, since our Denver live-shot is at 4:00pm. It's the day before Thanksgiving, and we're assuming traffic will be terrible.

We get there before some of the family. Apparently, they're out buying up most of the compact discs in town. Tom has discovered CDs and thinks they're the neatest thing invented during his captivity. When he arrives, he bounds up the steps to the house and shakes everyone's hand. He gives Lynn a hug and a peck on the cheek. You've gotta love this guy. He spends over six years chained to a wall, and now he's going on and on about the sound quality on a CD!

The family gathers and comes out on the front patio. Tom and Jean have a Thanksgiving message. It's sincere and emotional—good T.V. We get what we need and run for the car. It's now 2:30pm.

To our surprise, traffic moves well, and within a half-hour we're back at "The Dungeon." We snag an editing room, and Lynn views the tape while I call Denver about the live-shot. We want a shot from the roof of the building, with the city in the background, but the folks at KPIX won't promise anything. But after a few well-placed phone calls to CBS, KPIX becomes very accommodating.

We edit quickly and finish with ten minutes to spare. On the roof, the camera is in place, the IFB is perfect, and within moments, Lynn is live in Denver with a gorgeous shot of the Bay Bridge behind her. The station loves it, and we're happy campers.

We edit a new version of the story for the 10:00pm show and feed it to Denver via satellite. They don't want another live-shot, so by 8:00pm, our work is over. Time to explore the nightlife of Chinatown.

Our flight leaves Thanksgiving morning at 9:00am. We're eating turkey at home at 6:00pm.

Sunday—Fort Collins, Colorado: Today, Tom Sutherland finally comes home. At 11:23am, the Lear jet (donated by Anheuser-Busch) carrying the Sutherlands touches down at the Fort Collins/Loveland Airport. As the gangway is wheeled up to the plane, the station interrupts its regular programming. Lynn is anchoring the special report from the studio in Denver; I'm running the camera at the airport.

Sutherland pops out of the plane and, in a now-familiar move, throws his arms into the air. Hundreds of people are lined-up behind the fence surrounding the tarmac. They cheer as Sutherland hugs old friends.

A huge limousine decorated with American flags and a "Welcome Home Tom" banner waits nearby. Sutherland waves, gets in the car, then pops out through the sun roof. He grins and waves to the crowd, there are more cheers, and the motorcade is under way.

People are lined along the entire route. As the entourage slowly makes its way toward Moby Gym on the Fort Collins campus, we prepare to do more live television. We have three cameras at the gym—two to cover the proceedings and one for reporter Bill Clarke's live-shot. Our satellite truck, production truck, and an array of engineers are on location.

At 2:00pm, Sutherland enters the packed gym, and thousands of people send up a rafter-rattling cheer as Tom and his family make their way to the stage. Again, the station breaks into its regular programming for a live report. Lynn anchors from Denver, then turns it over to Bill Clarke. Clarke does a short introduction, then Sutherland begins to speak from the stage.

For the next hour, Sutherland regales the crowd with his wit, charm, and enthusiasm. He and Jean sing some old Scottish songs, Tom talks about his captivity, and finally, the sound of bagpipes signals the end of the festivities. We're live for over an hour, and everything goes well. The Sutherlands do one last press conference, and then they're on their way home. The Sutherland story would continue for weeks, but the first major chapter is over.

As I'm driving back to Denver, I get a call from the assignment desk. There's been a three-car wreck on Interstate 76. Could I check it out. . . ?

Is this a typical local news story? Hardly. Is this an average two weeks in the life of a television journalist? No, not even close. Then why recount it?

Several reasons: First, it is indeed possible to get sucked into the whirlwind of a major international story, even while working in local news. It's what true news junkies live for. If this type of manic behavior doesn't suit you, then you should consider another career. People in T.V. news, especially people in the "field" (reporters, photographers, etc.), are adrenaline-eaters. At least, the good ones are.

Second, the above diary provides insight into how television journalists cover a big, breaking story. Each day, they're faced with a thousand decisions, and they're not always going to decide correctly. Mistakes are facts of life in the news process. What separates the geniuses from the dopes in this job? It's simple. The geniuses make mistakes every day, but they make fewer than everyone else.

Third, this story had some real "moments." Most good news stories are based on some type of human emotion—anger, joy, fear, grief. Sometimes—and it doesn't happen often—one of these emotions crystallizes in time. It's only a flash, but for a "moment," an event (or even a lifetime!) can be distilled into a few revealing seconds of video. It's a privilege to witness a "moment," and it's an art to capture it and translate it to an audience.

The story of Tom Sutherland's release had several "moments." I will always carry the memory of the Sutherlands hugging each other on the balcony of the Army hospital. When a reporter asked Jean to describe her feelings, she replied, "No words— body language." The expressions on their faces said far more than any words could convey. That instant encapsulated the end of the entire six-and-a-half-year ordeal.

Fourth, this is a happy story. A lot of the big stories these days are based on tragedy, scandal, conflict, and violence. This was one of those rare joyful ones. You couldn't help but feel the ebullience radiating from the Sutherland family. More than once, I struggled to focus my camera because tears were obscuring my vision.

Finally, this story emphasizes the unpredictability and chaos of television journalism. To me, one of the great things about my job is that I never know what I'll be doing tomorrow. I might be shooting a feature story on mountain biking or scrambling to cover the destruction caused by a mid-winter avalanche. You've got to learn to love the uncertainty, the adventure, or you'll hate working in T.V. news.

It's a career that requires long hours and unflagging dedication. Twelve-hour days are common. You're always on call, and you'll work nights, weekends, and holidays. I can't count all the Christmases I've "celebrated" in the newsroom.

If your desire to work in television news remains undiminished after reading this diary, then continue reading this book, because it will give you an edge in nailing down a job. And in this business, having an edge makes the difference between winners and losers.

(And Lynn was a winner on this story. She received an Emmy for anchoring the live coverage of the Sutherlands' return to Fort Collins.)

Chapter 2

Who Does What

*"Television is an invention that permits you to be
entertained in your living room by people
you wouldn't have in your home."*
—David Frost

"In television news, you can't ever say 'I' did a story. You always have to say 'we'," Charles Kuralt wrote in *On the Road*. "The reporter depends on the skill of others who set up the lights just so, make pictures, record sound, and edit tape."

Like most of Kuralt's work, that's a dead-on accurate assessment of the process of making television news. If you're a loner, if you like to work on things by yourself, if you're not a "team player," then you won't like television news. Getting a news show on the air requires the efforts of a lot of people, and your success in television journalism will depend a lot on your ability to get along with your colleagues—and your ability to get them to do what you want them to do.

Many people are involved in the process, and they're all necessary in the production of a successful show. If one person in the long chain errs, it can damage the final product. On second thought, maybe "damage" is too kind. In fact, one mistake can *destroy* an entire day of work in an instant. I've heard a litany of excuses in my time: "We couldn't steer the live-shot in. . ." "I didn't realize that I'd put the tapes on the bulk eraser. . ." "I dropped the keys to the news car in the river. . ." "The script vanished into the computer, and I couldn't retrieve it in time. . ." "The machine ate the tape. . ." You get the idea.

Let's face it: shit happens. In television journalism, you must make dozens of decisions—instantly—every day. And since you're not perfect, no matter what your résumé says, you're going to make some bad ones. So are your co-workers. To make matters worse, television journalism relies on thousands of complex, persnickety machines, gadgets, and gizmos. Switches will break, the power will fail, and machines are going to ruin your life.

The keys to success in this job are simple: count on mistakes happening, keep your mistakes to a minimum, and learn to handle the mistakes other people make.

Of course, when you're part of a show that goes really well, there's an incredible elation and a satisfying bonding you'll share with your colleagues. Successful department-wide efforts—such as covering a disaster, a major election, or a Super Bowl—can produce an unmatched group euphoria. When local television news is done well, especially spot news, it's a beautiful thing to watch.

When you get your first job in T.V. news, you'll need to know what is expected of you and all those people around you. Of course, your first newsroom probably will be small, and many of the duties described below will be shared.

But let's take a look at the big picture. Imagine we're touring a large, fully-staffed newsroom—the operation of a station in a top-20 market. We'll see the offices of the head honchos, the newsroom, and the "behind-the-scenes" area, the control room. After all, they're the people who actually get the newscast on the air.

(*Note: Throughout the descriptions below, we have used the male pronoun to describe various people. However, this is only a convenience. Women comprise at least one-third, and proba-*

*bly more, of most T.V. news operations, from News Director
to photographer.)*

The Upper Crust

The **News Director** is the top banana of a television news operation. He's usually easy to recognize. For one thing, he'll have
an office. (There usually aren't many private offices in a newsroom.) He'll also be the person agonizing over the reams of
paper, provided by the Nielsen and Arbitron companies, that
contain the ratings and "share points" for the station's newscasts.
Plus, he'll probably be the guy using the most expletives when
the subject is money, whether it concerns an anchor's salary or
a reporter's arguing for that "absolutely necessary" trip to Japan.

The News Director is responsible for the overall direction of
the newsroom and the look of the newscast. In larger markets,
he'll spend more time pondering the station's future than worrying about which reporter should cover a train wreck. He'll be
calculating the next moves the newsroom needs to make to gain
market share and discerning the trends that will help him keep
the station #1 in the ratings—or at least move it from third to
second.

I tend to view News Directors as though they're baseball
managers or football coaches. They form the game plan and
call the plays, but they must rely on their players to perform.
Sometimes they make a bad call, sometimes the players screw
up, and sometimes the right play runs perfectly and the team
scores.

Like a coach, the News Director gets to pick his players. Probably, he'll be the person who will make the decision to hire
you—and maybe fire you later. You'll need to impress the News
Director to get a job, get a raise, and get the best assignments.
To extend the sports analogy, he's the guy who decides who
starts, who sits on the bench, and who gets cut.

The thought of being a busy, working journalist one day and
walking the street without a job the next is chilling. I think this
explains the subtle paranoia that exists between the people in

the newsroom and the News Director. Whether you have a contract or not, a News Director can fire you anytime. And whether the News Director is a truly fine person or a graduate of the Weasel School of Journalism, he controls your destiny.

On the other hand, News Directors usually don't last long. Barbara Frye, director of talent placement for Frank N. Magid Associates, tracks how many times News Directors change jobs among the affiliates in the 100 largest markets each year. The numbers are astounding: On average, slightly over 100 News Directors in the top 100 markets change jobs every year! Think about that. Since there are usually three stations per market, this statistic indicates that *one-third* of the newsrooms in the top 100 markets have a new boss this year. And next year. And the year after. The average Burger King probably doesn't have that much turnover. The good News Directors are building a reputation and moving up to more lucrative jobs; the bad or unlucky ones are getting dumped by station management. If the ratings take a tumble, the News Director, like the manager of a losing baseball team, will be the first to go.

One last point. When a News Director hires you, you become part of his chosen team. In most cases, this is a big advantage. When a News Director takes over a newsroom, he's usually faced with a group of people he didn't hire. So, to put his own stamp on the show, he will, over time, fire some people, shift some to different jobs, force some out, and hire some of his own people. It can be invaluable to be one of those hired under a new News Director, because you'll often be in a more favored position than the folks hired by the previous administration. Of course, if "your" News Director leaves—not a rare occurrence, as we've seen—you'll lose your advantage and join the ranks of the "hold-overs."

If you interview at a station at which the News Director seems secure in his job, and if you get a job offer, you should strongly consider it. A secure News Director usually means a secure job for you. Conversely, if you hear rumors about how the boss is on his way out, you should avoid taking a job there. Whenever a News Director leaves a station, it creates upheaval and change, and your position becomes tenuous.

As mentioned above, News Directors in larger markets rarely have an active role in the day-to-day news operation. They usually attend the morning meetings, where the day's news coverage is decided. And, when a major spot news event occurs, they often assume more prominent leadership. But overall, someone else in the department supervises the details of the daily routine. This "someone else" will have various titles and responsibilities, depending on the philosophy of the News Director. The most common titles are **Assistant News Director** and **Managing Editor**.

Typically, Managing Editor is the final stop in the news assembly line. His job can be compared to that of the line foreman in a manufacturing plant: It's his responsibility to ensure everyone's doing his job correctly and on time. In the newsroom, the Managing Editor enacts the policies of the News Director on a day-to-day basis, so he usually takes an active role in deciding the content of the broadcast. If the News Director decides that the station should increase its coverage of financial matters, for example, the Managing Editor must steer the reporters that way. He's also often charged with script approval. At most stations, reporters must have their scripts checked before their stories are edited, and the Managing Editor usually handles this chore. It's an important task, because he'll not only correct grammar mistakes and style flaws, he'll also be the final arbiter of the content of the story. He must double-check with the reporter to make sure the story's facts are correct, and he must delete statements that may be libelous or misleading.

The Managing Editor is troubleshooter, cheerleader, and disciplinarian. Often, however, the job tends to deteriorate into an "Enforcer" role. It's usually a difficult, no-win task.

Some stations may have both an Assistant News Director and a Managing Editor. In this case, the Assistant News Director often has more of a bureaucratic position—a liaison between the News Director, station management, and the newsroom—and the Managing Editor has a more hands-on role in the daily journalism.

There may be one last link in the upper management chain: **Executive News Producer.** This person could have one of two roles. He could be the person ultimately responsible for the final content of the news product, or he could be someone with an impressive-sounding title but no real power.

I'm always skeptical of any title with the word "Executive" in it. I'm just not sure what it means. I worked in one hapless newsroom in which *everyone* had a title—and they were all "Executive" something or other. In fact, the position of Assistant News Director was abolished, and the person occupying that office became Executive Producer of News Coverage. This person was the direct supervisor of the Director of News Operations. But just two months later, the Executive Producer of News Coverage was fired, and the Director of News Operations became the Executive Producer of News Coverage. At the same time, the position of Director of News Operations was abolished. I sure was relieved to hear that. Then, we also had an Executive Producer of Special Segments and an Executive Producer of Special Projects. In fact, the person who became the Executive Producer of Special Projects had been the Executive Producer for News. And the Executive Producer of Special Segments later became the Executive Producer of Sports.

Confused? I sure was. And anyone with a smidgen of rationality was cringing at this ridiculous game of title creation. As you might suspect, within a year or two, most of the people involved in this caper all had a single title: Unemployed.

One last note: In your first newsroom, many of these jobs probably will be combined. You'll definitely have a News Director and likely some sort of Managing Editor. But if you're working in a station that's not in the top 100 markets, they probably will be the extent of the bureaucracy. Job flexibility, not job proliferation, will be the key at a small station, where doing more with less is the name of the game.

In the Field or in the Office

The satellite truck engineer was neither happy nor amused. He'd worked hard to get a live-shot onto the satellite (a.k.a. the "bird") for a story that was painfully trivial. Someone back at the station had made a bad call and cut the story from the broadcast. "What can you expect?" he moaned. "They all work in rooms without windows."

It's a simple statement, but it highlights one of the profound dichotomies in television news: the difference between *covering* news and *gathering* news. When you cover news, you're at the scene of the tragic apartment fire; you're talking to the people who will be affected by a proposed toxic waste site; you're in the pressbox when Nolan Ryan fires another no-hitter. This is known as "working in the field." It's an essential component in getting the news on the air.

The news-gatherers, on the other hand, call the newsroom home. Most newsrooms are nothing more than an elaborate cluster of office cubicles, computer terminals (though many newsrooms still rely on that dinosaur, the typewriter), and high-tech gadgetry arrayed in a fashion conducive to news-gathering. This is known as "working in rooms without windows." News-gatherers are responsible for deciding just what really is the "news du jour." They compile all the various bits of information, videotape, graphics, and other items that are part of putting a news show together, and they're responsible for getting all of it on T.V. in the correct order. It's also an essential component in getting the news on the air.

So, there's a basic choice you must make early in your news career. And it's a very important choice, because the two areas lead in somewhat divergent directions, and your future career options will spring from this initial decision. So think about it carefully. Of course, if you start in a small market, you'll have ample opportunity to try out a lot of different hats, and you'll have time to decide between a hard hat and a Stetson.

As a photographer, of course, I'm partial to people who work in the field. Unlike the no-windows crowd, we never know just what we'll be doing, who we'll be seeing, and where we'll be going tomorrow. But I also know that such uncertainty and chaos—not to mention the long hours driving or just waiting for an event to unfold, in all kinds of weather—is not for everyone, so let's examine all the "outside jobs" and the "inside jobs."

Field Jobs

Reporters—The front line of television journalism, these folks venture onto the streets to create stories on the news and events of the day. A lot of people believe it's a glamorous job. After all, reporters get to do "stand-ups"—that part of the story where the reporter speaks on-camera, summarizing or introducing some part of the piece—and they get to badger elected officials, celebrities, or just plain citizens on the street because they brandish a microphone and pledge allegiance to a higher and greater good: the Truth and the Public's Right to Know.

Actually, reporters have a tough job. Good reporters are a driven, competitive lot. They not only want to be at the center of the storm, they *need* to be. They crave the big stories. It borders on an addiction.

Good reporters have a basic desire to probe, prod, and meddle. They can also think on their feet and get the story right. A good command of the language, which must eventually be honed into a personal style, is also essential.

Good reporters must be willing to get their hands dirty. A lot of news can't be covered in a Brooks Brothers or a Liz Claiborne suit. They've got to be willing to be blown around by a hurricane, to walk through the city landfill, to don a gas mask during combat, and to do a live report on traffic conditions on a dismal overpass above a nondescript highway during a snowstorm. In short, they've got to be prepared to go where the news is, no matter what the conditions, and then make some sense of it once they get there.

Of course, I'm referring to *good* general-assignment reporters. There are plenty—nay, a *glut*—of mediocre reporters in television, and many continue to get good jobs, though I can't tell you why. There's also a growing trend toward "beat" reporters who cover a special topic like education, health, politics, and consumer issues. Though you'll probably be a general-assignment reporter in your first job, you should consider focusing on a specific area for your next reporting job, especially if you have a keen interest in or knowledge of a hot topic.

Photographers—a.k.a. "photojournalists" (the term currently in vogue, though it sounds a bit self-important), "shooters" (the action term, though it sounds like you're a hitman or a drunk loading up on Cuervo), "photogs" (the folksy term), or "cameraman" (an archaic term used only by overpaid, overweight, cigar-smoking union guys at the big stations).

There wouldn't be much television news without photographers. Everything you see on your cathode-ray tube during a newscast that doesn't occur in the studio has been shot by a news photographer somewhere. News photographers are self-contained video factories and can cover news autonomously. A photographer can do a story without a reporter, but not vice versa. It's an essential position. At most large stations, there are more jobs for photographers than any other position.

It can be an exciting, adrenaline-pumping job at times. You are the eyes for your viewers, and it's your job to capture the facts *and* emotions of a story, while it's happening. Photogs tend to be crafty, street-smart, and hooked on action. Good photographers blend a healthy portion of personal creativity into the mix.

Many small stations make their reporters shoot their own stories, since spare photographers are a luxury the stations can't afford. That's okay. It'll give you a sample of both jobs, and you can pick which one you like better.

Photographers are paid less than reporters, and their job is often thankless. Everyone wants to meet or be seen with the reporter, not the photographer. But photographers have better opportunities for getting a job, especially women. There's a dearth of female photographers in the business, and women with talent move ahead quickly.

In this period of recession and cutbacks, the days of Max Headroom aren't far away. Remember Max? He was the computer-generated character in an ABC series in the mid-80's. Max, with a little help from the technology that existed in his world, could be a reporter and photographer at the same time, much of it on live television. Well, WTVJ, the NBC-affiliate in Miami, recently took a step toward Max's future.

The station had been waiting for just the right situation, and on June 4, 1991, they got it. The Assignment Editor learned that the windows on a 40-story building were blowing out, so he sent photographer Rob Pierce and a "live truck" (a vehicle with microwave equipment capable of transmitting T.V. directly; see below) to the scene. Pierce put a wireless microphone on himself and an eyewitness. The WTVJ anchors introduced the live-shot by saying "You're looking at a live picture of. . ." and then introduced Pierce and started to ask him questions. Pierce then walked over to a witness and let him explain what he'd seen to the camera.

It seems like a simple concept, but it was an unprecedented decision. Other stations are now experimenting with the same theme. In fact, KCNC in Denver has debuted a segment called "Point of View," which is basically a live-shot without a reporter. It's usually something that has a "soft" news edge, like a rally or street fair, and the photographer provides commentary while giving the viewers a P.O.V. look at what's going on around him.

(Editor's note: At press time, we learned of a news station that just debuted in New York City called "New York 1." The station has photographers *only*—no reporters—who conduct and photograph all the interviews by themselves. As the T.V. cliché goes: stay tuned. This may be the future of T.V. news.)

The photographer's role is expanding. As newsrooms tighten their finances, managers must use more creative approaches to cover the news. In Denver, considered one of the country's top markets for T.V. photographers, it has become a fairly standard procedure to send photographers to conduct interviews as well as take pictures. In fact, photogs will sometimes shoot the material for a "package" (a self-contained report from the field) and then have an anchor write and tape an audio track for it. Photographers will often shoot a "nat sound" package—a story that doesn't have a reporter's or anchor's narration, but instead relies entirely on the actual sounds of the event, interwoven with sound bites and interviews (and sometimes added music for transitions or to set a mood).

The point is, photographers will always have a place in the newsroom. And sometime soon, an enterprising T.V. photojournalist will become a star at a major spot news story. It's inevitable.

Live Truck Operators—Created in the early 1980's, vans capable of generating a microwave signal revolutionized the way news could be covered. "Live trucks," as they came to be known, are capable of transmitting ("feeding") tape from a remote location to the station or a live picture. The ability to "go live" from the scene has become an integral part of newscasts.

The live truck operator usually has an engineering background. He's responsible for getting to the location and "steering" in the shot. His ability to set-up quickly during a breaking story can make or break a newscast.

Since the mid-80's, a more dynamic form of live capability has evolved: the satellite truck, which, by linking up with a satellite in a fixed orbit, can feed tape or transmit a live picture from, literally, anywhere in the world. It has changed the complexion of the news business in ways that would require an entire book to explain properly.

A satellite truck operator needs to be one part truck driver, one part engineer, and one part journalist. It's a job that comes with a suitcase; the road is your home.

In the Rooms without Windows
Unlike people who work in the field, people who remain at the station throughout their work day never have to worry whether they should wear sunscreen, Gore-Tex, or layers of turtlenecks because of the weather. A newsroom can be an exciting place, but it's never as exciting as the field. However, it's always climate-controlled.

Indoor jobs are more numerous and varied than outdoor jobs. Let's start at the nexus of communication in a newsroom:

The Desk—No, you can't get a job as a piece of furniture, though some days you may feel like a doormat or a decorative plant. And, of course, a newsroom usually has lots of desks. But there's only one capital-D Desk: the Assignment Desk. And the person in charge of The Desk is usually the Assignment Editor or Assignment Manager.

The Desk's primary duty is to decide which stories will get covered and who's going to cover them. The Desk also makes sure the field crews know where they're going and what they're supposed to do. Once the crews have been sent out, The Desk acts as a dispatcher and information command center. All news cars are equipped with a much-dreaded two-way radio, which allows The Desk and the crews on the road to communicate with each other. Most of the information in the newsroom flows through The Desk in one form or another.

The Desk also has the unenviable task of monitoring the police scanners, the lifeline for learning about spot news. They're a fixture at every Assignment Desk in America—whether the Desk is at a television station, newspaper, or radio station. Scanners let you eavesdrop on fire departments, airports, ambulances, rescue teams, and even your competition. Unfortunately for The Desk, most of this electronic babble occurs simultaneously.

So, in addition to coordinating the crews and reporters, answering phones, sorting through faxes and mail, and so on, The Desk must isolate the occasional news item from the constant stream of mundane voice traffic on the scanners—an ugly proposition. And woe to The Desk that fails to hear about a big fire or wreck and gets scooped by the other stations. In fact, I knew an Assignment Editor who lost his job because he was an hour late in learning that a small farm town had been destroyed by a tornado. Losing an hour to the competition in a spot news story is an unforgivable sin.

The Desk is probably the most difficult, thankless, unappreciated job in the newsroom. When you talk to people in the business about working The Desk, they'll usually mutter something profound like, "Oh, that job really sucks." A good Desk person never relaxes, always haunted by the fear that he might be missing something important.

Of course, if you can handle The Desk, you will command a lot of respect in the newsroom. It's a good launching point for jobs in the upper management of the station.

Producers—Producers (or "Reducers," as we like to call them) are charged with organizing the many elements of a news show and putting them in the proper order (a.k.a. "stacking" a show). It sounds simple, but it's an art.

A Producer's greatest fear is that, when faced with three major stories, all of which could be the lead, he picks the wrong one. And Producers get instant feedback. If the other stations in town pick a different lead story, the Producer can look mighty stupid.

"What about individuality and creativity?" you ask. "Couldn't a different lead story *distinguish* the station instead of make it look bad?" Maybe, but never underestimate the lack of originality and creativity in the news business. Unless you've got an amazing exclusive, you want to have the same lead story as every other station in your market.

Not only do Producers need to determine which news stories are the most important, they also must create a "flow" to the broadcast. The "flow" —a hot buzzword in T.V. news these days—is simply the pacing of the show: how many times the anchors are on camera, how many tapes are used, how the story introductions and "teases" are set-up—in short, the structure of the newscast.

If your goal is to move into the ranks of news administration, the job of Producer is a good place to start. It's a position that requires a lot of contact with the people in the newsroom, and it provides a solid education in the myriad details of the news process.

Anchor—This position is the *raison d'être*, the meal ticket, the golden biscuit in television journalism.

The primary anchors—the folks who sit down each night at 6:00pm and 11:00pm (5:00pm and 10:00pm in the Heartland) and read the news—are the most identifiable images a newsroom has. They are beamed into your living room every night to tell you what's happening in your community and why it's important for you to know. For Mr. and Mrs. Joe Six-Pack, the anchors *are* the news. But for the people who work in the newsroom, the anchors are an anomaly.

Most viewers identify a news show with the anchors who "star" in the show. The countless people who work zillions of hours to create a good newscast mean nothing to the average viewer. John Q. Public knows that Peter Jennings is the anchor of ABC's evening newscast, but they sure as hell don't know—or care—who the show's Executive Producer is. (It's currently Paul Friedman, for all you above-average viewers out there.)

An anchor's importance in a newsroom is usually inversely proportional to the amount of work he actually performs. Most anchors in major markets are often little more than readers. Typically, they do very little writing, and they rarely leave the station and actually report a story (unless it's a ratings period and the news director decides to get the anchor into a high-profile series). In fact, they usually just give their scripts a once-over and check their hair and make-up.

Well, okay—that's a little strong. After all, Lynn is a weekend anchor, and she's one of the hardest working reporters I know. Many anchors do roll up their sleeves and get involved in the news process. They often assume the role of Managing Editor: overseeing, evaluating, and arranging the elements in "their" newscast. But to be sure, they're a minority. Instead of being working journalists, a lot of anchors are making appearances on behalf of the station at shopping malls and charity events, or deciding where to eat dinner, while the dreary process of putting the show together takes place.

There's sort of a cruel irony in the fact that the best-known—and usually the best-paid—people in a news operation have scant hands-on interaction with the news. Remember William Hurt in the movie *Broadcast News*? His role was a fairly accurate portrayal of a lot of anchors—an attractive, well-coiffured newsman with an ability to think on his feet. The fact that he didn't know much about the nuts and bolts of the T.V. news business didn't hinder his success. Neither did his lack of knowledge about world events. He looked natural on camera, and people were comfortable watching him—those were his keys to success.

Lately, though, one major trend has appeared in local news that puts the anchor in the center of a tough situation. When a jet crashes into a suburb or a riot erupts downtown, the anchors are getting thrust into a pivotal position, as many stations now put them in a newsroom setting when major spot news occurs. When all hell breaks loose and the station has interrupted *Wheel of Fortune* with an urgent news bulletin, the anchor must become the information conduit to anxious viewers. Not unlike the scene in *Broadcast News* where William Hurt deftly handles a fast-breaking story (with a lot of help from his Producer), today's anchors must be able to handle hot, chaotic spot news. Their ability to absorb a lot of often conflicting information and present it succinctly and accurately can make or break a station's coverage.

A few years ago, when a DC-9 crashed on take-off from Stapleton International Airport in Denver, the initial reports indicated that over 150 people were on board—and that all had perished. Our station confirmed this information with the Federal Aviation Administration in Seattle, and our anchor (who shall remain nameless) delivered this report, with all the usual qualifications attached.

Unfortunately, the information was completely inaccurate. In fact, there were 82 on board, 26 of whom died. Though the anchor corrected the error quickly, the damage had been done. Despite excellent coverage later, that one mistake haunted us, crippling our credibility. It also haunted the people who had friends and relatives on the ill-fated flight. Because their favorite news station had told them so, they thought for several minutes that their loved ones were dead. Obviously, we weren't their favorite news station after that.

Despite these risks and despite the grumbling (mainly from envy) of your colleagues, the anchor desk is the place to be for name recognition and glamor in television journalism. The workload may be light, but not everyone can stare steely-eyed into a camera, read often fast-changing copy without a flub, and convince the public he's trustworthy. And though anchors make the most money, their jobs are extremely tenuous. When the ratings plummet, News Directors will change anchors as a quick-fix. They're the most visible link to the community, but it's a fragile link.

The Supporting Cast—A variety of folks contribute to each newscast. I'll briefly describe these positions:

Writers: They assist with—what else?—writing the news.

Editors: They edit videotape, rather than news copy. Using the raw field tapes shot by photographers and the feed tapes sent via the network and various syndication sources, they edit and create the video package according to scripts written by reporters and writers.

Sports Producer: Most large newsrooms have one person responsible for coordinating the station's sports coverage.

Graphic Artist: This has become an extremely important position in today's newsroom. These people are versed in the art of using a rather complex device called an "Artstar" or a "Paintbox." With this piece of technology, they create all the graphics used during a newscast. If you watch a news program closely, you'll be amazed at the quantity (and, sometimes, the quality) of the graphics used.

E.N.G. Engineer: This person is a technician responsible for fixing and maintaining all the cameras, recorders, editors, etc. in a newsroom.

Playback: This person is responsible for ensuring that all tapes in a newscast are played in the correct order. This position is usually combined with additional responsibilities.

Feed Room: No, this isn't the station's cafeteria. The Feed Room is where all incoming microwave and satellite feeds are coordinated. Every live-shot must be "steered in" by the folks in the Feed Room. They adjust video and audio levels, and if there's any incoming tape, they record it here. The Feed Room can become a very hectic place an hour before a newscast.

The Control Room

The people in the Control Room, a bridge between the News Department and the Production Department, are responsible for actually putting the news on television. Since all T.V. news is done live, getting the show on the air can be a dicey proposition. People in the Control Room work in an environment that leaves no room for mistakes, because if you make a mistake it's immediately on T.V., and then the guy at home can sit on his sofa and make derogatory remarks about the morons at "Live at Five." Here's a rundown of the jobs in the Control Room:

Director—The dictator of the Control Room, the Director gives the commands to change camera angles, set up graphics, roll tape, etc. He is responsible for giving the show a clean look, free of technical errors.

On a day when everything is falling into place, the Director remains serene, and the task of putting a live show on the air seems easy. But when a late-breaking story on a gang shooting becomes the lead story only ten minutes before air, and they've got two live-shots from the scene plus fresh tape—well, maybe *some* tape, nobody's sure if it'll be edited in time to be useful—and the satellite remote from the crew at the nuclear power plant is in trouble because the truck has a mysterious power failure and they're not sure if they can get back on-line, and one of the tape playback machines just broke—this is when a Director earns his paycheck. It's this kind of "rock 'n roll television" that separates the good directors from the mediocre.

Technical Director—The "T.D." operates an elaborate piece of video technology called a "switcher," which lets him manipulate various video sources and effects and put them on the air. The T.D. takes all his cues from the Director. In smaller markets, the Director "switches" his own show—and on days like the one described above, he *really* earns his paycheck.

Audio—As the name implies, this person sits at an audio board and controls all the sound aspects of the show.

Chyron—This person types and controls all the "fonts" in a news show. Fonts resemble very brief captions beneath the picture, and they identify who's talking and where the story was shot. They usually appear in the bottom third of the screen and look like this:

Dr. Jane Doe
Psychotherapist

Or, they may be a simple geographic locator:

Bayonne, New Jersey

Finally, most reporters get a font at the beginning or end of each story:

Lynn Setzer

KMGH 7 News

E.S.S.—Short for "Electronic Still Store." At a large control room, one person may be responsible for a device that "captures" video images for use at a later time. Mostly, E.S.S. is used for graphics, but there are other uses.

Obviously, a newsroom offers a variety of jobs that require a multitude of skills. Whether your goal is to become an anchor, a graphic artist, or a News Director, we can offer one piece of advice: In your first job, become familiar with as many different jobs as possible. You may find you're more successful behind the camera than in front of it. And as you move up the T.V. news ladder, you'll be required to become more of a specialist, and you'll find it's harder to try out the various jobs—and the risks are greater if you screw up the job you've got.

A Day in the Life

> "We welcome almost any break in the monotony of
> things, and a man has only to murder a series of
> wives in a new way to become known to millions
> who have never heard of Homer."
> —Robert Lynd (1879-1949)

It's 1:00am in Denver, and in Los Angeles, the city is burning.

Nine hours after a jury delivered a controversial verdict in the trial of L.A. police officers accused of beating Rodney King, producer Glenna Stacer's adrenalin is pumping. Most of Denver is sleeping.

Stacer's workday starts at 1:00am, but she's been listening to the local talk radio station since 11:00pm. She knows the rioting in L.A. is getting worse, and her job is to get the story on the air by the time most people are rubbing the sleep out of their eyes.

"People will be waking up and hearing about this for the first time," she says. She wants her coverage to be informative, timely, and compelling. What she wants and what she gets is often different, but that's the way it is in the news business. She's gotten used to it.

The Early Morning Show

At 1:00am, Stacer is alone in the newsroom on the second floor

of the KMGH-TV building. The police scanners squawk intermittently; computer monitors glow, silent; the fax machine spits
out a press release now and then. She watches the 10:00pm
newscast from the night before, reads the wire service reports,
and calls the CBS network to request a live-shot from L.A. for
the 6:30am show. CBS says OK.

So far, so good.

At 4:00am, photographer Steve Kady walks in. He'll work
with the morning reporter, who should arrive soon. Stacer will
assign them to get "man on the street" reaction to what's happening in L.A., and she wants them to do a live report from
downtown Denver for the show.

But her plans change quickly after the phone call she gets at
4:30am—the morning reporter calls in sick. Stacer now has no
reporter for her show, so she sends Kady out to get the local
reaction by himself.

At 5:00am, the majority of the early morning staff arrives:
director Marthalea Krell pours some coffee and logs on to her
computer; anchor Anne Trujillo comes in looking fresh and
awake; video editors Mike LeClaire and Jim Barber settle into
their editing suites, turning on the equipment and pulling a fresh
supply of tapes.

At the other end of the second floor, the production staff is
gearing up as well: floor director Don McKnight (who points
the anchors to the correct camera and tells them to "stand by"),
technical director (T.D.) and E.S.S. operator Eric Hill, who heads
to the Control Room, where he is joined by audio expert Dave
Kintzele, Chyron operator Richard Yribia, robo-cam operator
Joe Contreras (more on the robo-cams below), and TelePrompTer
operator Liz Zachariah.

By 5:15am, everyone has logged on to a computer and is
reviewing what Stacer has planned for the show (a.k.a. "the
run-down").

Trujillo, the anchor, has discussed the newscast with Stacer,
and she begins to read the scripts Stacer has prepared. That will
consume most of her time until the show at 6:30am.

It's the job of the director, Marthalea Krell, to take what's on paper and translate it into T.V. She reviews the run-down as well, talking with Stacer about camera shots, graphics (the pictures that appear over the anchor's shoulder), and whether the story is a VO (voice-over) or a VO/SOT (voice-over into a sound bite). Krell calls the shots in the Control Room during the newscast, and she needs to be familiar with how the show is "stacked."

At 5:30am, the daytime assignment editor, Pat Ketchum, arrives, grabs a cup of coffee, and gets a briefing on what's happening. Though a list of possible stories for the day was compiled yesterday, she knows it will change. No one predicted the riots would get worse.

Stacer has been watching the other two Denver T.V. stations, and their networks' coverage of L.A. is riveting. "Everyone here was watching it as they came in to work," she said. "There was this incredible live-shot from an ABC reporter in L.A. You saw people starting to loot this shopping center, and then you saw wisps of smoke coming from the building."

But, unlike the competition, CBS doesn't deliver those compelling scenes—and they won't deliver the promised live-shot from L.A., either. Stacer learns this bad news at 6:00am, 30 minutes before air time. Once again, she scrambles. She and the anchor prepare a story using CBS footage transmitted to KMGH via satellite during the night. It's not as up-to-the-minute as the competition, but it will have to do.

It's 6:15am, 15 minutes before air time, and the Control Room is filled with people. Krell talks to the crew through headsets, Kintzele adjusts audio levels for the anchor's voice, the studio lights go full up, the cameras move into place.

At 6:25am, Stacer walks down to the Control Room to get her show on the air.

Trujillo is in the anchor chair and takes a quick look in the mirror. The floor director tells her to "stand by" and then cues her.

It's 6:30am—air time—and the show is quite different from the one Stacer envisioned five and half hours earlier. She says with a sigh, "I did what I could with what I had."

The Midday Show

The day in a T.V. newsroom is a continuous process of shifting gears, of making the transition from one story to the next, one newscast to the next. A half-hour after the early morning show ends, the 11:30am newscast and the 5:00pm show are under construction. The producer of the 11:30am show, Mark Durham, has been at the station since 5:00am. The first two "daytime" photographers arrive at 7:00am.

At 7:30am, Brad Remington, the managing editor, calls the Assignment Desk from his home. He wants Ketchum to start making phone calls, lining up Denver leaders to interview for their reaction to the verdict and the rioting. It's the first of many times during the day that he and Ketchum will confer. Ketchum gets on the phone to arrange for interviews and find out where the mayor, the police chief, and others will be during the day.

Remington is now in his car, on his way to the station. During his 25-minute drive, he considers which stories they should cover. He's switching his radio dial back and forth between the talk station and National Public Radio. He had already read one of Denver's morning newspapers over coffee at home.

By 8:30am, the newsroom is noisy with police scanners, ringing phones, and conversation. It's time for the morning meeting to begin. Reporters, a few photographers, Terri Simonich (producer of the 5:00pm show), Durham, Remington, Ketchum, and assistant news director Bill Gray all assemble around the conference table.

Remington runs the meeting, and Ketchum fills in the details: the mayor will be available at 10:00am, the police chief at noon, and other notables are being called.

Reporters are assigned, ideas are kicked around: How about sending a reporter and photographer to Denver's predominately black neighborhood, and have them ride with a cop assigned to the area? Remington and Gray like it, and reporter Pat Woodard gets the story, with photographers Perry Drake and Hank Bargine. Woodard is a fine reporter—one of the best "storytellers" around—and Remington knows he'll handle the piece with sensitivity and style.

Most of the local angles are covered, so someone suggests the obvious: Why not send a crew to L.A.? With its own people in place, the station wouldn't need to depend so much on the network. CBS had already gotten over 500 requests for live-shots from L.A. that day—and that was from U.S. stations alone. The suggestion is discussed for 15 minutes.

"Our main concern was the safety of the people we'd be sending there," Bill Gray says. "Plus, we didn't know if we could even fly into the L.A. airport. Cost was not really a factor. When it comes to spot news, the budget is a minor consideration."

The idea is nixed. The station management does not think it's safe. In addition, the station has a sister station, KGTV in San Diego, that can provide live-shots if necessary.*

Most of the reporters exit the station by 9:00am and start working on their stories.

Durham leaves the meeting and gets back to creating his show. He lands a lucky break—he'll get a live-shot from the CBS reporter in L.A.

A call comes in to the Assignment Desk. A community group has organized a rally at the State Capitol to protest the verdict, and they want the station to cover it. Ketchum decides to send a reporter and photographer, and Durham wants a live report for his show.

The scanners at the Assignment Desk are crackling and chattering, and the people at "The Desk" are listening closely for any reports of violence in Denver. Working the Desk is one of the most difficult jobs in the newsroom. At any given minute, Ketchum is answering calls from the public, talking to crews in the field on the two-way radio, and trying to monitor hundreds of frequencies on the police and emergency scanners. It's a bad job for someone prone to headaches. And today, there's increased tension—a minor traffic accident could escalate into a huge brawl. Ketchum wishes she had an extra ear—or at least an in-

---

*As it turned out, covering the riots overwhelmed KGTV (as well as most L.A.-area media), and they were unable to assist KMGH until the next day.

tern or two. Unfortunately, KMGH has only a sporadic internship program, and there are no interns at the station this month. (However, when the station does have interns, they often work at the Assignment Desk.)

By 9:30am, the morning meeting adjourns, and people scatter. Terri Simonich begins to format her 5:00pm newscast based on the topics discussed in the meeting, but she knows the show can change during the course of the day. In fact, she expects it. Her job will be to take the news of the day and cram it into about 12 minutes. (The rest of the air time will go for sports, weather, etc.) KMGH runs a half-hour newscast at 5:00pm, though its competition has one-hour shows. This is one of those days when everyone in the newsroom wishes the show had another 30 minutes.

Two hours later, the 11:30am broadcast is on the air, anchored by Trujillo. There's a live report from the riot area in L.A., a live-shot from the rally at the Capitol in Denver, and a series of reactions from leaders in Colorado and around the country. It's a good show.

At noon, the monitors in the newsroom are tuned to the other two Denver stations. Most people keep an eye on the competition during the day, and especially during newscasts. There's a sense in the newsroom that the other stations are handling the story better. "Around here, people felt that CBS was not doing as well as NBC and ABC covering this story," Remington said.

That's frustrating. As a local affiliate, the station is at the mercy of the network when it comes to video and live-shots outside Colorado. Of course, the station can cover the local scene as well as anyone, but what viewers wanted to see were pictures from L.A. And it really hurts when they can see great coverage on another station.

The Afternoon Show
There's a calm around lunchtime. Most of the reporters and photographers are out on stories, Simonich is busy writing, and Ketchum is still manning the Desk. Remington grabs a quick

lunch at Burger King and heads back to the station. He doesn't want to go far in case something major happens.

By 2:00pm, the quiet is replaced by a growing frenzy. Reporters and photographers are coming back from their stories, and the "night staff" arrives. On the news side of the second floor, the night crew is made up of a reporter, three photographers, one producer, a writer, an assignment editor, three video editors, and a live-truck engineer. On the production side, the night staff is a director, a T.D., an audio person, a Chyron operator, an E.S.S. operator, a floor director, a robo-cam operator, and a TelePrompTer operator.

The two principal anchors arrive at 2:00pm as well. They will handle the 5:00pm and 10:00pm broadcasts.

The afternoon meeting begins shortly after 2:00pm. Remington and Ketchum review what's been covered, who handled which story, and the status of each report.

At the meeting, Woodard says his "ride-along" with the cop in the black neighborhood turned out well. Photographer Hank Bargine had a run-in with some combative kids. They threatened him, he got it on tape, and the altercation will air in Woodard's piece. The march at the Capitol was peaceful, but vocal— another "minute-thirty package" (a story that will run one minute, 30 seconds). Plus, there are "re-acts" (reactions) from community leaders; Ketchum's early morning phone calls paid off. And during the day, a photographer shot video of a guy holding a protest sign on a street corner near Denver—one man's way of expressing his rage. That will make it onto the 5:00pm show, too.

The 10:00pm producer, Dave Mitchell, is taking notes, deciding which of the 5:00pm stories he'll use, and in what form. Remington suggests the night reporter, Lance Hernandez, get more reaction from Denver cops. And reporter Julie Hayden will contact a local gang counselor to see if she can interview gang members. Both will be fresh stories for the late newscast.

The afternoon meeting is over, and once again, the baton has been passed. As the day crew begins to wind down, the night staff is just warming up.

Andy Dudley is the director for the 5:00pm and 10:00pm shows. When he arrived at 2:00pm, he logged on to his computer and checked the run-down for the 5:00pm show. He also talked to Simonich about the graphics she'll want, and he begins to work on which camera shots to use and how he'll "block" the show.

At 3:00pm, the video editors' fingers are flying. Woodard sits in the editing suite with Kyle Burdash, overseeing the "cutting" of his story. Simonich checks on the progress of the 5:00pm show—Are the stories written? Have the scripts been approved by Remington? When will editing begin? Everything is going well except for one big element: Once again, CBS will not provide a live report from L.A. Hundreds of buildings in south-central L.A. are in flames, people are being beaten and killed, and CBS's Denver affiliate must settle for a voiced-over package. People in the newsroom utter silent, and some not-so-silent, profanities.

Throughout the afternoon, anchors Bertha Lynn and Ernie Bjorkman are reading scripts, updating information, and suggesting changes. A few minutes before air, they will apply their make-up, freshen their faces, and head to the set.

Simonich makes one last check. She has a tight show, time-wise, and needs the stories short, but good. She grabs her scripts and walks down to the Control Room, hoping all will go smoothly.

In the Control Room, the lights from dozens of T.V. monitors cast a flickering, somewhat eerie glow. This is the nucleus of the action during the newscast, but it's quiet and calm. Dudley is talking to technical director Jeff Hammond through his headsets, asking if the "effects" are ready. Hammond takes his cues from Dudley, pushing buttons to produce the special effects viewers will see on the screen. A good T.D. like Hammond is a blessing; a bad one can make a newscast look like it's being run by the Marx Brothers. Audio expert Dave Tessier sits alone in the "padded room," also called the "audio booth." The padding is sound-proofing foam. During the course of the newscast, Tessier will turn on the anchor's microphone when needed, and off when not needed. It's a crucial job, because when there's a mistake, the viewers can hear some pretty funny—and often embarrassing—stuff. In another part of the Control Room, Joanne Neale, the Chyron operator, is frantically typing the "fonts." Next to her lies an invaluable tool: a dictionary. Misspelled words and wrong sports scores are the stuff of Neale's nightmares.

In the studio, Bjorkman and Lynn are reviewing their scripts. Floor director Danny McClosky, who's worked in television news since the 1960's, is the anchors' link to the Control Room. If all hell starts breaking loose, he's the one who must keep the studio calm and focused. The robo-cam operator, Lynn Simonson, sits in the corner behind a bank of monitors. Many stations have replaced camera operators with robots. The huge robo-cams move by themselves across the floor and into position, and Simonson programs them and keeps them moving. Manning the studio cameras used to require three people; now it takes only one. Welcome to the brave new world.

The seconds tick by. It's 4:59:30pm, and the closing music of *Oprah* wafts through the studio speakers. McClosky tells the anchors, "Stand by—30 seconds." 5:00pm. The theme music for the newscast begins. "Now, live from Denver, KMGH 7 *News at Five*." McClosky cues the anchors. The show begins.

In the newsroom, people gather around the monitors and watch all three Denver stations. The discussion is a mixture of critique, praise, and relief. The local stories on KMGH are good, but what's missing, a lot of people think, is the "live presence" from Los Angeles. The competition has it. KMGH doesn't.

Dave Mitchell, the producer of the 10:00pm show, ignores the newsroom critics. He's watching the 5:00pm broadcast closely and sending computer messages to the reporters: Can they rewrite their story for 10:00pm? Can they cut their story down to a voice-over sound version that runs 45 seconds?

And, once again, a call is placed to CBS, requesting a live report from L.A. at 10:00pm.

By the time the 5:00pm newscast is over, reporter Julie Hayden and photographer Aaron Tomlinson are out on their story, and a preliminary run-down of the late show is in the computer. The night assignment editor Wayne Harrison replaces Ketchum, who goes home after a 12-hour day.

Remington and the other managers sit down to critique the 5:00pm show. Over all, they are pleased, and they don't regret the decision not to send a crew to L.A.

After the "postmortem" (what many stations call the critique of a show), Remington works on a story list for the next day, not knowing what will happen overnight in Los Angeles or Denver. Every evening, a list of possible stories is compiled for the next day. "Day files" (a file for each day of the month) are filled with story ideas and press releases—a tiny fraction of which will make it onto the newscast. But one of the great horrors of assignment editors is opening a day file and finding it empty!

By 6:00pm, reporters and photographers begin to drift out of the newsroom, heading home. For some, it's been a 10- or 12-hour day, and they fear tomorrow won't be any easier.

The Evening Show

Out in "the field," Hayden and Tomlinson are following the gang counselor, cruising, looking for gang members. They find them at their usual hang-outs. Hayden asks them what they think of the situation in L.A., and their responses are predictable. They're angry at the cops, but they say they'll keep their cool in Denver. It's good T.V., and Hayden and Tomlinson head back to the station with a solid story for the 10:00pm show.

As the evening progresses, the news from L.A. gets more tense. National Guard troops are called in, and the Associated Press wire is beeping almost constantly with alerts on the latest. There's a tension in the newsroom as people sense that at any moment the situation could get much worse. Because the news is changing so fast, some people stay past their usual quitting time to help Mitchell with the 10:00pm show. Weekend producer Chris Oldroyd volunteers to stay and help write the show. On a day like this, most news junkies don't mind working long hours. This is a huge, breaking story. If they can't be in L.A., then the newsroom is where most journalists want to be.

The night assignment editor Harrison keeps vigil over the scanners. There are reports of rioting in Atlanta, San Francisco, and Las Vegas. Like Los Angeles, Denver has a problem with violent urban gangs, and despite the gang members' assurances, violence could erupt at any time.

By 8:00pm, the late show is in the computer. Dudley takes a look at it and begins his work. The anchors start reading scripts.

CBS calls the producer and delivers bad news once again: no live-shot from L.A. for the 10:00pm show. They've just had too many requests. Mitchell will have to settle for another voiced-over report.

The night editors are frantically cutting video tape as it comes in. Hayden is in an editing booth, watching her story as it's cut. The production staff at the other end of the hall is preparing for the late broadcast, repeating the jobs they did for the 5:00pm show.

The 10:00pm show goes smoothly. The time allotted for sports and weather gets reduced a little to give more time to the L.A. coverage. There's no grumbling from the weatherman or the sports anchor on a day like today. The only missing element from the show is a live-shot. But it's too late to second-guess. Maybe tomorrow CBS will come through.

By 11:00pm, Mitchell, the anchors, and the news and production staffs are leaving. Mitchell leaves notes for Glenna Stacer. In two hours, her day will begin, and the process starts all over again.

This is a fairly comprehensive description of one particular day in the newsroom of a local television station. However, there is no "typical" day in a newsroom. Some days are frantic, some days are rather slow, but there's always a sense that, at any minute, things could change radically. That's why so-called "adrenaline junkies" get into the T.V. news business. No matter what job you hold in the newsroom, you must always be ready to change gears. What starts as a predictable, unexciting news day can end as a day you'll always remember. No one in this

Denver newsroom, from the news director to the floor direc-
tor, will forget the shock of the Rodney King verdict when it
hit the newswire, and no one will forget the pictures of Los
Angeles under siege.

It's 1:00am. Glenna Stacer rides the elevator to the second floor and walks into an empty newsroom. The police scanners squawk intermittently; computer monitors glow, silent; the fax machine spits out a press release now and then. She watches the 10:00pm newscast from the night before, reads the wire service reports, and calls the CBS network to request a live-shot from L.A. for the 6:30am show. In a few hours, the room will be filled with energy. Another day in the news business has begun.

"Television is the first truly democratic culture—
the first culture available to everybody and entirely
governed by what the people want. The most
terrifying thing is what the people do want."
—Clive Barnes, British drama critic

Chapter 4

A Tale of Two Stations

*"Television is a medium of entertainment
which permits millions of people to
listen to the same joke at the same
time, and yet remain lonesome."*
—T.S. Elliot (1888-1965)

Cheyenne, Wyoming sprouts from the high plains at the cross-roads of Interstates 80 and 25. Among other things, Cheyenne is the gateway to Curt Gowdy State Park. To get into town, you drive across a viaduct over the Union Pacific rail yards. The rail yard tower splits the roadway and rises above the town like an isolated sentry. One of the primary downtown streets, Lincolnway, is dotted with aging storefronts, home to businesses like The Wrangler and The Cheyenne Outfitter.

Though it's the state capital and the home of F.E. Warren Air Force base, Cheyenne is still very much a frontier town. The city lights do not burn brightly, as its nearly 50,000 residents continue to weather the devastating effects of an oil economy gone bust. There's no large university and no big sports teams, and major performers don't schedule Cheyenne on their concert tours. However, the rodeo has a big impact on the town, and cowboys are a fact of life there, not simply a tired gimmick in a jeans ad.

Cheyenne, the 195th-ranked television market, has only one

local television station. In T.V.-land, it's a remote outpost of civilization in the least densely populated state in the country. But—brace yourself—it's the type of situation you'll be looking at, maybe even *praying for*, when you're searching for your first job in television news.

The odds of your landing a first job at a station in New York, Miami, Seattle, or even Kansas City are slim. Actually, that's an overstatement. They're infinitesimal, microscopic, negligible. You'd be wise to get out your atlas and brush up on geography, because you'll have a much better chance getting a meaningful job in places like Augusta (Georgia), Monroe (Louisiana), and Fort Wayne (Indiana).

KGWN, a CBS-affiliate and a part of the Great Western Network, is the only T.V. station in Cheyenne. Headquartered in a solitary, boxy building on the eastern edge of town, KGWN employs a staff of 16 news people.

"We have a very aggressive attitude for a small market," Brian Olson, the News Director and co-anchor of the evening *Newsource 5 News Hour*, explains. "Due to our location,* we have to compete directly with Denver. In fact, five years ago, KUSA** was the highest rated 10:00pm news in Cheyenne. People here wanted to know why our newscasts didn't look like those coming out of Denver. We're faced with a situation where we have to satisfy champagne tastes with a beer budget."

To compete, Olson has taken a more formatted approach to the station's news coverage, adding daily health reports and more consumer features and commentaries. He's also taken advantage of a unique graduate program run by the Medill School of Journalism at Northwestern University, whose graduate students operate a bureau in Washington, D.C. Smaller stations like KGWN can subscribe to their program. Each semester, Medill assigns one student to the subscribing station to cover the national angles of Wyoming stories.

Editor's note: Cheyenne, about 100 miles north of Denver, has one of the highest cable T.V. penetration rates in the country, so its market is saturated with Denver stations.

**Denver's ABC-affiliate.

Olson thinks the program has been a great success. In fact, he's hired three Medill graduates to join his staff in Cheyenne. But here's where we get to the bad news for entry-level job seekers: "We stopped doing entry-level hiring four years ago," Olson says matter-of-factly. "We've been able to get experienced people."

This is a stunning statement. If I were a junior or senior in college, or anyone looking for that first job in T.V. news, Olson's comment would totally ruin my day. The sole station in the 195th market—for God's sake, there are only 210 markets out there in the whole U.S. of A.!—does not hire entry-level people. That is captial-U Ugly. It is, however, a harbinger of life in television news in the 1990's.

"I want 'gunners,' people who can hit the ground running," Olson says. "They have a basic knowledge of what they're doing, and we'll just refine them a bit. Sure, I can hire people who are adequate and keep them at the station for years. But I'd rather have good people who will stay here for a few years before moving up in the business.

"We work the hell out of them," he continues. "You'll find out if you've got the stuff to get past the first six months in the business. And this is where you'll find out what you're going to end up doing in news."

With a staff of only 16, each member of the KGWN news team gets to wear many hats. As noted above, Olson is both News Director and co-anchor of the 5:00pm show. The Assistant News Director, Glen Campbell, also works as a political reporter and the co-anchor of the 10:00pm newscast. Lisa Howell produces the 5:30pm show, does the on-camera newsbrief at 3:30pm, and creates a cutesy segment called "Li'l Orphan Animal." The weekend anchor, Janet Kohler, also produces the weekend shows (a common practice in small markets) and then works as a city-beat reporter during the week. Beth Hobbs, another weekday reporter, concentrates on county government, politics, and education. Diana Miller fills a seven-minute "healthcast" each day. A freelancer in Jackson, Wyoming contributes several stories a week.

In addition to the crew in Cheyenne, Ron Sniffen operates

as a "one-man band" in nearby Laramie, home of the University of Wyoming. (A "one-man band" is someone who photographs, writes, and edits his own stories.) Six interns assist Sniffen, but they aren't limited to minor, "go-fer" type roles. In fact, they can flesh-out their own stories and get them on the air. It's invaluable experience for a college student.

Sports and weather anchors round-out the on-air staff. Three photographers shoot most of the video for the two daily newscasts. Occasionally, though, the need will arise for a reporter to grab the gear and shoot his own story—a fact of life in a small market where people and resources are stretched as tight as they'll go.

The key to success at a station like KGWN is versatility. In the early stages of your T.V. career, you've got to know how to do as many things as possible. Specialization is for big staffs with big budgets. In the hinterlands, money and equipment will be in short supply. Your motto will always be: More with Less.

At a small station, a lot of things won't be working in your favor. Television is increasingly a high-tech endeavor, and each bell and whistle can cost thousands, or tens of thousands, of dollars. In a place like Cheyenne, you won't be using equipment on the cutting edge of technology. In fact, you'll be lucky if it's working at all.

The newsroom at KGWN is small and cramped. A few desks, shelves, and stacks of paper occupy most of the available space. Several computer monitors—part of the computerized Associated Press wire service—dot the room.

The news department has one "live truck," a vehicle from which reports from the field can be broadcast live or tape can be beamed to the station. But these days, one live truck isn't much. (For example, KMGH in Denver has four live trucks, a satellite truck, and a helicopter with microwave transmission equipment.) However, it does give the station a live presence, which is crucial in covering breaking stories. It also allows the reporters to gain experience doing live-shots, an essential skill in today's newsroom.

KGWN doesn't let its slim resources impede its aspirations,

though. In early 1991, the station expanded its 5:00pm news show to an hour. "We're very ambitious," Olson says. "At first, we weren't sure how we were going to fill an hour every day, but now our problem is that we're actually tight on time on most days."

Most assignments are posted the night before, and, unlike the practice at bigger stations, there is no set morning meeting. The crews call the newsroom each morning to see if there have been any changes or late developments.

Reporters at KGWN need to stretch their day, because they must write for two newscasts (5:30pm and 10:00pm). "If a story on our early newscast is important enough to run again at 10:00pm, it gets totally rewritten. We always have completely fresh material; we don't re-run any stories," Olson explains.

The day I visited the station, the show's lead story was a "reader" (a story without supporting video; the anchor simply reads copy on camera) about a small number of troops from the local Air Force Base being sent to the Persian Gulf. The second story was a local package concerning a change in the hours for the local public school system. A VO ("voice-over" —an on-air technique where the anchor reads a script while edited video is aired) on the temporary closure of the main gate at the Air Force Base and a VSV (more alphabet soup—this stands for "voice-over, sound, voice-over." The anchor reads a script while edited video airs until it hits a sound bite—a piece of an interview, usually— and then reads more script over edited video after the bite) about a school fundraiser followed. The final segment in the first section, provided by an intern, was about a peace activist appearing at the University of Wyoming. Let this emphasize both the importance of internships (a topic discussed in more depth later) and the flexibility of a small-market station. A student who can actually get his stories on the air has a great advantage when it's time to make the all-important job-getter, a résumé tape.

Next, "Hey, What's the Deal?" is KGWN's version of an investigative report, and it leads the second block of the newscast. Today, the story concerns some teenagers picketing a local Taco Bell. Their issue is sexual discrimination: the chain won't hire one of the boys because his hair is too long. The next story, also a local package, involves the American Legion's assistance to families involved in Operation Desert Storm. The rest of the hour is filled with sports, weather, national headlines, and a fairly long health segment.

The newscast is clean technically and without glitches. I'm surprised at the large number of local reports; they're a big effort for a small staff. Of course, no one is going to confuse the *News Source 5 News Hour* with the *CBS Evening News*, and on their best day, KGWN is not going to approximate even the worst newscast in a top-50 market.

But that would be a totally unfair comparison anyway, and for the 195th-ranked market, KGWN has a polished product. More importantly (from this book's perspective), the staff there is gaining terrific experience. Each day, they learn a little more about their craft and about television journalism, and they have daily opportunities to polish their skills. Of course, most of the staff makes a fairly meager wage, but that goes with the territory. No one makes much money in small markets. But one day, most of the people on staff at KGWN will land a job in a bigger, and better-paying, market. People have left this station for places like Albuquerque, Las Vegas, and even Chicago Cablevision. They moved up another rung on the T.V. news ladder, and for most people in the business, that's what it's all about.

A Top Station

The first thing you notice is that the traffic is moving at an alarming rate of speed. A mere 60 m.p.h. won't cut it here. In fact, I'm cruising along at 65 m.p.h., and I'm steadily losing ground. In response to the increasing congestion, cars are swooping into the breakdown lane, making it an *ad hoc* fourth lane. So what happens if you actually have a problem with your car and you need to pull over to the side of the road? The side of the road is not a safe place here.

I'm driving on Massachusetts 128, part of a beltway system around Boston and the East Coast version of Silicon Valley. Despite some retrenchment during the recent recession, this area remains a mecca of high technology.

As I approach Needham, one of the many towns around the perimeter of metro Boston, I notice a series of massive broadcast towers along both sides of the highway. They're so huge, they're almost surreal, and the steel skeletons seem to pierce the lower reaches of the atmosphere as they deliver their payload of television programming.

WCVB, nestled amidst the huge towers, offers a deceptively modest appearance. I drive down the short entrance road to the station, confronted with an array of satellite dishes and microwave towers. Among all this broadcasting hardware, I hardly notice the unobtrusive brick building that serves as the headquarters of one of the country's premier television outlets.

Inside, the station pulses with activity. This is the Big Time. Boston is the sixth-largest T.V. market in the country; its ADI* comprises over two million television households. And WCVB, an ABC-affiliate, has established itself as one of the best local stations in the country.

"It's a sophisticated market," Emily Rooney, the Vice-President of News for WCVB, explains. "This is a very staid community. People born here tend to live here all their lives. It's a very 'intune' populace, concerned with local politics and the issues that affect the city."

It's also an extremely competitive television market, and WCVB has the upper hand in the local news wars. They win in the morning, at noon, and at six. Only its late news occasionally loses to its primary competitor WBZ, an NBC-affiliate. WHDH, a perennial third in the Boston market, creates a respectable product—a show that many News Directors would kill for—but it's the annual loser in the ratings game.

Over 100 people work at WCVB's "Newscenter 5" —and this doesn't include the editing staff and other technicians affiliated with the news department. "Working here is sort of a lifer thing,"

---

*The Area of Dominent Influence, a geographic market design that defines each T.V. market. It was primarily based on the signal strength of the transmitters in each market, but now it's basically measured by audience viewing patterns. Additionally, there is no overlap in the markets.

Rooney says. "When people come here they tend to stay. A lot of people started here right out of college, and they've never left." In fact, 69 people have been with the station since it signed-on over 20 years ago.

The station is well-equipped to retain its leadership position in local news. The staff includes 18 full-time reporters and 15 photographers. They have two satellite trucks, three fully-loaded live vans, plus several more vehicles with a less-elaborate microwave system. However, WCVB has been hurt by the recent recession, which has hit New England especially hard. "We're not quite as global in our coverage as we once were," Rooney admits. "Our staff is smaller, but we haven't had to lay anyone off. We just haven't replaced those who have retired or left."

WCVB's coverage of the day's news usually starts the night before. "We pretty much know what we're going to do the next day and how we're going to cover it," Rooney says. "Of course, news is unpredictable, but the basic groundwork for the following day is finished the night before."

About 9:30am every day, Rooney presides over a well-attended morning meeting. The regulars at the morning session include the managing editor, the assignment editor, the producer of the noon show, the two producers for the 6:00pm show, a "special projects" representative, and any reporters who aren't out on an assignment. Often, the evening anchors will phone to see if there's anything they need to be aware of.

The agenda is extensive. There's usually a long list of both possible stories and stories in progress. And while the conversation usually starts on a pragmatic, "things-to-do-today" level, it often turns philosophical: what are the hot issues these days, which stories are more important, what are people laughing about or worrying over? "After that, it's a matter of going out and gathering news," Rooney concludes.

And WCVB churns out a lot of news. The first broadcast begins with *Eye-Opener* at 5:30am. This initial look at the news is on the air for an hour and a half (!) before yielding to *Good Morning America*. The station also runs a half-hour newscast at noon, a one-hour show at 6:00pm, and another half-hour at 11:00pm. The news department also collaborates with the extensive programming arm of WCVB to produce *Chronicle*, an early-evening magazine show dedicated to examining local events and issues.

It's an impressive undertaking, and they do it in an impressive manner. Some people argue that over the last decade, WCVB has been the best local television station in the U.S. They've certainly been one of the most prolific. By their own estimates, the station has devoted nearly 25% of its airtime to local productions. And it hasn't been a quantity-driven video factory, either. WCVB has won numerous prestigious awards, including the Edward R. Murrow Award for overall excellence, several Peabody Awards, a duPont-Columbia Award, numerous Gabriel and Iris Awards, and enough local Emmy Awards to fill a small warehouse.

Now, as you're reading this, you're probably thinking that there's no way in the world you could get a job at a major-market station like WCVB. But that's not necessarily true. "I don't have any words of discouragement," Rooney states. "In fact, I'm pretty encouraging toward entry-level people. Most talented people will find a way to get in the door."

At WCVB, three staff positions exist mainly to allow promising individuals a chance to break into the newsroom: weekend night assignment desk (say goodbye to a social life), weekday assignment desk assistant (say hello to "go-fer" work), and overnight writer (say hello to writer's cramp—this person sometimes writes 40 stories a night). Each is a tough job that will quickly dispel your notions of glamor in T.V. news. But those who demonstrate a proficiency at these jobs and a willingness to learn, work hard, and get along with their colleagues are poised to move up the newsroom ladder.

"I'm amazed by the number of people who will do any job in the newsroom just to get in the door," Rooney says. "Now, if you get in the door and can't do anything, you're in trouble. But I screen calls from hundreds of job-seekers, and with some examination, you can usually tell who's going to make it."

The lesson? You just never know. Certainly, landing a first

job at a big station like WCVB is a real long-shot, but top stations do hire entry-level people and put them in positions where they can prove their talent and ambition. Don't bet the ranch on it, but with luck and persistence, you *can* get your first job in a Top Ten market.

Chapter 5

The State of the Art

> *"It's true that bean counters have occasionally been useful in trimming away unnecessary fat, some of it life-threatening. But too often they mistake a healthy heart for a glob of fat. Especially in news. We must keep the heart."*
> —from an editorial in *Electronic Media*

Downsizing. Recessionary cutbacks. A weak advertising climate. Market uncertainty. A gloomy economic picture. Persistent advertising slump.

Call it whatever you'd like, but the recent woes of the American economy have had what is often described as a "chilling effect" on local T.V., especially local T.V. news departments. And when you factor the increasing impact of cable T.V. and the subsequent erosion of the networks' audience into the equation, well, you've got some serious problems.

Bluntly, in the last decade, commercial television's reign as a cash cow has been unceremoniously terminated. Sure, T.V. is still a money machine, but it's printing greenbacks at a much slower rate. And since news departments are usually the largest money hogs at a local station, they feel the effects of "retrenchment" and "downsizing" the deepest.

The picture is not pretty. To give you an idea of the scope of the cut-backs, let's look at some of the staff reductions that occurred during the latter half of 1991:

•In the summer of 1991, for the first time, a network affiliate chose to leave the local television business. WPTF, the NBC-affiliate in Raleigh-Durham, North Carolina, suspended its serious news operations. The station's new owners say they will have brief local news and weather updates throughout the day. The 30-person news department got a 30-day notice.

•In mid-September, WHDH-TV, the CBS-affiliate in Boston, handed out 41 pink slips. Over a period of 18 months, the station trimmed over 125 jobs. WHDH once employed over 300 people. Today it has a staff under 175.

•Also in September, WLNE, the CBS-affiliate in Providence, Rhode Island, announced it was putting on "hiatus" its one-hour newscast at 6:00am, its half-hour show at noon, and its early weekend newscasts. Twenty-two lay-offs were distributed among news personnel, production staff, and technicians.

•In November, stations in Portland, Maine took some hits. WCSH-TV (an NBC-affiliate) fired ten people. Two weeks later, WMTW-TV (an ABC-affiliate) announced the lay-offs of 14 full-time employees, and nine more full-timers were reduced to part-time status.

This is only a partial list of the impact of tough economic times on local news. Of course, it's also one-sided—plenty of stations hired new people in 1991, too. But overall, it was a tough year. And when you consider that most of the cuts occurred in a four-month span, you'll begin to understand the seriousness of the situation.

What does this mean to you? Basically, one thing: There are fewer jobs available in local T.V. news today than there were yesterday, and there are more people competing for the jobs that remain. And quite a few of those people are experienced reporters, photographers, etc. who were laid-off by another station.

Obviously, this is not good news for someone trying to get that first job in T.V. news. Unfortunately, the news isn't getting better. In June, 1991, the F.C.C. stated that the stations most

likely to be hurt in the next decade are those in small markets—
the most fertile ground for job-hunters. Further, the first stations to run into trouble will probably be the third-place operations in three-station markets—another good place for hiring,
since #3 stations usually have high turn-over. Already, a number of stations have dropped their late and weekend newscasts.
More will certainly follow.

Many experts in the industry believe that most markets will
be able to sustain only two local news operations. The revenue
from advertisers simply won't stretch far enough to maintain
three local newscasts.

Some of the blame for recent woes can be attributed to an
economy in recession. But much of the reason for longer-term
erosion of the local T.V. audience is cable T.V. With dozens of
channels and myriad viewing options, cable T.V. has splintered
the audience of the three major networks, creating a brutal
trickle-down effect on local affiliates. In fact, on July 9, 1991,
the networks achieved a dubious distinction: the Nielsen ratings
for the previous week of T.V. viewing revealed that the combined prime-time audience ratings of the "Big Three" were at
an all-time low. Of course, local stations depend on their networks for revenue and for shows that build an audience for their
news and other local programming. Thanks to cable, that
audience can flip from CBS to NBC to ESPN to HBO to CNN
to MTV in about five seconds. Few T.V. viewers receive only
the major networks these days, so fewer T.V. viewers are forced
to choose one of the local newscasts at 6:00pm or 10:00pm.

Now, as you're reading this, your hands might be getting
sweaty and your stomach may be forming a large knot. You're
thinking that it all looks sort of bleak and hopeless, and maybe
you should just settle for that job with your uncle's advertising
firm.

Well, it's bad, but it's not hopeless. We're not going to sugar-
coat the situation: It's tougher to get a job in local T.V. news
today than it has been in a long time, maybe ever. It's tough,
but it's not impossible.

However, it's essential for you to understand the state of the market. One key trait for a journalist is an ability to assess a situation realistically, without a varnish of fantasy and wish. You must know exactly what you're getting into. We didn't include this chapter to scare you away from T.V. news, but we do want you to be aware of the job climate in your chosen profession.

Remember: there are **always** job openings, and there always will be. The competition is tougher now, and you'll need to work harder to distinguish yourself, but you **can** get a job. And this book can help. Who knows—one of these days the economy might start to boom, and we'll be talking about the incredible expansion of local T.V. news.

---

*"You have debased (my) child . . .
You have made him a laughing-stock of
intelligence . . . a stench in the nostrils
of the gods of the ionosphere."*
—Dr. Lee de Forest (1873-1961),
American inventor of the audion tube,
to the National Association of Broadcasters

Chapter 6

Now That I'm Ready to Work, Where Do I Look? What Do They Expect of Me? What Should I Expect of Them? And What Am I Getting Myself into, Anyway?

"They won't get rich.
They'll work damned hard. But if it gets
in their blood, they'll never give it up."
—Peggy Carpenter, News Director
at KTXS-TV, Abilene, TX

"Choose another career."
—Martha Cameron, News Director
at WMGC-TV, Binghamton, NY

Please take a seat in a comfortable chair. Turn on your favorite music if you'd like. Take a deep breath. Relaxed? Okay, now think about Duluth, Minnesota.

Did you draw a blank? Well, try another city. Close your eyes and think about Yakima, Washington. Still nothing? How about Albany, Georgia? Strike three?

Why should you ponder these particular cities? Because they are representative of the places you'll be applying for your first job in T.V. news. Did I detect the sound of bubbles bursting? Sorry. Put away the dreams of starting your career in the Big Apple or the Windy City. You can cross off Los Angeles and

San Francisco, too. Even stations in more, er, obscure locales like Wichita and Toledo will be a reach for you.

Of course, you may be one of the fortunate few who lands a job at the station where you had an internship. Or maybe you'll be able to cash-in on a family connection and bypass the headache of hunting for that entry-level job. If so, appreciate your good fortune. If not, you're in the line to buy tickets for the unique torture that comes with the emotional roller coaster of trying to land that very first job in television. You thrill-seekers may want to start reading this book a little more carefully.

"I think if they knew how tough it would be, they'd really get into gear," Gigi Shervanick, a project coordinator at Don Fitzpatrick Associates*, warns.

It's tough to embellish such a pithy statement. You've probably been in college for the last four years, and you're ready to break out. All the training, the class projects, the internships (more on this later), the exams—all this has made you a prized broadcasting recruit, capable of shining in T.V. journalism and deserving of a handsome salary. Right?

Wrong.

The cold truth: you're one of thousands of people who have earned a journalism degree in the past year—a degree that comes with absolutely no guarantee of landing a job in journalism, let alone in T.V. news. In fact, the degree is just one of *many* assets you'll need to get a job.

It's discouraging, but it's reality. "I get depressed about the students that journalism schools are turning out," Shervanick says. "They aren't learning that the T.V. business is horribly competitive." There are hundreds of "mass communications" programs at universities throughout the country, and they are glutting the market with prospective employees.

You are part of the glut.

There are far more people who want jobs in television than

---

*Don Fitzpatrick Associates scouts on-air news talent from around the world, and when one of their clients needs a new anchor or reporter, the company sends them tapes of qualified candidates. They have a computerized library of over 9,000 on-air news, weather, and sports people. For more, see Chapter 8.

there are jobs available. Ever since Robert Redford and Dustin Hoffman starred in *All the President's Men*, journalism has been perceived as a glamor job. And though Woodward and Bernstein were reporters at the *Washington Post*, a newspaper, the wave of interest in the "romance" of journalism spilled into the broadcast ranks. More recently, the star-status achieved during the Persian Gulf War by NBC's Arthur ("Scud Stud") Kent and CNN's Peter Arnett increased the already overwhelming allure of television journalism.

But the simple fact is that there aren't enough jobs for everybody who wants to work in T.V. news. So, you need to develop some advantages that will lift you above the groveling masses. And there are some practical, effective things you can do to increase your chance of getting hired.

Recently, I mailed questionnaires to dozens of small-market News Directors. I chose smaller markets because that's where most of the entry-level jobs are. I received well over 100 responses from News Directors representing 82 markets in 39 states—a healthy cross-section of the nation's small markets. The responses contain a lot of valuable information, upon which I've based the bulk of this chapter and the next. Consider this advice carefully. It comes directly from the people who will be judging your résumé.

One note about my references to specific News Directors: Whenever I use a direct quote from a News Director, I also list the station and its market size. Of course, there's no guarantee that this person still works for that particular station or even in that market. News Directors are notoriously transient, and I've made no attempt to track them after receiving their questionnaire. The statements are true for that person while he/she was working at the station listed. Similarly, the market ranking is accurate only for that time. Rankings can change each year.

Where Do I Look?
"Go anywhere. Don't worry about money early." That's the succinct advice offered by Pete Michenfelder, News Director at WJBF-TV in Augusta, Georgia (ADI #112).

So, if you're not "dubbing for dollars," you should be weighing other factors in your job search. Look, you're not going to make much money in your first job. Period. (More on salaries and such later.) So perhaps one factor you should consider is geography.

Or is it? "Never say 'no' to *any* opportunity, no matter what the position," Mark Millage, News Director at KELO-TV in Sioux Falls, South Dakota (ADI #106), counsels. "Be prepared to take a job anywhere in the country, at any size market, at any time it's offered to you."

But it's a big country, so let's refine the possibilities of realistic regions for your first job.

First, check out the list of the primary markets in the United States (see page 141). There are 210 total markets, or ADI's— Arbitron's abbreviation for television's Areas of Dominant Influence. (Television has long been—and will forever be—an industry filled with such number-crunching jargon.)

Look at the top 50 markets. Now, scratch them off. Sure, there's a slim chance you could land a first job in one of these places, but it's a long shot. Hunting in this area will also consume two of your valuable resources: time and money. Besides, in terms of the "big picture" of your career and your experience, it's often more advantageous to start in a smaller market. People there will be more forgiving of mistakes; they'll even expect them. Large stations can't afford to shrug off the inevitable errors a rookie will make.

In one of the questions, I asked News Directors about the average experience level of new employees. From markets #50-80, about one-third of the job openings required only a person with a college degree and no professional experience. As you can see in the table, the odds of landing an entry-level job while having no previous experience get better as you move down in market size.

When you hire entry-level employees, what is their average level of experience?

Market size	50-80	81-100	101-130	131-165	166-up
Some college	0	4	3	6	0
College degree	32	37	56	46	64
One year experience	9	48	35	44	24
Two years experience	45	7	6	2	6
More than two years experience	14	4	0	2	6

(Numbers listed as a percentage of responses.)

Look at the list of the 210 T.V. markets again and concentrate on markets #100-210. This is your personal Promised Land, the most fertile ground for harvesting your first job.

Of course, there are no hard and fast rules. Market size does not always indicate whether you can land a job at a particular station. For example, a station in Charleston, West Virginia—the #55 market—will sometimes hire people with no T.V. news experience. Meanwhile, a news department in Boise, Idaho—the #142 market—requires applicants to have two years of professional experience just to be considered. In fact, a News Director in Corpus Christi, Texas (market #125) wrote, "If you are providing job referrals to inexperienced people, *do not* refer them to us. Tell them to get their first job in another market." Fortunately, that's not the situation everywhere. "Keep plugging away, and think small, but good, markets," Bruce Stein, News Director of WMTV in Madison, Wisconsin (market #92), advises.

How to Apply

Basically, there are two ways to get a job in television news. First, you can wait until a position is posted and the ads are in all the national trade magazines—which means you'll be sending your letter and résumé tape along with 100 other applicants. (Never underestimate the number of people eagerly applying for openings. One example: the National Press Photographers Association runs a computerized job bank, on which KTVK-TV in Phoenix listed a job for four weeks. They received over 130 résumé tapes! And this is a rather minor service offered to a small number of users, so you can imagine the response a national ad receives.)

Second, you can apply to stations in a targeted, logical fashion, in which case you need an advantage, an edge. First, ponder that list of markets and decide where (in markets #100-210) you'd really like to work. Use any criteria you wish—the reputation of a station, geographical location, network affiliation, or the number of days of sunshine a city receives annually. But keep the list of potential stations short (henceforth to be called the "short list" —clever, eh?). Next, according to Brian Olson, News Director at KGWN-TV in Cheyenne, Wyoming (ADI #195), "the best thing you can do is get in your car with a copy of Rand McNally's road map and go visiting. I'll see anybody if I have the time."

So, the first step in your job search is to **meet all the News Directors on your short list.** But before you call them or schedule an appointment, make sure you're armed with information. "Do your homework and learn about the station and the market before you interview," counsels Rick Willis, News Director of WBRZ-TV in Baton Rouge, Louisiana (ADI #95). Find out as much as you can about the markets and the stations where you want to work. Take out a map and look at the region the station serves and what type of community surrounds it. Is it primarily agricultural? Industrial? Is its economy prosperous? Depressed? Does the area have a university and cultural opportunities, or is it mostly rural and provincial? You get the idea.

Do the same with the specific stations. Make sure you know some basic facts, such as how many news shows the station airs each day, and what time they run. If possible, arrive in town the day before your interview, get a motel room, and watch the evening broadcasts. Ask the locals what they think of the station's coverage and how it could improve. You'll do a much better job convincing a News Director that you deserve a place at his station if you know what its news product looks like and if you can converse with some authority on local issues.

After you've educated yourself on the station and its community, it's time to press the flesh, to get out and shake some hands. As Valerie Calhoun, News Director at WHOA-TV in Montgomery, Alabama (ADI #110), puts it, "A handshake is worth a thousand résumés."

Meeting the News Director will give you an edge. "Shake as many hands as possible," counsels Michael Sullivan, News Director at KTUL-TV in Tulsa, Oklahoma (ADI #58). "Résumés just become stacks of paper in my office. Unsolicited tapes, especially when there's not an opening, are just as bad. It's more likely you'll be remembered if you've met the News Director before he/she ever has an opening." Brian Olson puts it succinctly: "I've never seen a résumé tape shake hands and say, 'I'll kill for you'."

So review your short list, get on the phone, and make some calls. Contact the News Director and schedule an appointment. It's also not a bad idea to send a letter introducing yourself first, then call for an appointment. Sonja Bennett, News Director at WRBL-TV in Columbus, Georgia (ADI #121), adds this note of caution, "Never say 'entry-level'. This immediately sends up a red flag that tells me this person is not experienced and an interview would be a waste of time."

Most News Directors in the smaller markets will be happy to see you. They never know when they'll spot a "diamond in the rough," so they frequently schedule appointments with potential applicants. If you can get in the door, don't miss the opportunity, even if there aren't any job openings at the time. *Especially* if there aren't any job openings at the time! Remember, you're trying to cultivate a contact so you'll be in position to act when an opening does arise. You're also trying to establish a favorable impression, which will give you a step on the competition. "Network with as many industry people as possible," advises Jim Shaver, News Director at WDBJ in Roanoke, Virginia (ADI #65).

If you're unable to visit the station in person, then call to ask if there are any job openings. Regardless, ask if the News Director will review your résumé tape. If so, don't hesitate to send it. Be absolutely sure to send the tape to the correct person—and make sure you spell his name correctly. A misdirected letter or a misspelled name will ruin your shot at a job immediately. If you can't get in touch with the News Director, talk to a producer, reporter, or anybody who works in the newsroom—just to find out what the place is like and learn where you might fit in.

Whether you visit in person or mail your tape, always follow up your initial contact. Call occasionally to see if anything new has transpired and to keep your name in the News Director's mind. Of course, the problem here is defining "occasionally." How often you should call is a tough thing to quantify. Allen Martin, News Director at KHOG-TV (great call letters!) in Fayetteville, Arkansas (ADI #118), says, "Be persistent but don't be a pest." Brian Olson says, "Callbacks tell me that the person is persistent." Only you can determine when persistence becomes a liability instead of an asset, but staying in regular contact to some degree is essential.

Of course, you can't personally visit and phone every single News Director in 110 different markets. You'll also need to use some basic job-seeking methods. Sending an unsolicited letter and a résumé tape is one of the most typical methods of getting your foot in the door. But—in the questionnaires, I asked News Directors how they find most of the applicants for their jobs. The percentage citing unsolicited résumé tapes is not encouraging. It does, however, increase as market size decreases. Smaller newsrooms simply have smaller resources, and an unsolicited tape has a slightly better chance of finding its mark.

When you have a new job opening, how do you find most of the applicants for the position?

Market size	50-80	81-100	101-130	131-165	166-up
Word of mouth	30	13	25	13	0
Ad in local paper	0	7	11	4	4
Ad in trade magazine	30	33	25	25	33
Unsolicited résumé tapes	21	17	11	29	47
Newsroom intern	4	17	22	21	14
Other	15	13	6	8	4

(Note: Responses are represented in percentages. Some news directors named more than one source.)

Sending Résumé Tapes

Résumé tapes can get expensive. So can postage. And you can never count on getting the tape returned. I worked at one station that recycled unwanted résumé tapes. They simply bulk-erased them and gave them to their photographers to use as field tapes. Clearly, sending out tapes *en masse* to newsrooms across the country is costly and ineffective. The number of résumé tapes arriving in each newsroom in America every day is staggering. Most of them get stacked in a corner, where they gather dust for a long time. After I'd been working at KMGH in Denver for three years, a competing Denver station returned one of my old résumé tapes with a letter apologizing for the delay! They probably never looked at the tape, and I'm sure they didn't realize who had sent it.

If you've got the money and you feel compelled to send your tape out to the Great Unknown, at least be sure you're mailing it to the right person. The most critical piece of information you need is simple but—amazingly—often neglected by most applicants: **the name of the current News Director at the sta-**

tion to which you're applying. Mailing your package to a News Director who left the station two years ago is dumb, and most News Directors will discard your tape immediately. After all, if you can't figure out who should get your tape, you'll obviously make a lousy journalist. Ditto for spelling names correctly. I've seen countless letters from job-seekers who have misspelled the name of the person who might hire them! Think about it. How do *you* feel when you get mail and your name is spelled wrong?

So where do you find this basic information? First, beginning on page 146, we have listed each newsroom in the country, with its address and phone number. However, you may want to cross-reference our list with the information in the *Broadcasting & Cable Market Place*, published by R.R. Bowker. (It should be in your library.) This directory, updated annually, contains the names, addresses, and phone numbers of all the radio and television stations in the U.S. and Canada. It also lists the name of the News Director at each station, but *don't trust this information,* because News Directors move frequently. Always call the station to confirm the current News Director before sending your tape.

Competing with the Masses

There are several conventional avenues you can take to finding that first job in television news. Let's take a look at some of the more popular routes:

The Trades

Many News Directors hunt for job applicants by placing an ad in a trade magazine. The chart on page 85 clearly indicates the popularity of this method.

It doesn't require sophisticated detective work to decide what to do at this point. Simply, you need to get as many trade magazines in your hands as possible.

Broadcasting Magazine is probably the trade journal News Directors use most often. Its back pages are usually crammed with Want Ads, and, since it's a weekly publication, the jobs are current. You can also place a "Job Wanted" ad, but there's no data on how successful such ads are.

There is a snag, though. *Broadcasting* provides a comprehensive review of the important events and developments in the industry every week. Therefore, its subscription price is quite expensive—probably prohibitive for most people reading this book. Fortunately, most libraries receive *Broadcasting*, though sometimes a little later than the industry. So, find out what day your local library receives its copy, and make sure you get your butt down there on that day.

Also, **RTNDA** publishes a bi-weekly listing of current job openings. RTNDA is a clumsy acronym for "Radio and Television News Directors Association." Their membership of 3,600 includes about 1,200 radio and T.V. News Directors, who relay the information on the job listings.

The good news: you don't have to be a member to receive the jobs newsletter. The bad news: the newsletter comes out only twice a month, and it costs $16.00 for four issues. If you're interested, contact RTNDA at 1000 Connecticut Ave. N.W., Suite 615, Washington, DC, 20036; phone 202-659-6510.

Dialing for Dollars

Several major job banks are available by simply picking up your phone and making a call. But these services, of course, are not free. Either you'll pay an up-front fee to gain access to the job bank, or you'll dial one of those somewhat unsavory, pay-as-you-go 900 numbers.

The primary advantage of a telephone job bank is immediacy. The listings are usually updated daily, so you know the positions are fresh. You won't be applying for a job that was filled two months ago.

Medialine, one of the largest media phone services, has offered a dial-a-job operation since 1986. Medialine charges you a fee for access to its job bank (currently $30 for six weeks). The concept is simple: When you call their number, you'll get an automated voice-prompt, which will ask for your access code. After you punch in your code, you'll gain entry to the main menu, where you can select the areas that interest you. Areas currently listed are anchors/reporters, sports, weather, producer/assignment desk, photographer/editor, and production. The folks at Medialine say the anchor/reporter, photographer/editor, and production categories are usually flush with job offers. The other three areas have an unpredictable ebb and flow of listings.

Medialine learns about job openings directly from the source. Various management folks from stations around the country call in and list their current positions available—sort of like a Want Ads by telephone (or maybe more like a phone dating service!). In a good week, each category will have 15-20 new job listings; a poor week will see only five or six new entries. Each listing runs for only one week, then it's deleted. That way, you won't accrue a huge long-distance bill while listening to job openings you heard a month ago.

Medialine has one additional feature that rookies should note. On Monday, Wednesday, and Friday, it offers a separate category consisting only of entry-level jobs. So, you can get right to the goodies, and you won't waste time and money listening to the most recent need for a weekend sports anchor in Dallas or similar high-level jobs that you don't have a prayer of getting.

If you're interested in Medialine's service, the number to call is **408-648-5200.**

Somewhat similar, **Pipeline** is a 900-number service offered by Don Fitzpatrick Associates of San Francisco, one of the largest job placement (a.k.a. "headhunter") agencies in the country (more on this later).

Pipeline's job listings are updated daily. The service is free to News Directors, which encourages them to call in with their job needs. Pipeline's staff also scours the trade magazines for new listings.

Pipeline is easy to use. After you dial their number, you'll receive a menu of job listings, much like Medialine's menu. Pipeline, however, offers a two-tier system. When you choose a category, you'll hear a brief version of each entry, and, if a particular job interests you, you can dial-up a longer, more detailed account of the opening. However, Pipeline does not have an entry-level-only category, so you'll be on the phone longer, and your charges will add up.

Currently, the fee for Pipeline is $1.95 for the first minute and ninety-five cents for each additional minute. If you want to avail yourself of their service, call 1-900-456-2626.

Broadcast Jobline, a Chicago-based 900 phone service, compiles new job listings from around the country. They use a variety of sources, including word-of-mouth, News Directors, and trade journals.

The listings are updated daily, and unlike Pipeline, they offer a separate category with only entry-level jobs. However, Broadcast Jobline is fairly expensive. They charge $2.29 a minute— yep, the first minute and every minute thereafter.

Broadcast Jobline also has services that list job openings in the print and radio fields. Their number is 1-900-786-7800.

Jobphone, a 900 number run by Keith Mueller, a former producer at NBC, has been operating since 1988. Updated daily, it lists both radio and T.V. jobs, and it has an entry-level category. The Jobphone connection costs $1.99 per minute.

In addition to job listings, Jobphone offers a "Talking Résumé" —the vocal equivalent of a "Situations Wanted" print ad. You can call up and leave your résumé and job desires with the service, in the hope that a News Director will call Jobphone in search of applicants. Mueller says that the Talking Résumé has had only limited success, but it might be worth a few bucks. To reach Jobphone, call 1-900-726-5627.

Headhunters

Headhunters are basically the matchmakers of industry, compiling large pools of available talent and trying to match people with companies. Most headhunters are hired by a station (not by individuals) to find an appropriate person to fill a specific job.

Many large headhunter agencies will not accept résumé tapes from people with little or no experience. However, there are three exceptions:

Don Fitzpatrick Associates
Ghirardelli Square
900 North Point, Suite D-404
San Francisco, CA 94109
phone: 415-928-2626

Audience Research & Development
8828 Stemmons Freeway North, Suite 600
Dallas, TX 75247
phone: 214-630-5097

Frank N. Magid Associates
Talent Placement Services
One Research Center
Marion, IA 52302
phone: 319-377-7345

These agencies will view and evaluate your résumé tape and, if you meet their criteria, they'll add you to their talent pool. It's important to remember that they are not working on your behalf. Their clients are News Directors and other station management who are looking for new talent. If you happen to get a job through a headhunter, you'll be sort of an indirect beneficiary of their efforts. In most cases, you will incur no fee for their services, because they are paid by the stations looking for that hot new reporter or anchor.

Vacation Relief
Don't overlook this route to a full-time job. If you get hired as vacation relief (a.k.a. "VR"), you'll be filling-in for someone who, obviously, is on vacation or an extended leave of absence. Though it's a temporary position and as shaky as the San Andreas Fault, a VR job is a great way to gain experience, get a chance to shine, and be immediately available for a more permanent job, should one arise.

It's how I got my first job in the T.V. business. While working on my Master's Degree, I took a VR spot in production at a small station in Springfield, Massachusetts. Mostly, I ran the

TelePrompTer and operated a studio camera. (Ironically, these duties are automated at many stations today.) The pay was lousy, the hours stank, but the VR job got me in the door. By the end of the summer, I was offered a full-time production job. Six months later, I got a position as a photographer in the news department. The rest, as they say, is history.

Vacation relief jobs often resemble a paid internship. In larger markets, however, the positions require a degree of expertise, so they may be out of your reach. For example, KMGH in Denver hires a VR photographer every summer—but always someone with several years of experience. Smaller stations will hire rookies, though, and you probably won't need much experience to be considered. A willingness to learn, cooperate, and pitch in wherever necessary may be all that's required.

Since most VR jobs are available in the summer, start calling the stations in your area in March. Find out if the station will be hiring summer relief workers, and ask what the requirements are. Then get yourself in the door for a handshake while you drop off your résumé.

Salaries

By now, you're probably wondering just what kind of money you're likely to make in your first job. Well, as we've seen, the odds of landing a first job aren't great, and, while I don't want to raise your anxiety level much higher, you should realize that you won't need to be studying Porsche or BMW brochures just yet.

The ugly reality is that you'll probably make much less money than you expect. *Much* less.

But what about all those exorbitant salaries you hear about in the television business? Dan Rather makes about $500 million a year, right? Well, such salaries do exist, but they're in short supply. Sure, network stars make millions, and even in Denver, some anchors take home about 400,000 cool ones a year. But they are exceptions.

Once you move up the ladder of local T.V., you will make

enough money to live a pretty nice life. You won't be interviewed by Robin Leach anytime soon, but you'll be able to afford a nice home, a decent car, and an annual vacation. Lynn and I live comfortably on our combined salaries, and we've got local T.V. news to thank for that. But it wasn't always this way.

When I broke into television in the late 1970's, I made a whopping $6,000 a year. I know that was years ago, and I understand inflation and all that, but even then it was a paltry sum. The bad news is, entry-level salaries haven't gotten any better.

So take this advice: limit your expectations. If you're going into T.V. news because you think it's a nifty get-rich-quick scheme, then you'll be mighty disappointed. The demands and challenges in the news business are too great for someone just looking to make a fast buck. The only reason to make television news a career is because you want to be a journalist or a technician. Maybe, probably, a decent wage will come later.

In the questionnaire, I asked News Directors to provide their basic starting salaries for producers, reporters, and photographers. While the individual numbers varied widely, some general trends did emerge.

This should be pretty obvious, but, clearly, people make more money in larger markets. Generally, in markets #50-80, the average starting salaries range from $20,000-$25,000 a year. At some stations, producers earn more than reporters, but this doesn't hold true across the board. Almost without exception, photographers make a few thousand dollars less than their colleagues. However, their lower salary is often offset by other perks. For example, many stations let their photographers take their news car home. Also, photographers have more opportunity to earn additional income by freelancing (providing video services to corporations, shooting "how-to" tapes, and even taping an occasional wedding).

From markets #80-110, salaries drop, sometimes precipitously. For example, one station in the low 90's starts reporters and photographers at $13,500 and producers at $11,500. A station in a mid-80's market offers producers and reporters $14,000 per year and photographers $13,000 per year. But, there's a midwest station in the low 100's that starts producers at $19,000, reporters at $20,500, and photographers at $16,250. As you move through the markets in the 100's, salary levels generally move into the low teens, sometimes down to $10,000 a year. In some cases, the jobs are paid by the hour.

As you can see, salaries can fluctuate widely, so any comments about pay must be very broad. Salaries are very station- and market-specific. One thing's for sure, though: you'll never get rich working in small-market T.V. news.

"Journalism will kill you,
but it will keep you alive while you're at it."
—Horace Greeley (1811-1872),
American newspaper editor, politician

Chapter 7

The Right Stuff

"Entry-level candidates are a lot like marathon runners a mile into the race. They're still very much bunched up, and there's no way to tell the eventual winners from the losers. The top 60% all look alike."
—Tim Sharp, News Director at WCHS-TV in Charleston, SC

Your heart is set on a career in television news, and you think you've got the right combination of talent, grit, and perseverance to be a success. But what are the traits that News Directors are looking for?

Well, here are the answers, straight from the horses' mouths, so to speak. The following list is a compilation of responses that News Directors provided when I asked what were the most important qualities they sought in job applicants. The responses are listed in a random order, so "delivery" is *not* the most important trait. Rather, News Directors look for *all* these attributes in applicants:

1. Delivery.
2. Appearance.
3. Intelligence.
4. Attitude (defined as drive, energy, aggressiveness, etc.).
5. Curiosity.
6. News judgment.
7. Personality; the ability to work with people.

8. Experience.
9. Writing ability.
10. Strong work ethic.
11. Common sense.
12. Story-telling ability.
13. On-air presence.
14. Honest understanding of the business.
15. Knowledge of current events.
16. Depth of life experiences.
17. Capacity to be honest and caring.
18. Resourcefulness.
19. A concern for the profession.
20. Enthusiasm.
21. Commitment to journalism.
22. Self-confidence.
23. Maturity.
24. Composure (how well you handle pressure).
25. Information-gathering skills.
26. Motivation.
27. Past success.
28. Ability to shoot and write to video.
29. Dynamic on-camera skills.
30. Innovative mind.
31. Initiative.
32. Ability to take coaching.
33. Versatility; "jack of all trades."
34. Well-rounded education.
35. Ability to listen.
36. Vocal qualities.
37. A genuine interest in journalism (rather than someone who just wants to be "on T.V.").
38. Charisma.
39. Burning desire to learn.

Are some of these qualities more important than others? Yes. Several skills, abilities, attributes—whatever you want to call them—kept recurring in the responses to the questionnaire. I've distilled them into a "must" list, the top four traits you absolutely must possess before you will be taken seriously when applying for a position.

1. Writing Ability.

Without a doubt, News Directors cited this as the most important skill for a prospective television journalist. Forget about good looks, a great voice, a gung-ho attitude—if you can't write, you're not meant to work in the news business.

Almost every News Director stressed strong writing skills as the cornerstone of an applicant's abilities. And the related art of story-telling tags close behind. A lot of television news can be considered a process of forming and telling little stories. Condensing the complexities of an event and relating it in an interesting and credible manner is far more difficult than it appears. It's a talent highly prized by most News Directors.

2. Attitude.

News Directors said over and over that they want individuals who possess the "right journalistic stuff" —all those intangible personal qualities that can make or break an applicant. Also known as: Attitude. But how does one define that?

Curiosity and aggressiveness head the list. A person with an unquenchable desire to discover every facet of a story in the time available will be a good journalist. News directors want people motivated to unearth everything relevant to a piece. They want people who can take the initiative on stories, people who are enterprising, whether it's with hard news or soft features. And when a big story happens, they look for people who want to "own" the story. When the floodwaters hit or the mayor is indicted, a News Director needs someone who will develop the story faster, advance it further, and explain it better than the competition.

Let me add a note of caution here. Don't confuse being aggressive with being unethical. The news business is intensely competitive, but there's absolutely no room for someone who will break, or even bend, journalistic ethics. Getting a reputation as a sleazy journalist will **not** work in your favor. I've known my share of reporters who used questionable or underhanded tactics to get a story. Their reputations are common knowledge, and word spreads quickly. Most of them are no longer reporters; they're in public relations or advertising or some such purgatory. Television news is a relatively small industry, and its gossip network moves faster than the latest news about a sex scandal. Build your reputation carefully, because it will always precede you in this business.

3. Hands-On Skills.

Most News Directors in smaller markets are looking for individuals who can do it all—write, shoot, edit, and produce. Versatility is your key to a job in small-market T.V. news. Learn to do as many things as you can, and take advantage of every opportunity to acquire a new skill. "I look for someone with a well-rounded understanding of a news operation," Kevin Cobb, News Director at KVHP in Lake Charles, Louisiana (A.D.I. # 174), explains. "With such a small staff, I need people who can wear more than one hat."

4. Strong Work Ethic.

Dick Pompa, News Director at KFBB-TV in Great Falls, Montana (ADI #182), provided a classic description of the dedication News Directors seek in an employee:

"Be willing to make a very strong commitment to your work for the first couple of years. That means chasing stories at all hours of the day and working as a one-man (or one-woman) band, if necessary. Don't be a clock-watcher. Eat, sleep, and breathe news. Spend extra time practicing in front of a camera. Observe those in the media you admire—not to imitate them, but to pick up pointers."

As I've repeated *ad nauseum*, this is not a profession for the timid. About the only thing I can add to Pompa's advice is that the commitment doesn't end after "the first couple of years." If you're working in the trenches of T.V. news, your hours will always be long. Though I've been in the business over a decade, I still work an endless number of 16-hour days. And I still study the work of people I respect. The quest to get better never ends.

Chapter 8

Cover Letters, Résumés, & Résumé Tapes

*"It is better to know some of the questions
than all of the answers."* —James Thurber

"Most people applying for television jobs do a poor job of marketing themselves," Don Fitzpatrick, owner of Don Fitzpatrick Associates, asserts. "They're sloppy and lazy. They must prove that they're better than the other 19 people applying for the job. But many don't pay attention to details. They need to sit down and create a decent résumé and résumé tape."

This sentiment is echoed by most News Directors. Most job applicants, they say, make a number of major mistakes when they create their résumé and résumé tape. Some are conceptual errors—an applicant simply demonstrates poor judgment in the way he presents himself. Others are procedural errors—a person makes grammar mistakes, misspellings, or worse. The latter category is easy to correct; the former presents a more difficult challenge.

When you're searching for a job in T.V. news, in most cases you'll contact a News Director in writing before you actually meet him in person. And you'll usually send him a package of information about yourself. Typically, the package consists of three elements: a **cover letter**, a **résumé**, and a **résumé tape**.

You should think of these three items as your own set of specialized tools. With these tools, either you can build a positive presentation of yourself and your work, or you can dismantle any hope of getting a job. It all depends on what specific features you plan to build into your package—and the condition of your tools.

The Cover Letter

The cover letter is your personal introduction to a News Director. It definitely will make an impression—usually the first impression a News Director will form about you. Of course, you want to guarantee it's favorable, so by all means consider carefully the structure of your cover letter and its contents.

"Most people don't take advantage of the opportunity a cover letter offers," observes Cris Johnson, a former recruiter at Cable News Network. (For more information on opportunities at CNN, see Chapter 11.) "In a cover letter, I want you to tell me about yourself and demonstrate something about your character and expectations. I'm impressed by people who are focused and highly interested in the news process."

"The cover letter is actually much more important than the résumé," John Denney, News Director at KOLN-TV in Lincoln, Nebraska (ADI #98), maintains. "Applicants seem to spend a lot of time on their résumés, and then they write a two-paragraph letter that does little to 'sell' me. And it's often written improperly. Every applicant should learn the proper way to write a business letter, with date, inside address, close, etc."

If you need to take a refresher course in the fundamentals of proper letter-writing, then *do it*. There are standard, accepted methods of letter construction, and you should know what they are. This is basic stuff, so get it right. Don't let elementary mistakes defeat your chances for success at the very first step.

(There are a number of books available on writing cover letters and résumés, and most bookstores and libraries will have a variety of titles. In particular, guides published by Bob Adams, Inc. [260 Center St., Holbrook, MA 02343; 800-872-5627] and Peterson's Guides [Box 2123, Princeton, NJ 08543; 800-338-3282] are considered top-notch.)

Never misspell words or make grammar errors in a cover letter. Always ask a few friends to proofread your letter before you send it. A dangling participle, a misplaced semi-colon, or an incorrect spelling can speed your entire application into the dumpster. "There is nothing worse than a spelling error or grammatical mistake on a résumé," notes Ashley Webster, News Director at KTVH in Helena, Montana (ADI #208), "and you'd be surprised how often they occur."

Another crucial point: Be sure your letter is addressed to the station's current News Director. Addressing your application to "The News Director" or—horror of horrors!—to the *former* News Director at a station is a fatal *faux pas*. Your package will be jettisoned immediately into the garbage can. If you send a letter that starts with "Dear News Director," you can expect to receive a letter that starts with "Dear Applicant." After all, what kind of journalist could you be if you can't even uncover the name of your potential boss?

This means a little more work for you. It means that when you drag out the *Broadcasting & Cable Market Place* to get information on television stations and their addresses, you'll need to do more than just copy the News Director's name and insert it into your letter. It means you'll need to copy down the station's phone number, too. And it means you'll need to call the station to confirm the News Director's name (and its correct spelling) and the station's address.

(Of course, we've listed all the stations in all the markets—plus their addresses and phone numbers—starting on page 146. But you should drag out *Broadcasting & Cable Market Place* anyway.)

What else should you know about your cover letter? The best advice comes from News Directors around the country:

- "Keep it short—the cover letter must *sell*. If it doesn't, the rest of the résumé is a waste of time."

- "Don't profess a desire to become an anchor or work in a top-50 newsroom in a year—or three."

- "Never start a cover letter with 'Dear Sir or Madam,' 'Dear News Director,' or any other generic greeting. Such letters go directly into my garbage can."

- "Lay off talking about the big market you interned in. Talk experience and dedication instead."

- "Tell me why you will improve my newscast."

In brief, your cover letter should be one page, and it should sell you to the News Director. Don't try to be cute or folksy—just be sincere and straightforward. Explain to the News Director why you want to work for him and what assets you bring to the job. Be succinct. The cover letter is not an essay contest; it's more of a statement of purpose.

"Tell them what you want to do," Don Fitzpatrick advises. "If you want to be a news reporter, say so. Statements like 'I'll do anything' will get you nothing."

"Make it brief and to the point," offers Dana C. Beards, News Director at KMIR-TV in Palm Springs, California (ADI #170). "Don't be weird and try to grab the News Director's attention. The tape sells the applicant. The résumé and cover letter should entice me with basic information to view the tape."

By the way, always have your résumé printed professionally. It will cost a few bucks to have it done right, but the results are worth the investment. For some variation, have your résumé printed on an attractive colored paper instead of plain white bond. Just don't choose anything too ostentatious or wacky.

Also, if you're interning or working at a station, **never** type your cover letter on its stationery. "It's tacky. Very tacky," Fitzpatrick says. "You're sending out signals that you're looking for a new job on your current employer's time." Rather, go to a stationery store and spend a few bucks on some tasteful paper. Again, try a subtle color instead of plain white.

Writing a great cover letter is the first of many steps you must take to land a job. It should be an easy step—after all, as a journalist, you should have a knack for writing—but a lot of people self-destruct at this point through carelessness and ignorance.

You want to ensure that even in a worst-case scenario (e.g., there are no jobs available at the station, yours is the 12th cover letter the News Director has read that day, etc.), the News Director is simply neutral about you and will therefore look at your tape.

Remember, the whole point of a cover letter and résumé is to get the News Director to watch your tape. John Denney aptly sums it up: "A great résumé can't overcome a bad cover letter; however, a great résumé tape *can*."

The Résumé

Brevity is your ally when you compose your résumé. College students often approach their résumés in the same way they approach an essay or a class project. That is, they fill it with loads of unnecessary information and irrelevant detail, thinking that the longer it is, the more important it must be.

While this might fool a beleaguered teaching assistant, it won't work with a résumé. Your résumé must be concise and to the point. Let's face it—if you're applying for an entry-level job, you won't have a whole lot to put on your résumé. So remain focused and *cut the crap*. You won't fool anyone by loading your résumé with exaggerated descriptions of insignificant jobs and experiences. Well, actually, that's inaccurate. You will fool one person—yourself. You'll fool yourself into thinking you can get a job by blowing a lot of smoke at a News Director.

So if you don't have much relevant detail to pad a résumé with, what should you do? Cal Hunter, News Director at KRCR in Redding, California (ADI #130), offers a good starting point: "Like a good story, your résumé should be short, simple, and *accurate*, with references." Here's more advice from your future employers:

- "Don't fill it with phony baloney. Internships at 'big' stations don't impress me. Keep it to one page. List three good references, with phone numbers. Don't misspell."

- "Put the most recent experience at the top. I don't care if you worked at McDonald's. Keep it clear and concise, and don't add items to fill up the page."

- "Put education at the bottom, not the top. Otherwise, it says 'rookie.'"

- "Understand that it's going to be compared with résumés from more experienced folks. Overstatement and fine detail (coursework, etc.) are liabilities. A résumé should be an honest summary of your life experience."

- "Get to the point, and don't make stuff up to make it look good."

- "Be honest. Give me some detail, but don't write a book."

- "Make it as concise as possible and explain reasons for leaving a job or any gaps in employment."

- "Don't use gimmicks. Unless you have extensive professional experience, keep it to a maximum of two pages. Include references—why be secretive?"

- "Be neat, brief, and give references, with phone numbers. Make sure grammar and spelling are flawless."

- "One page. No gimmicks. No fancy three-fold jobs. No folders or binders."

- "Don't brag about glitzy internships at top-10 markets. Show genuine journalistic talent, with emphasis on experience in the field."

- "Leave off hobbies. Who cares if you like to swim or put model airplanes together? I want to know how you can help our show."

- "Don't include beauty contests. Undersell rather than oversell."

- "Leave off the fraternity and sorority stuff—who cares? If it's not related to the job you're seeking, drop it."

- "Don't lie. If you were an 'intern,' then say so! Don't claim you were an 'associate producer.'"

- "Include broadcast experience first and demonstrate a proven track record for hard work."

The News Directors' comments point to two key factors you must consider when composing your résumé:

1. Be brief—keep your résumé to the point. If an item doesn't contribute to an assessment of your skills as a journalist, *leave it out*. And keep your résumé to one page. At this stage in your career, there's no need for more.

2. Dont' lie—don't even think about it! Don't exaggerate, don't embellish, don't create fiction. If you've been fired from a job, explain why. "If you lie, I'll catch you," warns Kirk Winkler, News Director at KETV in Omaha, Nebraska (ADI #73). So will everyone else, eventually.

Four items **must** be a part of your résumé:

1. Your personal information: name, address, and telephone number.
While these details may seem obvious, people make mistakes even in this essential area. Make sure you provide a phone number that will be answered. If you're hard to reach by phone, get an answering machine, and be sure to check it several times a day. Make it easy for a News Director to contact you—how many times will he call before moving on to someone else? And leave off the cute, funny, or weird greetings on your phone machine. Your friends might think you're clever, but a News Director might think you're a wing-nut.

2. Experience.
List all relevant experience that you have, including internships. If you've had a job outside of broadcasting, list it if it demonstrates a positive character trait. This is especially true if you've been out of school for some time or if you're making a career change.

3. Education.
Remember, stick to the basics. No one cares about your History Club Award in 10th grade. Just list where you went to col-

lege and the degree you received (or will receive). Include your grade point average only if it works in your favor. If you graduated with honors, note the honor, but keep it brief. You could list a major academic honor, too, but be sure it's relevant.

4. References.
Include at least three references. Don't try to play it cool by writing, "References available upon request." News Directors need the pertinent information about you *now*. They're busy people, they don't have time to wait. Always list a phone-number with the reference. News Directors usually check your references, especially at this stage of your career. You're not going to scam anyone by listing Dan Rather as a reference just because you shook his hand when he spoke to your journalism class.

You may also want to include a short **goal** or **objectives statement**. The News Directors I've contacted are split on the need for something like this. Some think it's a valuable part of a résumé, giving them greater insight on the applicant. Others feel that it's a waste of time. It's your choice, but if you do include it, make sure it is pithy and appropriate.

As a final option on your résumé, you could list the television equipment you know how to operate. (And, no, listing "Nintendo" or "a remote control" is not hilarious.) Small-market newsrooms especially require versatility, and they need people who possess a variety of skills. Even if you want to be a reporter, an ability to shoot and edit may help you get your first job. But, only list equipment that you truly know how to use. Don't say you can operate a Chyron just because you saw somebody use it once. Even small-market technology is getting quite complex, and you can't bluff your way through the operation of an editor or a still store, so don't try.

Now, after all this about your résumé, don't forget: Your cover letter and résumé act only as a lure to your résumé tape. In broadcasting, your résumé tape is your *real* résumé, and it becomes increasingly important as your career advances. At the higher levels of local television, News Directors just glance at a résumé and assume the résumé tape will say it all. Michael Sullivan, News Director at KTUL-TV in Tulsa, Oklahoma (ADI #58), said, "The résumé is just a reference tool to let me know the person's background, address, and telephone number. However, the audition tape—that's *everything*."

The Résumé Tape

A résumé tape should demonstrate in living color just what your abilities are. A good tape will take weeks, if not years, to create. Is there any way to avoid the painful hell of putting together a résumé tape? Not if you want to work as a reporter, photographer, producer, or graphics person in T.V. news.

What do News Directors look for in a résumé tape? First, let's review some of the qualities they seek in every applicant, and then we'll discuss how to package these traits into the elements required for a good résumé tape. (Remember, most of these responses are weighted toward people who will work on-air.)

1. Good writing.
2. Delivery.
3. Presence.
4. Consistency.
5. Range of ability.
6. Creativity.
7. Accuracy.
8. Depth.
9. Story structure.
10. Motivated stand-ups. (This doesn't mean showing a lot of enthusiasm in your stand-up. News Directors look to see if there is a *reason* for a stand-up. Is it necessary, and is it in the right place in the story?)
11. Credibility.
12. Authority.
13. Ability to use video tools: natural sound, graphics, editing techniques, etc.

Now, how do you display your proficiency in these areas in the most appealing and efficient manner? Before we discuss the particulars, let's digress and discuss **Don Fitzpatrick Associates,** one of the major players in the world of television jobs.

Throughout this book, we've quoted Don Fitzpatrick several times. Fitzpatrick recruits talent for both local News Directors and network news executives. In the industry, he's commonly called a "headhunter" or, in a gentler parlance, a "talent scout." Officially, he and his seven-person staff are television news and programming "brokers." Simply put, T.V. stations come to him to find news talent. His firm has retainers with such notable clients as CBS News, CNN, and over 100 local stations, including KGO and KRON in San Francisco, KYW in Philadelphia, WLS and WGN in Chicago, WSB in Atlanta, and KING in Seattle. When Fitzpatrick and his staff can match a news talent to a station, Fitzpatrick's firm makes money.

To assist in his search, Fitzpatrick has a computerized video library of over 12,000 on-air news, weather, and sports people. Every year, Fitzpatrick gets videotapes of newscasts originating in markets #1-165. He and his staff view the tapes and rank each newscaster, and they ask those who receive a high score to send an audition tape.

This video library also includes hundreds of résumé tapes sent "on spec." Fitzpatrick welcomes tapes from anyone, even a lowly college student with no professional experience. Though it's only a fraction of his business, Fitzpatrick does conduct talent searches for News Directors in small markets. But if you send his firm a tape, don't expect a critique. Rather, his staff will rank your tape like all the others, and if you show promise, you'll make it into the library computer. If you don't, your tape will be dumped on the heap (unless you include return postage, of course).

Obviously, Fitzpatrick has tremendous experience in evaluating talent and résumé tapes. He's got a lot of good advice for prospective job-seekers, and I'll be referring to him frequently as we discuss résumé tapes.

"Most talent audition tapes are poorly constructed, especially considering they're done by people in the business of communicating," Fitzpatrick says. "Many of these tapes are sending out the wrong signals. They demonstrate a lack of ability on the part of on-air people to market themselves properly. And it costs many talented people better jobs."

Like the cover letter and the résumé, the résumé tape has its own internal protocol. Let's attack the résumé tape dilemma from two angles: packaging and presentation.

Packaging Your Tape

"I'm amazed at the number of tapes I receive that have sloppy labels on the tape box and no label on the tape. If the applicant is sloppy putting together his résumé tape, is he going to be sloppy labeling story tapes for air at my station?" questions John Denney, News Director at KOLN-TV in Lincoln, Nebraska (ADI #98). "I think that the person who sends me a neat, well-labeled, well-edited résumé tape is a person who is careful and who pays attention to details. When I send a reporter out to cover a story, I want a reporter who pays attention to details."

The first detail to get right is tape format. Should you dub your résumé tape in a Beta, VHS, or ¾" format? Overwhelmingly, the answer is ¾". Most stations have a ¾" machine that lost too many battles in the news wars and has been retired with honors to the News Director's office. VHS is out of the question. Most News Directors have their VHS machines at home, and they certainly don't want your tape stinking up their elegant living rooms. The Beta format provides the best quality, but most News Directors don't have a Beta player. If you have the equipment to make Beta dubs, then you'll have one more question when you're on the phone confirming the current News Director and the station's address: Ask if the News Director will accept a Beta résumé tape. If so, go for Beta.

The next detail: tape labeling. Type your name, address, and telephone number on the front of the tape box. "This may sound obvious," Fitzpatrick says, "but you'd be surprised at how many unlabeled tapes we receive." Next, make sure the tape itself is labeled with your name, address, and phone. A News Director has a zillion tapes lying around his office, and an unlabeled tape will be quickly recycled or discarded.

Creating Your Tape

Now to the tape. Just what should you include, and what should you avoid?

The first thing on your tape should be a slate with your name, address, and phone number. "A nice, clean slate with that information will be most helpful," Fitzpatrick notes. "And should your résumé or cover letter get separated from the tape—it happens more often than most News Directors would like to admit—the News Director can still track you down."

Two caveats before we move on: Don't put color bars on your tape, and don't put tone on it, either. I don't know one News Director on this planet who is going to fiddle with his T.V. set to adjust it to your color bars. Tone is even more annoying. Also, color bars and tone waste time, and time is precious, especially when you consider the Thirty-Second Rule.

"Some people say it should be a Ten-Second Rule," Fitzpatrick admits. "In any case, it's the amount of time you have to sell your skills to the News Director before your tape becomes a victim of the EJECT button. I know it sounds as though the News Directors of America are more interested in form over substance, appearance over intelligence. But the fact is, you have thirty seconds to arouse interest from your next potential News Director."

So, you can't waste any time at all, and you want the beginning of your tape to be hot—red hot. Where do you start?

"Most college students can't gather enough material for a complete résumé tape," Fitzpatrick states. "They just don't have the facilities or the stories to do the job."

So you must improvise to an extent. "A good tape could have a student introducing his own package," Fitzpatrick counsels. "He can use an anchor set-up as a way to get to one of their stories."

This gives you two shots at getting a News Director's attention, and it lets you display your skills in two different settings. But keep the anchor-intro portion short. A lot of local News Directors said they don't want to see any anchor stuff on an audition tape, because they need people who can do the nuts and bolts of news reporting. They can always make you an anchor later if you show potential.

The first story on your tape should be your best story. No exceptions.

Well, actually, one exception. If your best story is a soft feature, consider leading with something newsier. In your first job, whether you're a reporter, photographer, or newsroom go-fer, you'll need to pull your weight in hard news. An ability to create a good feature is valuable, but most News Directors want to see how you handle the day-to-day, down-and-dirty news stories. "News Directors have biases," Fitzpatrick warns. "Some believe an audition tape full of features or soft stories is a person's way of admitting he can't report news." John Denney agrees. "Show me a routine report. You're not going to be covering major fires every day, so show me what you can do with a city council meeting."

Make sure there is a stand-up in your first story, because News Directors want to see what you look like, and they want to see it early. Don't disappoint them. Also make sure there is some logical motivation for your stand-up. It should serve some purpose other than to comply with the truism that every story should have a stand-up (which I don't believe is true).

Next, if you have a live-shot, put it here. "With television news in satellite heaven these days, more and more News Directors want to see live-shots," Fitzpatrick asserts. Of course, if you're a college student or an entry-level applicant, it will be tough, if not impossible, for you to get an opportunity to do a real live-shot. If you have one, great. If you don't, then don't sweat it.

Your next story could be a feature or another hard news story. Include both, but put whichever is better in front of the other.

"Many young reporters load up an audition tape with lighter material," Fitzpatrick says. "You might want to include one—no more than two—features on a résumé tape, but concentrate on the harder news. And don't lead an audition tape with a feature piece unless you are absolutely convinced it will blow the socks off the News Director."

Finally, if you have footage of yourself working as an anchor, and if it's *good*, include it at the end of the tape. It will show a News Director that you can anchor but that it's not your priority.

Your tape should have four or five elements, tops. An "element" can be considered a story, an anchor segment, or a live-shot. Ideally, you want to demonstrate your diversity of skills, and you want to pique the curiosity of a News Director.

You don't want to be guilty of the major pet peeves of News Directors. Fitzpatrick's firm did a survey on the miscues and mistakes most frequently made on audition tapes. The results:

What's wrong with today's video audition tapes?

Problem	% Citing It
Color bars/tone at head of tape	80%
Tape opens to intro of newscast	60%
(Anchors only): Change of clothes after each story read	50%
On-camera bio's ("Hi, I'm Bob Smith and I want to work for you.")	35%
Voice-over bio's	15%
Anchor/reporter sending only anchor work	10%

Your tape should run about ten minutes—and shorter is better than longer. A News Director has seen several thousand résumé tapes, and he'll usually form an opinion about your work quickly. If you've got four stories you're considering, and one is markedly weaker than the others, *leave it out*. Don't include a piece just to fill time.

One more major "don't": Don't re-track a package that has already aired. Sometimes interns, especially at larger stations, get the bright idea of erasing the reporter's track and inserting their own. That's basically fraud—video plagiarism—and it's a very dumb move. A News Director will recognize quickly that it's not your writing and not your style. Now, if you're working at a station and get to go out on a story, and you cajole the photographer to shoot a stand-up for you, then you're okay.

Take the raw tape, write your own script, track it, and edit the piece yourself. Then, it's your work.

Several more hints: If you haven't gotten a job in six months, start making changes to your application package. Perhaps your cover letter needs to be rewritten. Maybe your tape should be edited differently. A News Director will rarely rewind a résumé tape. So when you get your tape back without a job offer attached, note where it was ejected. If it's at the end of the tape, you'll at least know your tape's OK. If it's in the middle of a story, then it's time to reconsider some things.

Finally, if you want your tape returned, include a stamped, self-addressed envelope. It won't guarantee you'll get your tape back, but it will increase the possibility. In an age of "downsizing," don't take anything for granted—even the cost of returning a tape.

"Let's face it—there are no plain women on television."
—Anna Ford, British television personality

Chapter 9

So You Want to Be on the Air?

"I was a real reporter once, but I was not suited for it by physique or temperament. Real reporters have to stick their noses in where they're not wanted, ask embarrassing questions, dodge bullets, contend with deadlines, and worry about the competition. I did all these things, while trying to figure out an easier line of work." —Charles Kuralt

(This chapter written by Lynn Setzer.)

It was great spot news—lots of fire trucks, ambulances, rescue workers, and spotlights. A truck filled with propane had careened off a steep ravine and tumbled into a rushing mountain stream. The accident had happened hours ago, but the emergency crews couldn't move the truck until they removed the propane. It might take all night.

I had just finished a live report for the 10:00pm broadcast, when the Assignment Desk told me to stay with the story until the propane was gone. I groaned. Propane was the least of my worries.

You see, nature called, and I had nothing but nature and rescue workers around me. No houses. No stores. No Porta-Johns. Nothing. There was only one thing I could do. I walked up the dirt road until I was out of sight, hiked up my skirt, and emptied my aching bladder. Ahhhhhhhh.

My relief ended when I felt my foot getting warm.

Tears of laughter and frustration welled up in my eyes as I realized what I had done. I had just urinated on my foot. In my shoe. The shoe I had to wear until the damn propane was gone.

I gritted my teeth and squished back down to the news site. Who says T.V. isn't glamorous?

If you're intent on a career in television news because you think it's sexy and dazzling, you're very, very wrong.

It's a career that requires you to work—hard—innumerable nights, weekends, and holidays, in all kinds of weather. You'll melt in the heat, shiver in the snow, sneeze in the drizzle, and you'll wonder why in God's name you ever went into television news. You'll barely scrape by on a salary that a Burger King trainee would reject, while your peers are making a legitimate, adult wage—and you'll wonder why in God's name you ever went into television news. People will say you're a vulture whenever you cover a tragedy, they'll call your profession superficial and dumb, and they'll blame your medium for the End of Civilization—and you'll wonder why in God's name you ever went into television news.

The answer is easy. At times, it's the best job in the world. You'll meet and interview people who are fascinating, famous, unforgettable. You'll travel to big cities and small towns, getting a glimpse of life only a T.V. camera can capture. If you're lucky, you'll be *doing* what everyone else can only talk about. It's vicarious living at its best.

I've found that my job is rarely dull. I might cover an abortion protest at the State Capitol in the morning, and, in the afternoon, report on the tornado that just swept through town.

I covered the release of hostage Thomas Sutherland in Germany. I did Bourbon Street in New Orleans with the Republican National Convention in 1988 (you Democrats might think that sounds like Hell on earth, but it was really a blast), and I was shoved around at a neo-Nazi demonstration in Atlanta during the Democratic National Convention. I've covered floods, helicopter crashes, restaurant explosions, hurricanes, and the best hot dogs in Connecticut. I covered visits of Presidents Carter, Reagan, and Bush, and I followed (though not as closely as the *Miami Herald!*) Gary Hart on the 1988 campaign trail. What a great job!

I love using the Ted Baxter line when someone asks me how I got into T.V.: "It all started in a 10,000-watt radio station in Fresno, California." Actually, for me it all started at a big Washington, D.C. radio station, WASH-FM, where I had an internship during college. After I graduated, I bugged the people there incessantly until they gave me a job. (I majored in Medieval History, by the way—so much for a journalism background.)

The job at WASH paid $10,000—big bucks in 1977—and I even had a title: "Traffic Manager." I wish I could say I flew around in a helicopter during rush hour giving fender-bender reports. Hardly. As Traffic Manager, I scheduled all the commercials that ran on the station—probably the most tedious job in broadcasting. But it gave me a chance to hang around the newsroom.

It took me a year before I got my "big break." A friend knew a friend who worked at a radio station in Rome, Georgia, and they had a job opening. Within a month, my U-Haul was packed and I was on my way to Dixie and my first "on-air" job.

When you're trying to get your first job, knowing someone who knows someone always helps. Like any other industry, television is a business of friendships and personalities, favors and old ties. T.V. journalists are notoriously nomadic and peripatetic, so you try not to burn bridges with your colleagues. At your next job, they may be your bosses.

Internships are also a great way to get the proverbial foot-in-the-door. It may not land you the job you really, really want, but it's a good way to start forming the friendships and contacts with people who can help you later.

My time in radio was a lot of fun, and I highly recommend it as a way of getting on-air experience. It's a good way to learn how to write in "news-style," and it's a great way to develop an "on-air" voice.

Unfortunately, fewer and fewer radio stations have vital news departments these days. But if you can find a station that does news, and you need a job while you're waiting for the break into T.V., take it.

I was working at a radio station in Gainesville, Florida when I was asked to interview for a job at the local T.V. station. I got the job—and I owed a lot to my time in radio.

Gainesville is now the 165th market. When I worked there, it was #177. It wasn't the bottom, but you could see it from there. But it was, and is, a great place to learn.

There were no photographers, so we worked on the buddy system: two reporters worked together in the field. We shot our own video, so I had to learn the basics of photography. In my case, I learned how to focus and get a white-balance, and occasionally I would get usable pictures and sound. If you needed a stand-up, your partner shot that for you.

At some stations, reporters work alone. To do stand-ups, they mark a spot, focus the camera on it, turn the camera on, stand in their spot, and talk. That's known as a "one-man band" operation. It isn't the best way to do news, but at some small-market stations, it's the only way. At some big-market stations, too: One Denver station has a bureau reporter who sometimes shoots, writes, and edits his own stories. And Denver is the 21st market.

That's why small-market T.V. experience can be invaluable. The more you know how to do, the better chance you'll have of beating someone else for a choice job. You'll also be a better reporter, because you'll know what it takes, mentally and physically, to get the story done. Photographers love reporters who come from small markets, because they're usually not afraid to get their hands dirty.

When my "partner" and I had completed our stories, we would come back to the station, write them, and edit. By the time I left Gainesville, I could shoot, edit, produce, report, and anchor. I couldn't do all of them brilliantly, but I could manage. And by trying all those skills, I could better decide which I should pursue.

Getting out of Gainesville was a lot harder than getting in.

It took two years of hard job-hunting before I got another job. Here's how I did it (but remember, everyone has a different story):

First, I read the "Help Wanted" ads in *Broadcasting Magazine*, and I sent tapes to the jobs that looked interesting. I got nowhere. So, with my résumé tape tucked into my well-worn briefcase, I spent every vacation day I had looking for a job. I picked an area of the country—the Northeast—and I went hunting, using my famous "critique approach": I would call a T.V. station in advance and tell the News Director or an assistant that I would be in their city in a few weeks. I tried to set up an appointment with the News Director. If he said he had no job openings, I asked for a few minutes of his time to look at and critique my tape. Sometimes—most times—I was blown-off. They didn't have the time or the interest. But in Harrisburg, Pennsylvania, I had two interviews, two critiques. A year later, one of the stations offered me a job.

If you catch a News Director on a good day, he is often happy to sit down, watch your tape, and give you feedback. Don't expect more than 10 or 15 minutes, though. But more important than the time he gives you is the chance you'll have to make eye contact and shake hands with the person who could hire you. It's an opportunity to form a good impression and make a "friend."

In my case, I looked a whole lot better in person than I did on my résumé tape. The studio cameras in Gainesville tended to make me look a little green around the gills.

By scheduling appointments and asking for critiques, I got in to see News Directors in Jacksonville, Providence, Harrisburg, and New Haven, Connecticut. About 18 months after I first met the News Director in New Haven, he hired me. I called him every few months just to keep in touch and keep my name in his mind.

He told me later that my sheer persistence convinced him to hire me. He wanted a reporter who was dogged and insistent, and those qualities outweighed my novice résumé tape. I will always be grateful to him for looking beyond the tape.

Moral of the story: Don't be discouraged if your tape isn't the world's greatest. There are ways to compensate; you just have to keep trying.

I worked nights and weekends in New Haven for three years, and I learned a lot. I didn't always appreciate the teachers, but I can look back now and be grateful to the people who kicked me in the butt when I screwed up. Most of what I learned can be summarized in four simple lessons:

Lesson #1: Always try to look good.
T.V. is a visual medium—pretty simple concept, but one I often chose to ignore when it came to my appearance. You've got to look your very best no matter what the circumstances. Even in a blizzard, with your hands, feet, and lips frozen, take time to put on lipstick, comb your hair, straighten your tie, etc. The audience—and your boss—will marvel at how good and "composed" you look under trying conditions.

In New Haven, I figured the story was more important than my appearance. I was set straight. While I still believe putting together a good story and getting it on the air is the most crucial thing I do, I have also learned that some make-up and decent clothes will give me credibility—without which the story can flop. Whom would you rather look at, a reporter in a nice suit with a good haircut, or one who looks like Herb from WKRP? Which journalist would you believe?

Never be afraid to get your hands dirty, but never let the viewers see the dirt.

Lesson #2: If you can't write well, either learn or find another line of work.
Though I thought I knew how to write when I arrived in New Haven, I needed help. Fortunately, I got it from producers who would look at my copy and rip it apart. After they were done, I wanted to rip them apart—but the final product was much better.

I studied what they changed and why, and I tried to learn and improve. Unless you currently write like Charles Kuralt, you'll need to write better. (For one thing, News Directors will look for well-written stories on your résumé tape.)

For help, turn on any of the network news shows, close your eyes, and *listen* to the reporters' stories—the rhythm and texture of the words, the way soundbites and natural sound are used, etc. And, by all means, watch *CBS Sunday Morning* with Charles Kuralt. You'll learn a helluva lot, and the show will restore your faith in television journalism. I think it's the finest 90 minutes of T.V. on the air.

I have learned to avoid using the "official" sound in my stories. Tell the who, what, when, where, and why in your copy, then let the soundbites give the story its resonance. The copy and the soundbites should be interwoven like a tapestry. Unfortunately, most of what you see on local (and sometimes national) news is a factory-made, standard-issue weave—that's just the realities and limitations of journalism.

Lesson #3: Use your voice.

Some people are blessed with mellifluous pipes; others must work on their voices every day. My voice changes depending on how much sleep I've had, what I've had to eat, the time of day, and whether I've peed in my shoe.

Your voice and delivery can enhance the story or ruin it. If viewers hear a voice that squeals like fingernails on a chalkboard, they'll simply pick up the magic remote control and change channels. If a News Director hears it, he'll toss your résumé tape in the trash.

Don't be discouraged if you don't sound like Diane Sawyer or Walter Cronkite. Tom Brokaw has a speech impediment, and he's at the top of the network heap.

I learned a great deal about using my voice and improving my delivery by listening hard to reporters and anchors I respected. So find one or two you like and study them. If you need additional help, take voice lessons. You'll learn fairly simple, effective tricks and techniques that will give you the all-important edge in the job application game.

Lesson #4: Keep your ego in check.
Television news feeds on ego, and it's easy to lose your perspective. Remember, there is always someone willing to work a little harder and a little cheaper than you. And he may have more talent. That should be a pretty humbling thought.

Just because you're on T.V., you're not a star. You're a reporter, covering the news, issues, and lives in your community and presenting them to your audience in an objective, balanced fashion. Though an occasional feature story may be about you, most of your work should put you in the background and your topic up front. If you're looking for stardom, take a bus to Hollywood.

The T.V. news business will have very few superstars in the years to come. It will have a driven, hard-working crew of journalists who can perform more than one job.

Of course, there are moments when I forget my own advice, and I begin to feel pretty smug. It's great to be recognized at a restaurant or in a shop. It's wonderful when a total stranger comes up and asks, "Aren't you that lady on T.V.?" I usually blush, nod my head, grin, and feel great. And that's when they deliver the ego-crushing blow. "Gosh," they'll say, "you look a lot better in person."

Chapter 10

Internships

"Journalism consists largely in saying 'Lord Jones Dead' to people who never knew Lord Jones was alive." —G.K. Chesterton (1874-1936)

This is a short chapter. That's because the message is simple: **Get an internship. If you have the time, get two.** It can only help you.

"I can't emphasize how important an internship is," Cris Johnson, a recruiter for Cable News Network, said. "Even if you go to a school like Northwestern or Emerson, you must have an internship on top of it."

Most television stations sponsor some type of internship program. In fact, over 90% of the news departments I contacted in my survey offer internships, and most run their programs throughout the year, so you can work as an intern during summer break or on a semester's leave.

The Advantages

Internships offer three huge advantages:

First, an internship lets you experience the "feel" of a newsroom. You'll learn the routines that make the place work, the buzzwords of electronic journalism, and the camaraderie necessary for a successful show. You'll discover (far better than you can from this book) what the different jobs in a newsroom entail, and you'll begin to see whether T.V. news really is a career you want to pursue for the next 50 years.

Second, an internship lets you make contacts. I can't stress the importance of "networking" (no pun intended) in this business. Despite its gargantuan influence on our daily lives and its huge revenues, T.V. news is a still a small, gossipy, incestuous industry, and you'll keep running into the same people over and over. "Many of our interns use people here as references," states JoAnne Wilder, the internship coordinator at WCAU-TV, a CBS-owned and -operated station in Philadelphia. "Former interns will come back and visit, and the contacts are invaluable."

Finally, an internship gives you an opportunity to make a résumé tape, which is the key to getting a real job.

Where and How
So, your question is never, "Do I want an internship?" Instead, ask yourself *where* you want one and *how* you're going to get it. You do have some options.

The first decision: Should you apply at a local station or a network?

A network can offer a range of experiences that are not available at the local level. In fact, a large outlet like Turner Broadcasting offers internships at CNN, WTBS, and TNT, and their internship opportunities range from CNN's "Environmental Unit" to *Larry King Live*. They even offer housing assistance during the intern's tenure.

Of course, since most internships do not include a wage—in fact, *The MacNeil/Lehrer Newshour* has the only paid internship I know about—you might not have the bucks to uproot yourself for a three-month hitch in Atlanta. New York and Washington, D.C. are other internship meccas, but the cost of living in these cities may be prohibitive.

While a network may offer a greater quantity of opportunities, its internships may not be of the highest quality. The same goes for big-market versus small-market local stations. A small station may *need* your services as an intern, while a large station might see you as just a "go-fer." Many News Directors advised that an internship at a small station will provide more chances for "hands-on" experience. Instead of watching someone do something, you'll learn to do it yourself.

At larger stations, there's also a greater chance you'll run into union snags. CBS, ABC, and NBC are heavily unionized, as are many stations in the larger markets. To protect their membership, the unions restrict who can do what in a newsroom. In a union shop, the operation of any equipment by someone not in the union is strictly *verboten*. So at a large-market station, you may lose the opportunity to learn how to edit, operate a camera, or run Chyron.

There's also more at stake at a large-market station. The people in a major newsroom are not going to trust an intern with anything of major importance. Mostly, you'll be relegated to performing menial chores, though you'll still have front-row seats to the drama of putting together a big league news show.

Apply Early

Many internships are offered on a first-come, first-served basis, so make sure you get your applications in early.

Gigi Shervanick, a project coordinator at Don Fitzpatrick Associates, thinks you should take the process one step further: "After your internship is over, offer to *volunteer* at the station. Everything is so tight these days, who wouldn't want a volunteer? Let them see your face, see your face, see your face. Let them know how valuable you are. If you're good, you're going to stand out."

What about Journalism School?

One final note. The discussion of internships leads to another obvious question: Do I need to enroll in a journalism school or major in a journalism program to get a job in T.V. news?

It's a good question. Lynn majored in medieval history at a small private college in Pennsylvania. Now she's a successful reporter and anchor. I transferred to Syracuse University as a sophomore and graduated from its Newhouse School. Now I'm a successful news photographer. Of course, Newhouse gave me only the fundamentals of journalism. I didn't take a single course in photography or electronic news-gathering there. In fact, I mostly took writing classes.

I really never considered a job in television. Rather, I thought I'd end up writing for a magazine. Most people in the business today have taken similar, circuitous routes to their present careers. So I can't really tell you, based on my own experience, whether majoring in journalism is the best thing to do. Certainly, the reputation of Newhouse opened some doors for me, but it's hard to say whether what I learned there has been particularly useful for me.

But the competition today is a lot fiercer than when Lynn and I first broke into T.V. news, so you'll need every advantage to get your first job. If you're really committed to getting a job in broadcasting, then enroll in the best broadcast journalism program that you can. It certainly can't hurt.

"Almost universally, journalism schools do a good job of prepping people in T.V. production," Cris Johnson says.

However, while a T.V. curriculum will teach you the basics of doing T.V., it won't provide much knowledge about the world around you. So I strongly advise you to consider a double major. History, political science, and economics are good companion fields for a broadcast journalism student.

Of course, there's considerable debate about the merits of broadcast journalism schools in general. I won't go into this too deeply here—there's enough material to write an entire book on the topic—but let's just say that not everyone believes in the value of a journalism program.

"I get depressed about the kind of students the journalism schools are turning out," Shervanick states. "Students aren't learning that the business is horribly competitive."

John Hurt, the News Director at KJAC-TV in Port Arthur, Texas (ADI #134), feels strongly about the issue. "The best advice I can give a prospective applicant is to stay away from a degree in broadcasting. The courses are worthless, usually taught by individuals who have been out of the industry for years, and they don't adequately prepare students for this business. Universities, despite their loud protests to the contrary, are teaching students the *science*, but not the *art*, of broadcasting. Most of the kids just want to be 'T.V. stars' and are not willing to educate themselves about the world around them."

There's one more option to consider: the so-called "trade schools"—schools that specialize specifically in radio/television education.

For example, the National Education Center in Minneapolis offers a nine-month certificate program and an Associate of Applied Science degree in radio/television broadcasting. They're fairly typical of a journalism trade school. "I have my best chance of getting someone a job in television when they've taken our certificate course *after* completing their four-year college degree—and have added as many internships as possible," Mike Kronforst, the Placement Director, advises.

"I would guess that about six or seven percent of our annual graduation gets an entry-level job in television," he continues. "I've seen the market tighten up over the 13 years I've been doing placement for broadcasting. There's no longer a chance to walk into a T.V. station and be discovered."

There are myriad choices you need to make concerning your education. There's simply no single best way to get into television. But, without a doubt, an internship is a building block that is absolutely vital to your career.

Chapter 11

CNN

*"The reason I stayed in Baghdad is quite simple.
Reporting is what I do for a living. I made the full
commitment to journalism years ago. If you ask,
'Are some stories worth the risk of dying for?' my
answer is yes—and many of my journalist friends
have died believing that. I revere their memories,
and I would betray them if I did anything less
than continue a full commitment to coverage."*
—CNN reporter Peter Arnett

"When you become a VJ, they tell you the job is like being
a waiter, but you don't get the tips," Bruce Jacobs says with a
laugh. After graduating from college with a history degree and
briefly trying a variety of career paths, Jacobs landed an entry-
level job with Cable News Network, which calls his position a
"video journalist," or "VJ."

Of course, the phrase "entry-level position" is a euphemism
for "starting at the bottom." CNN likes to start employees at the
bottom, indoctrinate them into the CNN system, and then let
them grow into more responsible positions as their abilities and
ambitions dictate. "There's more of a spread of upward mobili-
ty at CNN," explains Steve Haworth, Vice-President of Public
Relations for the network. "People often remark on how many
young people are working in responsible positions. A 30-year-
old here will get a lot more experience as say, a producer, than
his 45-year-old counterpart at one of the Big Three networks.

There's simply more news product here to get experience with."
At CNN, you really can start at the bottom and work your way
to the top of a network now on the cutting edge of broadcast news.

The Scene in Atlanta

The newsroom at CNN's headquarters in Atlanta is a study in
controlled chaos. Large scoop lights hang from a huge grid suspended high above the room, showering the newsroom with constant illumination. Producers and writers, crammed around three
circular desks, are connected to their news lifelines: computer
monitors and telex headsets. Their job is to make sense of the
day's events around the world. They must distill thousands of
pieces of information and hundreds of television images, and then
write and arrange it all into a coherent show.

The assignment editors and other shift managers sit at a long
desk that bisects the newsroom, flanked by the international and
national desks. The long back wall, which houses countless rout-
ers and tape decks, is where all the video feeds from around the
world are "steered in" and recorded. Tiny editing booths line the
outer corridors. A plexiglass wall above the newsroom reveals
an endless stream of gawking visitors taking the popular CNN
tour. In the control room, crammed into one corner of the newsroom, endless rows of monitors line the front wall, their images
flickering and changing as the Director reviews the current run-
down. A harried producer crushes a can of Coke. "Just the first
of many," he says with a grin.

Over 1,700 people around the world work for CNN in a news-
related job. In Atlanta alone, the network employs over 1,000
people in jobs directly related to getting the news on the air.
Another 250 people work for *Headline News*, and 450 are scattered throughout CNN's 24 news bureaus. These journalists are
faced with the task of filling a bottomless news hole. It's a for-
midable challenge, but most CNN employees seem happy to be
there. It wasn't always that way.

CNN Comes of Age

CNN used to have a terrible reputation. Called the "Chicken Noodle Network" in its early years, it was not a place an aspiring television journalist wanted to spend a lot of time, let alone build a career. Sure, if you showed some promise you could get a job, and with a little luck, you might work your way to a sexy bureau like Paris or Rome. But you couldn't make a living while you were doing it. That was the catch.

"CNN has really grown-up," explains Cris Johnson, former head of video journalist recruiting. "Things have changed dramatically. We used to be known as a poor-paying place where you could get some experience. Now our attrition rates are much lower."

Why? In the wake of Operation Desert Storm and the L.A. riots, CNN has exploded to the forefront of the news business. It has abandoned its reputation as a stripped-down, no-frills club for news junkies and now owns the bragging rights for getting breaking news on the air first, no matter where it's happening in the world.

From the very first moments of the Gulf War, CNN owned the story, and its reporters Bernard Shaw, Peter Arnett, and John Holliman pulled off the journalistic coup of the decade. With the aid of a device called a four-wire, they were able to broadcast live the first (and only) extensive accounts of the Allied air assault on Baghdad. CNN had an extraordinary exclusive. In the world of television news, exclusive coverage of the first major battle of a war involving the United States is about as good as it gets. Within hours, CNN had forged a new reputation. According to Cris Johnson, "CNN has become a neat place to be."

The Job Situation

It's also become the focal point for all the eager young people who want to work in T.V. news. "At the height of the Gulf War, we were getting about 450 applications a month. Now we're back down to 100 or 200 a month," Johnson says.

As you might expect, there's good news and bad news in this. The good news: CNN is hiring. And they're hiring people for entry-level jobs. In fact, CNN hires more people in entry-level positions than any other broadcast news operation in the world.

The bad news: The competition for jobs at CNN is more intense than ever. Not only does CNN get applications from the usual pool of college students, it's also flooded with applications from seasoned T.V. journalists who have lost their jobs in the recent recession. Highly qualified people from both local television and the national networks are pounding on CNN's door.

To maintain their policy of promoting from within the company, CNN established the entry-level "video journalist" (VJ) position. The majority of the field producers, technicians, editors, technical directors, master control personnel, associate producers, supervisors, desk assistants, and assignment editors at CNN—as well as producers and writers at *Headline News*—start as video journalists. However, most VJ's do **not** advance to on-air positions—a fact that CNN makes very clear from the start.

As you may suspect, VJ's do most of the grunt work. All the VJ's are based at CNN's headquarters in Atlanta, and all start on the floor crew. According to the network, most VJ's spend five to ten months on the studio floor before being promoted.

The entry-level VJ does get to make a few decisions, which can be pivotal to his career. First, a VJ must decide whether to take a technical track or an editorial track. The technical track takes the employee through a variety of positions, with the ultimate goal of being either an on-air director or a field photographer and editor. The editorial route moves the VJ through jobs like associate producer, copy editor, and tape production coordinator on the way to becoming a supervising or line producer.

Promotions to these positions are based solely on merit and are awarded through an evaluation process—and often a written test is thrown in for good measure. Though CNN cautions that promotions are not guaranteed, most VJ's advance to higher positions. You'll also be happy to learn that there are provisions for salary raises within most positions—and you'll certainly need them. Even though it's growing, CNN keeps its salary structure lean. VJ's receive a whopping $15,000 a year, based on a 40-hour work week.

Applying for the VJ Job

CNN takes the selection of its video journalists seriously. In fact, a three-person office is dedicated entirely to recruiting people for the various VJ positions. "We used to have a hard time finding enough qualified applicants, but that's not the case anymore," Johnson states. For example, in 1991, Johnson received over 3,700 video journalist applications. In "the old days," she says CNN hired about six VJ's a week. Today, they hire only four or five VJ's a *month*. Of those 3,700+ applicants in 1991, just 67 became CNN VJ's.

All job applicants at CNN must meet three basic requirements:

- A Bachelors or Masters degree in broadcast journalism (or a communications-related field) from a school that emphasizes both television production skills and news writing.

- Additional television production, studio, and/or newsroom experience—usually from internships in a professional television setting.

- A subjective trait CNN refers to as "news background." They feel a good candidate is interested in the news and has a strong awareness of—and involvement in—current events.

If you didn't graduate from some sort of communications program, you can still be considered for a VJ position. In fact, backgrounds of current VJ's include history, health, English, and law. However, CNN notes that these atypical VJ's have supplemented their degrees with a significant amount of newsroom internship experience.

Of course, those are just the minimum requirements. "We process all applicants with a writing test, where we ask candidates to rewrite long wire stories," Johnson explains. "We can screen out a lot of applicants this way. We're looking for people who have the skill to distill a long, complex story into 25 seconds or less." Last year, CNN administered over 600 such tests.

And what is Johnson looking for when she and her colleagues review the test? First, they're looking for people who have spent some time polishing their writing skills. "Most students feel it's a lot more fun to be in the field, holding a microphone and asking questions," she laments. "They feel it's more fun than working on your writing. But writing is what will get you a job here." Johnson looks primarily for three traits in an applicant's writing:

- Knowing what's important—the candidate must be able to cut through the clutter and get to the critical elements of a story.

- Style—the writer should be developing a personal style of writing.

- Originality—the applicant should be able to use his own words to tell a story. He must do more than simply edit the wire copy.

In face-to-face interviews, CNN's recruiters quiz applicants on their knowledge of current events and issues. And they don't ask vague questions like, "What do you think of the upcoming election?" or "How do you feel about abortion?" These interviews get specific. You'll not only need to know who Hosni Mubarak is, you'll also need to be able to discuss his relative importance and impact on the world.

The recruiters also try to determine how people will react to pressure. "If things are tense and people get yelled at," Johnson explains, "we want to know: Will they get flustered? Will they cry? Or will they show a capacity to react well under what are often difficult circumstances?"

Meet the VJ's

The people who make the final cut are highly qualified with impressive résumés. In fact, most of them are over-qualified.

Yasmin Ghahremani is an example. Ghahremani majored in advertising at the University of Texas, worked for two and a half years as a copywriter in New York, then got a graduate degree in international affairs from Columbia University. For good measure, she passed the State Department's foreign service exam.

"I sent CNN a résumé, but I didn't really know if I wanted to do it," she explained while munching a sandwich in the compact lunchroom at *Headline News*. "I was offered a position as a VJ, but I put it off. I couldn't imagine living on $15,000 a year."

A short time later, CNN offered her the VJ job again. This time she took it. "I didn't want to do just local news," she said. "My interests are international in scope. I'll definitely stay here for a while. I'd eventually like to get out of day-to-day news and do longer pieces."

Four months after starting as a video journalist, Ghahremani got her first promotion. She was moved into *Headline News*, where the career track moves a little quicker. Two or three days a week, she pulls scripts and does other basic chores for the show. On the other days, she's involved in what's called "write training," and she writes on-air stories for *Headline News*. She has a lighter load than a full-fledged staff writer would handle, but it's a start. And her work receives regular critiques—perhaps the most valuable part of the job. Trainees like Ghahremani will learn how to correct their mistakes, and they get a lot of personal attention as they refine their writing.

Bruce Jacobs took a more circuitous route. Jacobs graduated from the State University of New York at Binghamton with a history degree, but his ambitions were vague. He took a year off and traveled, working as a waiter in London and living on a *kibbutz* in Israel. When he returned to the U.S., he got a job in publishing but quit after two months. Then he got a job as—believe it or not—a shoe salesman. "The money was good, but I sort of got upset," Jacobs recounted. "I just knew I didn't want to be a shoe salesman. I sat down and thought about just what I wanted to do."

He decided to take the State Department's foreign service exam, but he flunked it. He then decided to try broadcasting and applied to USC's graduate school. "I wanted to get some connections in the biz, and I figured USC would be great for that," Jacobs said.

He was right. Jacobs, one step ahead of the crowd, investigated internships early in his first semester. "I pretty much had the run of them because I got started early," he recalled. After several dead ends, he landed an internship at KCBS, the CBS-affiliate in Los Angeles.

At first, he worked as a "news planner." In other words, he

opened the mail. "But I was just glad to be there," he said. "I was probably the only one there who would be happy to do that job. Going to school and interning gave me a new lease on life."

During the Christmas break, the station was short on available staff, and Jacobs jumped in to fill the void. "On Christmas Day, they asked me if I could work, and I said I'd be glad to work around the clock. And that's what I did. Then they taught me how to run the overnight desk, and I did that on New Year's. I eventually worked through the holidays and the semester, and then all the way the way through August."

Jacobs parlayed this experience into a job as a VJ at CNN. Like Ghahremani, he landed a slot at *Headline News* within four months of arriving in Atlanta. "This is a pretty secure place to be," Jacobs said. "It's a good learning experience. I can always take my risks later. If I put in my time here, I might try to get a job as a reporter somewhere else, but that's well in the future."

Applications for the video journalist position are screened continually, and new VJ's are hired as openings occur. If you'd like to apply, send a cover letter and résumé to

CNN Recruiter
CNN Human Resources
One CNN Center
Box 105366
Atlanta, GA 30348-5366

If you do send an application, don't send it to Cris Johnson. She's decided to go back into news as a producer for CNN International. "I just got the news bug again," she says with a smile.

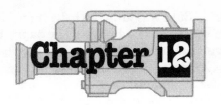

Chapter 12

That's the News . . .

"Doctors bury mistakes. Lawyers hang them. But journalists put theirs on the front page."
—anonymous

Let's assume you're all set. You've dotted all your i's and crossed all your t's on your résumé and cover letter; you've created a killer résumé tape; and now, armed with confidence, ambition, and the priceless information in this book, you're ready to impress News Directors all over North America with your broadcasting brilliance.

That's all great, but before you spend a lot of time and money pursuing a job, there's one final thing you must do. You've got to ask yourself *why* you want to make television news your career. Really: *Why?*

Sure, it sounds kind of silly, like one of those goofy "self exploration" exercises you did in church Youth Group when you were 14. However, before you take your first step on this career path, it's essential that you carefully, seriously appraise your commitment to the business of television news. It's a very tough profession.

Yes, there are many difficult professions, and we're certainly not suggesting that T.V. news is the only career that exacts a high cost. After all, many people spend years at medical school, in the bowels of a law library, or on the assembly line at a machine tools factory, and they'd say T.V. journalism looks mighty comfortable in comparison. But you must never underestimate the dedication the job will require and the ferocious competition within the industry.

At present, there are 1,131 commercial T.V. stations and 358 educational stations in the U.S.—a grand total of 1,489 stations. Throw in the networks, including the cable networks, and that's your entire job universe. And, of course, not all of these stations have viable news departments.

The simple truth is, the number of jobs in television news is fairly small. When you consider the facts that 1. colleges across the country are churning out thousands of eager journalism/communications/broadcasting graduates each year, and 2. hundreds of experienced television journalists have been laid off in the last few years and are looking *anywhere* for a job, you'll begin to see the problem you're facing.

Still feeling sanguine about your chosen career? OK then, next you need to assess whether you've got the "right stuff" for the job. This is a little tougher. While the people in the T.V. news work force come from all walks of life and span the range of personality types, those at the top of the profession tend to share certain attributes. Though we've covered some of this in earlier chapters, consider the following as more of a personal viewpoint, a brief primer on Gritty Personal Traits and Other Relevant Thoughts and Musings. These views, solely the opinions of the authors, are totally unsupported by anything as tedious as facts or empirical data.

Trait #1: Intensity

In general, journalists (and anyone in the news business) tend to live a little on the edge. Most, for example, crave spot news, which always makes newsrooms shift into a higher gear and causes a communal adrenaline surge.

Maybe it's a bit warped, but the possibility of a raging hurricane or a big plane crash will make any good journalist's pulse quicken. A major spot news story is a newsroom's call to action. It means working at a frantic pace in conditions that are unknown or constantly changing. In short, it's probably the biggest challenge in the business. And people in this business thrive on challenges.

Spot news also puts the journalist at the center of activity. Good newspeople all want to cover the biggest story of the day, every day. That's impossible, of course, but the desire is always present. In fact, good newspeople not only want to cover the biggest story of the day, they want to handle it so well that their competition *cries*.

So it's only right that spot news is the acid-test of any news department. It's when news departments strain their resources to be the first and the best. How a station performs during times of crisis and catastrophe goes a long way toward forging an image with its audience.

Let's face it, when bombs land on Baghdad and Los Angeles erupts in riots, millions of people become glued to their televisions. There's an undeniable fascination in watching such things unfold. Well, working in T.V. news gives you a ringside seat to these events, and it's your job to translate them into a coherent story—a thrilling, awesome responsibility.

We've been covering news since the late 1970's, and our jobs have provided us with a lot of unique experiences in a lot of unusual, and sometimes difficult, situations. We've covered hurricanes, train wrecks, myriad automobile accidents, fires of all kinds, police shootings, gang riots, Ku Klux Klan rallies, floods, bank robberies, avalanches, and countless homicides.

Did we enjoy covering all these stories? No. Did all of them provide a rush of adrenaline? No. Did we always make the competition cry? No. Did we cry? Sometimes. But they all came as part of the job. And a big part of the job is gritting your teeth and doing your job as well as you can while you cover things that are grim, tragic, or distasteful. It's all part of the territory, and the territory requires intensity.

Of course, T.V. news is not all mayhem and tragedy. In fact, we get annoyed when people call us "ambulance chasers." Sure, we do cover a lot of murders and fatal car wrecks, but such stories comprise only a small part of our work in a given week or month. We also handle plenty of upbeat features, boring city council meetings, and community notables. They all require intensity, too.

It's considerably harder to get pumped up for a story on a new zoning law than it is for a piece on a hostage situation in a crack house. But you've got to muster the same intensity, the same level of dedication, tenacity, and attention to detail for both stories. It's how "professionalism" is defined in television journalism.

Trait #2: Curiosity

Being a news photographer and a reporter offers the opportunity to be a voyeur of life and a license to poke around in the nooks and crannies of strangers' lives. You get to see everything from how a homeless person survives to how a space shuttle gets launched.

For whatever reasons, a T.V. camera and a microphone open doors closed to the general public. We usually find it pretty interesting to get behind those doors. Indeed, we *love* getting behind those doors. We've been inside maximum security prisons, nuclear weapons plants, and the Denver Broncos' locker room after a Super Bowl loss. We've ridden in fighter jets, on hydroplanes, and even on a bobsled. We've stood just beneath the President as he gave a speech and at the bottom of the Olympic downhill ski run at Val D'Isere. All in the name of T.V. news— and *local* news, at that.

Good journalists have an innate desire to get to the bottom of things, whether it's proving that local Public Works employees are goofing off most of the day or discovering why a 90-year-old barber still clips hair in the prairie town where he was born.

Working in T.V. news requires a large dose of curiosity—from people who work both in the field and in the newsroom. Often, the best information in a story is uncovered by a lot of phone-calling and paper-trailing—activities that aren't as glamorous as waving a microphone under some big shot's nose.

Curiosity is required in both hard news and soft features. Feature stories provide more flexibility and need more creativity, but they demand the same degree of probing as the day's lead story. Any good story needs two things: people and emotion. A well-crafted feature capitalizes on a person's character traits; discovering those traits requires an interest in your subject. And you'll get your answers only by asking lots of questions and getting to know the people in your story.

If you're usually satisfied with the status quo, then you should consider a different profession. Good journalists have a thousand questions, and they're not happy until they get an answer to each and every one.

Trait #3: Competitiveness

It's come up more than once in these pages: Good journalists want to win. They want to be the best. They hate getting beat on a story. And they're usually willing to expend the enormous effort required to stay at the top of the heap.

Mostly, that effort translates into hours, thousands and thousands of hours on the job. News is not just a career, it's a lifestyle. You never know when your beeper will go off or when the phone will ring. A working journalist often has absolutely no idea what he'll be doing tomorrow, where he'll be doing it, or how long he'll be there. It's a career that demands great flexibility and considerable understanding from your family and friends.

In a sense, we have it easy, since we each married someone who works in television news. We don't have to explain why a gang shooting means that we'll be late for dinner, or why we have to wake up at 0-dark-30 to get out by sunrise because that's when the light is good.

The journalism lifestyle has caused more than one divorce. And, in these recessionary times, the demands on journalists are increasing. Every station and every network is trying to do more with less. This means you'll be spending more time at work and less time at home. When a big story breaks, News Directors and Assignment Editors don't want to hear about your dinner reservations or your daughter's kindergarten play. They want you to go out and cover the story. That's your job.

And the news never stops. Like doctors, police officers, and 7-Eleven clerks, you'll have the privilege of working holidays, nights, and weekends. There are plenty of brutal shifts in this business. We worked either nights or weekends—or both—for our first five years in television. We've missed so many Thanksgiving and Christmas dinners that we've forgotten how turkey and dressing tastes. It's a tough profession for the sentimental.

People in T.V. news are usually highly motivated and highly driven. And we all have a sizeable ego. If you ever doubt the degree of ego and competitive fire in this business, then just consider the number of awards contests for T.V. journalists. Just in Colorado, we annually compete in the Emmy Awards, the Associated Press Awards, the Sigma Delta Chi Awards, and the Colorado Broadcaster's Association Awards. On a national level, there are the Dupont Awards, the Peabody Awards, the Scripps-Howard Awards, the National Press Photographers Association Awards—and the list goes on. Only the military gives out more medals.

There's probably not a more self-promoting profession, either. Indeed, there's a danger that television journalism will drown itself in a flood of promotional hype and backslapping. Simply broadcasting a quality news show isn't enough to survive today. No, your station must also sponsor an endless series of parades, health fairs, tree plantings, fun runs, and the like—all in the name of being a good "community partner."

Yes, to survive in the 90's, T.V. stations (especially the news departments) play a game called "We Are a Vital Part of Your Community." The strategy is simple: If you sponsor enough community events, the community will repay you by watching your station. The more viewers you attract, the more money you can charge advertisers. It's a fairly harmless game, though it does tend to blur the line between reporting the news and creating it.

T.V. stations also want you to become dependent on them for information—and we're talking more than just the who, what, when, where, and why of the day's news events. Stations want you to learn about the risks of high blood pressure or the precautions to take in a thunderstorm from those helpful reporters on the evening news. And, of course, there's an address on the screen where you can write and get a handy pamphlet on the warning signs of melanoma.

It's hard to say whether this is good or bad, but you should know that it's an integral part of today's local television news environment. Some anchors and reporters love to make station-sponsored appearances at retirement homes or shopping centers; others simply bite their tongues and do the deed. In a fiercely competitive environment, anything that gives you and your station an advantage will be part of your job profile.

Conclusions

Like any other career, television news will offer things you love and things you detest. It's all a matter of tipping the scales in the right direction.

We still enjoy our jobs enormously. Sometimes we think it's the greatest thing since the Mets won the '69 World Series, and sometimes we feel like we're stuck in a never-ending cycle of car wrecks, toaster fires, and talking heads.

It can be tedious and mundane, and it can also be thrilling and rewarding. Spot news aside, when we hear about a story with a lot of compelling elements, we're eager to get out and do it. It can range from a family divided by the abortion rights issue to a small town's horse race on the High Plains. Doing a good story is something we all savor. Doing a good story that has some meaningful impact is even better.

Television news is not just a job, it's a craft. It takes years to learn and refine the skills necessary to create a good story or produce a good newscast. And, like many crafts, it insists that you use your creativity every day. There is no right or wrong way to do a story or produce a newscast. There are simply things that work, and things that don't work. The options—and the challenges—are infinite. If you can maintain a high level of intensity, curiosity, and competitiveness over time, you'll make increasingly better decisions.

Working in T.V. news can be incredibly exciting and genuinely rewarding. It can also be totally frustrating and thoroughly disheartening.

Is it the right profession for you? Only you have the answer. Good luck!

Television Markets Ranked by Size*

Market—Population of ADI

1. New York—6,749,500
2. Los Angeles—4,883,200
3. Chicago—2,999,700
4. Philadelphia—2,637,400
5. San Francisco/Oakland/San Jose—2,208,000
6. Boston—2,126,300
7. Washington, D.C.—1,718,100
8. Dallas/Fort Worth—1,763,400
9. Detroit—1,719,000
10. Atlanta—1,456,800
11. Houston—1,452,000
12. Cleveland—1,421,800
13. Minneapolis/St. Paul—1,380,100
14. Seattle/Tacoma—1,379,400
15. Miami/Ft. Lauderdale—1,286,300
16. Tampa/St. Petersburg—1,243,100
17. Pittsburgh—1,139,600
18. St. Louis—1,110,900
19. Sacramento/Stockton—1,045,700
20. Phoenix—1,021,500
21. Denver—1,008,200
22. Baltimore—963,900
23. Orlando/Daytona Beach/Melbourne—926,900
24. Hartford/New Haven—925,600
25. San Diego—911,200
26. Indianapolis—853,200
27. Portland (OR)—839,900
28. Milwaukee—765,300
29. Kansas City—762,900

*Source: 1991-92 Arbitron Television ADI Market Rankings

30. Cincinnati—759,000
31. Charlotte—740,000
32. Raleigh/Durham—729,300
33. Nashville (TN)—720,900
34. Columbus (OH)—691,300
35. Greenville/Spartanburg/Asheville—657,900
36. Buffalo—629,400
37. Grand Rapids/Kalamazoo/Battle Creek—612,700
38. Norfolk/Portsmith/Newport News/Hampton—607,500
39. Memphis—597,000
40. New Orleans—595,400
41. San Antonio—584,900
42. Salt Lake City—584,600
43. Providence/New Bedford—571,700
44. Oklahoma City—564,900
45. Louisville—549,700
46. West Palm Beach/Ft. Pierce/Vero Beach—546,800
47. Harrisburg/York/Lancaster/Lebanon—542,900
48. Greensboro/Winston Salem/High Point—527,400
49. Wilkes Barre/Scranton—518,500
50. Birmingham (AL)—505,100
51. Albany/Schenectady/Troy—503,500
52. Albuquerque—502,000
53. Dayton (OH)—498,900
54. Jacksonville (FL)—471,500
55. Charleston/Huntington—462,200
56. Flint/Saginaw/Bay City—451,500
57. Little Rock—449,100
58. Tulsa—443,600
59. Fresno/Visalia—441,700
60. Richmond (VA)—436,900
61. Wichita/Hutchinson—423,200
62. Knoxville (TN)—420,900
63. Mobile/Pensacola—410,200
64. Toledo—401,300
65. Roanoke/Lynchburg—389,300
66. Syracuse—381,500
67. Green Bay/Appleton—380,700
68. Austin (TX)—375,200
69. Portland/Poland Spring (ME)—368,800
70. Des Moines—368,000
71. Shreveport/Texarkana—362,600
72. Rochester (NY)—358,300
73. Omaha—356,700
74. Lexington (KY)—342,300
75. Paducah/Cape Girardeau/Harrisburg—333,000

75. Springfield/Decatur/Champaign—333,000
77. Springfield (MO)—318,900
78. Tucson—311,200
79. Las Vegas—310,700
80. Spokane—310,000
81. Chattanooga—306,900
82. Cedar Rapids/Waterloo/Dubuque—298,800
83. Davenport/Rock Island/Moline—298,100
83. Johnstown/Altoona—298,100
85. Bristol/Kingsport/Johnson City (TN)—295,100
86. South Bend/Elkhart—295,000
87. Columbia (SC)—289,100
88. Huntsville/Decatur/Florence—285,400
89. Jackson (MS)—276,100
90. Ft. Myers/Naples—275,200
91. Youngstown—269,300
92. Madison (WI)—265,200
93. Evansville—258,200
94. Waco/Temple/Bryan—250,200
95. Baton Rouge—249,500
96. Springfield (MA)—247,700
97. Burlington/Plattsburgh—240,800
98. Lincoln/Hastings/Kearney—238,600
99. Colorado Springs/Pueblo—238,100
100. El Paso—237,800
101. Savannah—232,000
102. Fort Wayne—231,500
103. Lansing—226,300
104. Greenville/New Bern/Washington—225,900
105. Charleston (SC)—223,100
106. Sioux Falls/Mitchell—218,600
107. Peoria/Bloomington—217,000
108. Fargo—212,800
109. Santa Barbara/Santa Maria/San Luis Obispo—209,000
110. Montgomery/Selma—208,000
111. Salinas/Monterey—207,900
112. Augusta—203,300
113. Tyler/Longview/Jacksonville—199,800
114. McAllen/Brownsville—196,800
115. Tallahassee/Thomasville—195,300
116. Reno—191,400
117. Eugene—190,300
118. Fort Smith—186,600
119. Lafayette (LA)—181,600
120. Macon—180,200
121. Columbus (GA)—179,700

122. Traverse City/Cadillac—179,500
123. La Crosse/Eau Claire—173,500
124. Columbus/Tupelo—170,100
125. Corpus Christi—169,400
126. Duluth/Superior—168,200
127. Amarillo—166,000
128. Monroe/El Dorado—165,700
129. Yakima/Pasco/Richland/Kennewick—164,900
130. Chico/Redding—161,600
131. Wausau/Rhinelander—160,400
132. Bakersfield—158,600
133. Binghamton—158,300
134. Beaumont/Port Arthur—158,200
135. Rockford—155,000
136. Terre Haute—154,400
137. Sioux City—151,900
138. Florence/Myrtle Beach—151,000
139. Wichita Falls/Lawton—150,900
140. Erie—150,300
141. Topeka—150,100
142. Boise—149,000
143. Wilmington—146,100
144. Wheeling/Steubenville—142,400
145. Joplin/Pittsburg—137,900
146. Bluefield/Beckley/Oak Hill—134,800
147. Lubbock—134,600
148. Rochester/Mason City/Austin—134,400
149. Medford—133,900
149. Minot/Bismarck/Dickinson/Glendive—133,900
151. Odessa/Midland—133,400
152. Columbia/Jefferson City—132,600
153. Albany (GA)—131,400
154. Sarasota—129,300
155. Bangor—123,900
156. Quincy/Hannibal—108,700
157. Abilene/Sweetwater—107,100
158. Biloxi/Gulfport/Pascagoula—106,600
159. Clarksburg/Weston—104,900
160. Idaho Falls/Pocatello—104,800
161. Utica—103,900
162. Panama City—96,700
163. Salisbury—95,300
164. Laurel/Hattiesburg—94,300
165. Gainesville—90,000
166. Dothan—88,900
167. Harrisonburg—88,000

168. Watertown/Carthage—86,400
169. Elmira—86,300
170. Palm Springs—85,700
171. Rapid City—84,600
172. Billings/Hardin—84,000
173. Alexandria (LA)—83,600
174. Lake Charles—80,400
175. Greenwood/Greenville—73,700
176. Jonesboro—71,800
177. Missoula—71,300
178. Ardmore/Ada—69,500
179. Grand Junction/Durango—67,400
180. El Centro/Yuma—67,300
181. Meridan—64,900
182. Great Falls—61,800
183. Jackson (TN)—57,400
184. Parkersburg—56,600
185. Tuscaloosa—55,900
186. Marquette—55,700
187. Eureka—53,400
188. San Angelo—48,900
189. St. Joseph—48,700
190. Butte—48,600
191. Bowling Green—46,000
192. Hagerstown—45,200
193. Lafayette (IN)—45,100
194. Anniston—43,000
195. Cheyenne/Scottsbluff—41,600
196. Charlottesville—40,800
197. Casper/Riverton—39,800
198. Lima—38,900
199. Laredo—38,000
200. Twin Falls—35,600
201. Ottumwa/Kirksville—33,600
202. Presque Isle—30,500
203. Zanesville—30,400
204. Mankato—29,900
205. Flagstaff—29,400
206. Bend—28,500
207. Victoria—25,800
208. Helena—18,300
209. North Platte—17,500
210. Alpena—15,700

Addresses of U.S. Television Stations with News Programs

(listed by market size)

1. New York, NY

WABC-TV
7 Lincoln Square
New York, NY 10023
212-456-7777

WCBS-TV
524 West 57th St.
New York, NY 10019
212-975-4321

WNBC-TV
30 Rockefeller Plaza
New York, NY 10020
212-664-4444

WNYC-TV (non-commercial station)
One Centre St.
New York, NY 10007
212-669-7800

WNYW
205 East 67th St.
New York, NY 10021
212-452-5555

WPIX
11 WPIX Plaza
New York, NY 10017
212-949-1100

WWOR-TV
9 Broadcast Plaza
Secaucus, NJ 07096
201-348-0009

2. Los Angeles, CA

KABC-TV
4151 Prospect Ave.
Los Angeles, CA 90027
310-557-7777

KCAL
5515 Melrose Ave.
Los Angeles, CA 90038
213-467-9999

KCBS-TV
6121 Sunset Blvd.
Los Angeles, CA 90028
213-460-3000

KCET (non-commercial)
4401 Sunset Blvd.
Hollywood, CA 90027
213-666-6500

KCOP
915 North La Brea Ave.
Los Angeles, CA 90038
213-851-1000

KMEX-TV (Univision)
6255 Sunset Blvd., 16th Floor
Hollywood, CA 90028
213-960-3313

KNBC-TV
3000 West Alameda Ave.
Burbank, CA 91523
818-840-4444

KTLA
5800 Sunset Blvd.
Los Angeles, CA 90078
213-460-5500

KVEA
1130A Air Way
Glendale, CA 91201
818-502-5700

KWHY-TV
5545 Sunset Blvd.
Los Angeles, CA 90028
213-466-5441

KTTV (Fox)
5746 Sunset Blvd.
Los Angeles, CA 90028
213-856-1000

3. Chicago, IL

WBBM-TV (CBS)
630 North McClurg Court
Chicago, IL 60611
312-944-6000

WCIU-TV
141 W. Jackson Blvd.
Chicago, IL 60604
312-663-0260

WFLD (Fox)
205 North Michigan Ave.
Chicago, IL 60601
312-565-5532

WGN-TV
2501 Bradley Pl.
Chicago, IL 60618
312-528-2311

WLS-TV (ABC)
190 North State St.
Chicago, IL 60601
312-750-7777

WMAQ-TV (NBC)
454 North Columbus Dr.
Chicago, IL 60611
312-836-5555

WSNS (Telemundo)
430 West Grant Pl.
Chicago, IL 60614
312-929-1200

4. Philadelphia, PA

KYW-TV (NBC)
Independence Mall East
Philadelphia, PA 19106
215-238-4700

WCAU-TV (CBS)
City Ave. & Monument Rd.
Philadelphia, PA 19131
215-668-5510

WPVI-TV (ABC)
4100 City Line Ave.
Philadelphia, PA 19131
215-878-9700

WTXF-TV (Fox)
330 Market St.
Philadelphia, PA 19106
215-925-2929

---

*"I hate television. I hate it as much as peanuts.
But I can't stop eating peanuts."* —Orson Welles

5. San Francisco/Oakland/ San Jose, CA

KDTV (Univision)
2200 Palou Ave.
San Francisco, CA 94124
415-641-1400

KGO-TV (ABC)
900 Front St.
San Francisco, CA 94111
415-954-7777

KPIX (CBS)
855 Battery St.
San Francisco, CA 94111
415-362-5550

KRON-TV (NBC)
1001 Van Ness Ave.
San Francisco, CA 94109
415-441-4444

KTSF
100 Valley Dr.
Brisbane, CA 94005
415-468-2626

KTVU (Fox)
Box 22222
Oakland, CA 94623
510-834-1212

KICU-TV
1585 Schallenberger Rd.
San Jose, CA 95131
408-298-3636

KNTV (ABC)
645 Park Ave.
San Jose, CA 95110
408-286-1111

KSTS (Telemundo)
2349 Bering Dr.
San Jose, CA 95131
408-435-8848

6. Boston, MA

WBZ-TV (NBC)
1170 Soldiers Field Rd.
Boston, MA 02134
617-787-7000

WCVB-TV (ABC)
5 TV Place
Needham, MA 02194
617-449-0400

WGBH-TV (non-commercial)
125 Western Ave.
Boston, MA 02134
617-492-2777

WHDH-TV (CBS)
7 Bulfinch Place
Boston, MA 02114
617-725-0777

WLVI-TV
75 Morrissey Blvd.
Boston, MA 02125
617-265-5656

7. Washington, D.C.

WETA-TV (non-commercial)
Box 2626
Washington, D.C. 20013
703-998-2600

WJLA-TV (ABC)
3007 Tilden St., N.W.
Washington, D.C. 20008
202-364-7777

WRC-TV (NBC)
4001 Nebraska Ave., N.W.
Washington, D.C. 20016
202-885-4000

WTTG (Fox)
5151 Wisconsin Ave., N.W.
Washington, D.C. 20016
202-244-5151

WUSA (CBS)
4100 Wisconsin Ave., N.W.
Washington, D.C. 20016
202-895-5999

8. Dallas/Fort Worth, TX

KDFW-TV (CBS)
400 North Griffin
Dallas, TX 75202
214-720-4444

KXTX-TV
3900 Harry Hines Blvd.
Dallas, TX 75219
214-521-3900

WFAA-TV (ABC)
606 Young St.
Dallas, TX 75202
214-748-9631

KFWD (Telemundo)
3000 West Story Rd.
Irving, TX 75038
214-637-5200

KTVT
5233 Bridge St.
Fort Worth, TX 76113
817-451-1111

KXAS-TV (NBC)
3900 Barnett
Fort Worth, TX 76103
817-536-5555

9. Detroit, MI

WDIV (NBC)
550 West Lafayette Blvd.
Detroit, MI 48231
313-222-0444

WGPR-TV
3146 East Jefferson Ave.
Detroit, MI 48207
313-259-8862

WJBK-TV (CBS)
Box 2000
Southfield, MI 48037
313-557-2000

WKBD (Fox)
26905 West 11 Mile Rd.
Southfield, MI 48037
313-350-5050

WXON
27777 Franklin Rd., Suite 1220
Southfield, MI 48034
313-355-2900

WXYZ-TV (ABC)
20777 West 10 Mile Rd.
Southfield, MI 48037
313-827-7777

10. Atlanta, GA

WAGA-TV (CBS)
1551 Briarcliff Rd. N.E.
Atlanta, GA 30306
404-875-5555

WGNX
1810 Briarcliff Rd. N.E.
Atlanta, GA 30329
404-325-4646

WSB-TV (ABC)
1601 West Peachtree St. N.E.
Atlanta, GA 30309
404-897-7000

WXIA-TV (NBC)
1611 West Peachtree St. N.E.
Atlanta, GA 30309
404-892-1611

11. Houston, TX

KHOU-TV (CBS)
1945 Allen Pkwy.
Houston, TX 77019
713-526-1111

KHTV (Independent)
7700 Westpark Dr.
Houston, TX 77063
713-781-3939

KPRC-TV (NBC)
Box 2222
Houston, TX 77252
713-771-4631

KRIV (Fox)
3935 Westheimer Rd.
Houston, TX 77227
713-626-2610

KTRK-TV (ABC)
3310 Bissonnet
Houston, TX 77005
713-666-0713

12. Cleveland, OH

WEWS (ABC)
3001 Euclid Ave.
Cleveland, OH 44115
216-431-5555

WJW-TV (CBS)
5800 S. Marginal Rd.
Cleveland, OH 44103
216-431-8888

WKYC-TV (NBC)
1403 E. 6th St.
Cleveland, OH 44114
216-344-3333

WQHS
2861 W. Ridgewood Dr.
Parma, OH 44134
216-888-0061

WUAB
8443 Day Dr.
Cleveland, OH 44129
216-845-6043

13. Minneapolis/St. Paul, MN

KARE (NBC)
8811 Olson Memorial Hwy.
Minneapolis, MN 55427
612-546-1111

KITN-TV (Fox)
7325 Aspen Lane North
Minneapolis, MN 55428
612-424-2929

KMSP-TV (Independent)
6975 York Ave. South
Minneapolis, MN 55435
612-926-9999

KSTP-TV (ABC)
3415 University Ave.
St. Paul, MN 55114
612-646-5555

KTMA
1640 Como Ave.
St. Paul, MN 55108
612-646-2300

WCCO-TV (CBS)
90 S. 11th St.
Minneapolis, MN 55403
612-339-4444

14. Seattle/Tacoma, WA

KING-TV (NBC)
333 Dexter Ave. North
Seattle, WA 98124
206-448-5555

KIRO-TV (CBS)
2807 Third Ave.
Seattle, WA 98111
206-728-7777

KOMO-TV (ABC)
100 4th Ave. North
Seattle, WA 98109
206-443-4000

KSTW
Box 11411
Tacoma, WA 98411
206-572-5789

15. Miami/Ft. Lauderdale, FL

WCIX (CBS)
8900 N.W. 18th Terrace
Miami, FL 33172
305-593-0606

WPLG (ABC)
3900 Biscayne Blvd.
Miami, FL 33137
305-576-1010

WSVN (Fox)
1401 79th St., Causeway
Miami, FL 33141
305-751-6692

WTVJ (NBC)
316 N. Miami Ave.
Miami, FL 33128
305-379-4444

16. Tampa/St. Petersburg, FL

WFLA-TV (NBC)
905 E. Jackson St.
Tampa, FL 33602
813-228-8888

WTOG
365 105th Terrace N.E.
St. Petersburg, FL 33716
813-576-4444

WTSP (ABC)
11450 Gandy Blvd.
St. Petersburg, FL 33702
813-577-1010

WTVT (CBS)
3213 W. Kennedy Blvd.
Tampa, FL 33609
813-876-1313

17. Pittsburgh, PA

KDKA-TV (CBS)
One Gateway Center
Pittsburgh, PA 15222
412-392-2200

WPXI (NBC)
11 Television Hill
Pittsburgh, PA 15230
412-237-1100

WTAE-TV (ABC)
400 Ardmore Blvd.
Pittsburgh, PA 15221
412-242-4300

18. St. Louis, MO

KMOV (CBS)
One Memorial Dr.
St. Louis, MO 63102
314-621-4444

KPLR-TV
4935 Lindell Blvd.
St. Louis, MO 63108
314-367-7211

KSDK (NBC)
1000 Market St.
St. Louis, MO 63101
314-421-5055

KTVI (ABC)
5915 Berthold Ave.
St. Louis, MO 63110
314-647-2222

19. Sacramento/Stockton, CA

KCRA-TV (NBC)
3 Television Circle
Sacramento, CA 95814
916-446-3333

KCSO (Univision)
Box 3689
Modesto, CA 95352
209-578-1900

KOVR (ABC)
2713 KOVR Dr.
West Sacramento, CA 95605
916-374-1313

KRBK-TV
500 Media Pl.
Sacramento, CA 95815
916-929-0300

KTXL (Fox)
4655 Fruitridge Rd.
Sacramento, CA 95820
916-454-4422

KXTV (CBS)
400 Broadway
Sacramento, CA 95818
916-441-2345

20. Phoenix, AZ
KPHO-TV
4016 N. Black Canyon
Phoenix, AZ 85017
602-264-1000

KPNX (NBC)
1101 N. Central Ave.
Phoenix, AZ 85004
602-257-1212

KTSP-TV (CBS)
511 W. Adams St.
Phoenix, AZ 85003
602-257-1234

KTVK (ABC)
3435 N. 16th St.
Phoenix, AZ 85016
602-263-3333

KTVW-TV (Univision)
3019 E. Southern Ave.
Phoenix, AZ 85040
602-243-3333

21. Denver, CO
KCNC-TV (NBC)
Box 5012
Denver, CO 80217
303-861-4444

KMGH-TV (CBS)
123 Speer Blvd.
Denver, CO 80203
303-832-7777

KUSA-TV (ABC)
500 Speer Blvd.
Denver, CO 80203
303-871-9999

KWGN-TV (Independent)
6160 S. Wabash Way
Englewood, CO 80111
303-740-2222

22. Baltimore, MD
WBAL-TV (CBS)
3800 Hooper Ave.
Baltimore, MD 21211
410-467-3000

WBFF (Fox)
2000 W. 41st St.
Baltimore, MD 21211
410-467-4545

WJZ-TV (ABC)
TV Hill
Baltimore, MD 21211
410-466-0013

WMAR-TV (NBC)
64009 York Rd.
Baltimore, MD 21212
410-377-2222

WMPB (non-commercial)
11767 Owings Mills Blvd.
Owings Mill, MD 21117
410-356-5600

**23. Orlando/Daytona Beach/
Melbourne, FL**

WAYQ
944 Sea Breeze Blvd., Suite 940
Daytona Beach, FL 32018
904-238-0026

WCPX-TV (CBS)
4466 John Young Pkwy.
Orlando, FL 32804
407-291-6000

WESH (NBC)
211 N. Ridgewood Ave.
Daytona Beach, FL 32115
904-226-2222

WFTV
490 E. South St.
Orlando, FL 32801
407-841-9000

WOFL (Fox)
35 Skyline Dr.
Lake Mary, FL 32746
407-644-3535

24. Hartford/New Haven, CT

WFSB (CBS)
3 Constitution Plaza
Hartford, CT 06103
203-728-3333

WTIC-TV (Fox)
One Corporate Center
Hartford, CT 06103
203-527-6161

WVIT (NBC)
1422 New Britain Ave.
West Hartford, CT 06110
203-521-3030

WTNH-TV (ABC)
Box 1859
New Haven, CT 06508
203-784-8888

WTWS
216 Broad St.
New London, CT 06320
203-444-2626

25. San Diego, CA

KFMB-TV (CBS)
7677 Engineer Rd.
San Diego, CA 92111
619-571-8888

KGTV (ABC)
Box 85347
San Diego, CA 92186
619-237-1010

KNSD (NBC)
8330 Engineer Rd.
San Diego, CA 92171
619-279-3939

KUSI-TV
4575 Viewridge Ave.
San Diego, CA 92123
619-571-5151

XEWT-TV (Tijuana, Mexico)
8253 Ronson Rd.
San Ysidro, CA 92073
706-684-5185

26. Indianapolis

WISH-TV (CBS)
1950 N. Meridian St.
Indianapolis, IN 46207
317-923-8888

WRTV (ABC)
1330 N. Meridian St.
Indianapolis, IN 46202
317-635-9788

WTHR (NBC)
1000 N. Meridian St.
Indianapolis, IN 46204
317-636-1313

WXIN (Fox)
1440 N. Meridian St.
Indianapolis, IN 46202
317-632-5900

27. Portland, OR

KATU (ABC)
2153 N.E. Sandy Blvd.
Portland, OR 97232
503-231-4222

KGW-TV (NBC)
1501 S.W. Jefferson St.
Portland, OR 97201
503-226-5000

KOIN-TV (CBS)
222 S.W. Columbia St.
Portland, OR 97201
503-464-0600

KPTV
Box 3401
Portland, OR 97208
503-222-9921

28. Milwaukee, WI

WISN-TV (ABC)
Box 402
Milwaukee, WI 53201
414-342-8812

WITI-TV (CBS)
9001 N. Green Bay Rd.
Milwaukee, WI 53217
414-355-6666

WMVS (non-commercial)
1036 N. 8th St.
Milwaukee, WI 53233
414-271-1036

WTMJ-TV (NBC)
720 E. Capitol Dr.
Milwaukee, WI 53201
414-332-9611

WVTV
4041 N. 35th St.
Milwaukee, WI 53216
414-442-7050

29. Kansas City, MO

KCTV (CBS)
4500 Shawnee Mission Pkwy.
Fairway, KS 66205
913-677-5555

KMBC-TV (ABC)
1049 Central
Kansas City, MO 64105
816-221-9999

KSHB-TV (Fox)
4720 Oak St.
Kansas City, MO 64112
816-753-4141

WDAF-TV (NBC)
Signal Hill
Kansas City, MO 64108
816-753-4567

30. Cincinnati, OH

WCPO-TV (CBS)
500 Central Ave.
Cincinnati, OH 45202
513-721-9900

WKRC-TV (ABC)
1906 Highland Ave.
Cincinnati, OH 45219
513-763-5500

WLWT (NBC)
140 W. 9th St.
Cincinnati, OH 45202
513-352-5000

WXIX-TV (Fox)
10490 Taconic Terrace
Cincinnati, OH 45215
513-772-1919

31. Charlotte, NC

WBTV (CBS)
One Julian Price Pl.
Charlotte, NC 28208
704-374-3500

WCCB (Fox)
One TV Place
Charlotte, NC 28205
704-372-1800

WCNC-TV (NBC)
1001 Wood Ridge Center Dr.
Charlotte, NC 28217
704-329-3636

WSOC-TV (ABC)
1901 N. Tryon St.
Charlotte, NC 28206
704-335-4999

32. Raleigh-Durham, NC

WPTF-TV (NBC)
3012 Highwoods Blvd.
Durham, NC 27604
919-876-0674

WRAL-TV (CBS)
2619 Western Blvd.
Raleigh, NC 20606
919-821-8555

WRMY
126 N. Washington St.
Rocky Mount, NC 27801
919-985-2447

WTVD
Box 2009
Durham, NC 27702
919-683-1111

33. Nashville, TN

WKRN-TV (ABC)
441 Murfreesboro Rd.
Nashville, TN 37210
615-259-2200

WSMV (NBC)
5700 Knob Rd.
Nashville, TN 37209
615-749-2244

WTVF (CBS)
474 James Robertson Pkwy.
Nashville, TN 37219
615-244-5000

34. Columbus, OH

WBNS-TV (CBS)
770 Twin Rivers Dr.
Columbus, OH 43215
614-460-3700

WCMH (NBC)
3165 Olentangy River Rd.
Columbus, OH 43202
614-263-4444

WSYX
1261 Dublin Rd.
Columbus, OH 43216
614-481-6666

WWAT
1281 River Rd.
Chillicothe, OH 45601
614-775-3578

35. Greenville/Spartanburg/Asheville

WLOS (ABC)
288 Macon Ave.
Asheville, NC 28804
704-255-0013

WSPA-TV (CBS)
250 International Dr.
Spartanburg, SC 29304
803-576-7777

WYFF-TV (NBC)
505 Rutherford St.
Greenville, SC 29602
803-242-4404

36. Buffalo, NY

WGRZ-TV (NBC)
259 Delaware Ave.
Buffalo, NY 14202
716-856-1414

WIVB-TV (CBS)
2077 Elmwood Ave.
Buffalo, NY 14207
716-874-4410

WKBW-TV (ABC)
7 Broadcast Plaza
Buffalo, NY 14202
716-845-6100

37. Grand Rapids/Kalamazoo/ Battle Creek, MI

WUHQ-TV (ABC)
5200 W. Dickman Rd.
Battle Creek, MI 49016
616-968-9341

WOTV (NBC)
Box B
Grand Rapids, MI 49501
616-456-8888

WZZM-TV (ABC)
645 Three Mile Rd. N.W.
Grand Rapids, MI 49504
616-784-4200

WGVK (non-commercial)
301 W. Fulton St.
Grand Rapids, MI 49504
616-771-6666

WWMT (CBS)
590 W. Maple St.
Kalamazoo, MI 49008
616-388-3333

38. Norfolk/Portsmith/Newport News/ Hampton, VA

WAVY-TV (NBC)
300 Wavy St.
Portsmouth, VA 23704
804-393-1010

WTKR-TV (CBS)
720 Boush St.
Norfolk, VA 23510
804-446-1000

WVEC-TV (ABC)
613 Woodis Ave.
Norfolk, VA 23510
804-625-1313

WGNT
1318 Spratley St.
Portsmouth, VA 23704
804-393-2501

39. Memphis, TN

WHBQ-TV (ABC)
485 S. Highland Ave.
Memphis, TN 38111
901-320-1313

WMC-TV (NBC)
1960 Union Ave.
Memphis, TN 38104
901-726-0555

WREG-TV (CBS)
803 Channel 3 Dr.
Memphis, TN 38103
901-577-0100

40. New Orleans, LA

WDSU-TV (NBC)
520 Royal St.
New Orleans, LA 70130
504-527-0666

WVUE (ABC)
1025 S. Jefferson Davis Pkwy.
New Orleans, LA 70125
504-486-6161

WWL-TV (CBS)
1024 N. Rampart St.
New Orleans, LA 70116
504-529-4444

41. San Antonio, TX

KENS-TV (CBS)
5400 Fredericksburg Rd.
San Antonio, TX 78299
512-366-5000

KMOL-TV (NBC)
1031 Navarro Rd.
San Antonio, TX 78205
512-226-4444

KSAT-TV (ABC)
1408 N. Saint Mary's St.
San Antonio, TX 78215
512-351-1200

KVDA (Telemundo)
6234 San Pedro Rd.
San Antonio, TX 78216
512-340-8860

42. Salt Lake City, UT

KSL-TV (CBS)
Broadcast House
Salt Lake City, UT 84110
801-575-5500

KTVX (ABC)
1760 Fremont Dr.
Salt Lake City, UT 84104
801-972-1776

KUTV
2185 South, 3600 West
Salt Lake City, UT 84119
801-973-3000

**43. Providence, RI/
New Bedford, MA**

WJAR (NBC)
111 Dorrance St.
Providence, RI 02903
401-455-9100

WLNE (CBS)
10 Orms St.
Providence, RI 02904
401-751-6666

WPRI-TV (ABC)
25 Catamore Blvd.
East Providence, RI 02914
401-438-7200

44. Oklahoma City, OK

KETA (non-commercial)
7403 N. Kelley
Oklahoma City, OK 73113
405-848-8501

KFOR-TV (NBC)
444 E. Britton Rd.
Oklahoma City, OK 73114
405-478-1212

KOCO-TV (ABC)
1300 E. Britton Rd.
Oklahoma City, OK 73113
405-478-3000

KOKH-TV
1228 E. Wilshire Blvd.
Oklahoma City, OK 73111
405-843-2525

KWTV (CBS)
7401 N. Kelley Ave.
Oklahoma City, OK 73111
405-843-6641

45. Louisville, KY

WAVE (NBC)
725 S. Floyd St.
Louisville, KY 40203
502-585-2201

WDRB-TV (Fox)
Independence Square
Louisville, KY 40203
502-584-6441

WHAS-TV (ABC)
520 W. Chestnut St.
Louisville, KY 40202
502-582-7840

WLKY-TV (CBS)
1918 Mellwood Ave.
Louisville, KY 40206
502-893-3671

46. West Palm Beach/Fort Pierce/ Vero Beach, FL

WTVX
Box 3434
Fort Pierce, FL 34954
305-464-3434

WPBF (ABC)
3970 RCA Blvd., Suite 7007
Palm Beach Gardens, FL 33410
407-694-2525

WPEC (CBS)
Box 24612
West Palm Beach, FL 33416
407-844-1212

WPTV (NBC)
622 N. Flagler Dr.
West Palm Beach, FL 33401
407-655-5455

47. Harrisburg/York/ Lancaster/Lebanon, PA

WHP-TV (CBS)
3300 N. 6th St.
Harrisburg, PA 17110
717-238-2100

WHTM-TV (ABC)
3235 Hoffman St.
Harrisburg, PA 17110
717-236-2727

WITF-TV (non-commercial)
1982 Locust Ln.
Harrisburg, PA 17109
717-236-6000

WGAL (NBC)
1300 Columbia Ave.
Lancaster, PA 17604
717-393-5851

WLYH-TV (CBS)
Television Hill
Lebanon, PA 17042
717-273-4551

48. Greensboro/Winston Salem/ High Point, NC

WAAP
Bass Mountain Rd.
Snow Camp, NC 27349
919-376-6016

WFMY-TV (CBS)
1615 Phillips Ave.
Greensboro, NC 27405
919-379-9369

WGHP-TV (ABC)
2005 Francis St.
High Point, NC 27263
919-841-8888

WXII (NBC)
700 Coliseum Dr.
Winston-Salem, NC 27116
919-721-9944

49. Wilkes-Barre/Scranton, PA

WBRE-TV (NBC)
62 S. Franklin St.
Wilkes-Barre, PA 18773
717-823-2828

WNEP-TV (ABC)
16 Montage Mountain Rd.
Moosic, PA 18507
717-346-7474

WYOU (CBS)
415 Lackawanna Ave.
Scranton, PA 18503
717-961-2222

50. Birmingham, AL

WBMG (CBS)
2075 Goldencrest Dr.
Birmingham, AL 35209
205-322-4200

WBRC-TV (ABC)
1720 Valley View Drive
Birmingham, AL 35209
205-322-6666

WVTM-TV (NBC)
Box 10502
Birmingham, AL 35202
205-933-1313

51. Albany/Schenectady/Troy, NY
WNYT (NBC)
15 N. Pearl St.
Albany, NY 12204
518-436-4791

WRGB (CBS)
1400 Balltown Rd.
Schenectady, NY 12309
518-346-6666

WTEN (ABC)
341 Northern Blvd.
Albany, NY 12204
518-436-4822

52. Albuquerque, NM
KGGM-TV (CBS)
Box 1294
Albuquerque, NM 87103
505-243-2285

KGSW-TV (Fox)
1377 University Blvd. N.E.
Albuquerque, NM 87102
505-842-1414

KLUZ-TV (Univision)
2725 F Broadbent Pkwy. N.E.
Albuquerque, NM 87107
505-344-5589

KOAT-TV (ABC)
3801 Carlisle N.E.
Albuquerque, NM 87107
505-884-7777

KOB-TV (NBC)
Box 1351
Albuquerque, NM 87103
505-243-4411

KVIO-TV (ABC)
1092 N. Canal St.
Carlsbad, NM 88220
806-372-5555

KBIM-TV (CBS)
214 N. Main St.
Roswell, NM 88201
505-622-2120

KOBR (NBC)
124 E. 4th St.
Roswell, NM 88201
505-625-8888

53. Dayton, OH
WDTN (ABC)
4595 S. Dixie Ave.
Dayton, OH 45439
513-293-2101

WHIO-TV (CBS)
1414 Wilmington Ave.
Dayton, OH 45420
513-259-2111

WKEF (NBC)
1731 Soldiers Home Rd.
Dayton, OH 45418
513-263-2662

WPTD (non-commercial)
110 S. Jefferson St.
Dayton, OH 45402
513-220-1600

WTJC
2675 Dayton Rd.
Springfield, OH 45506
513-323-0026

54. Jacksonville, FL
WJKS (ABC)
9117 Hogan Rd.
Jacksonville, FL 32216
904-641-1700

WJXT (CBS)
4 Broadcast Place
Jacksonville, FL 32207
904-399-4000

WNFT
1 Independent Dr.
Jacksonville, FL 32202
904-355-4747

WTLV (NBC)
1070 E. Adams St.
Jacksonville, FL 32202
904-354-1212

55. Charleston-Huntington, WV

WCHS-TV (ABC)
1301 Piedmont Rd.
Charleston, WV 25301
304-346-5358

WOWK-TV (CBS)
555 Fifth Ave.
Huntington, WV 25701
304-525-7661

WSAZ-TV (NBC)
645 Fifth Ave.
Huntington, WV 25721
304-697-4780

56. Flint/Saginaw/Bay City, MI

WEYI-TV (CBS)
2225 W. Willard Rd.
Clio, MI 48420
517-755-0525

WJRT-TV (ABC)
2302 Lapeer Rd.
Flint, MI 48503
313-233-3130

WNEM-TV (NBC)
107 N. Franklin St.
Saginaw, MI 48606
517-755-8191

57. Little Rock, AR

KARK-TV (NBC)
Box 748
Little Rock, AR 72203
501-376-4444

KATV
401 S. Main
Little Rock, AR 72201
501-324-7777

KTHV (CBS)
720 Izard St.
Little Rock, AR 72202
501-376-1111

58. Tulsa, OK

KJRH (NBC)
3701 S. Peoria
Tulsa, OK 74105
918-743-2222

KOKI-TV (Fox)
7422 E. 46th Pl.
Tulsa, OK 74145
918-622-2300

KOTV (CBS)
302 S. Frankfort
Tulsa, OK 74101
918-582-6666

KTUL-TV (ABC)
Box 8
Tulsa, OK 74101
918-446-3351

59. Fresno/Visalia, CA

KAIL
1590 Alluvial Ave.
Clovis, CA 93612
209-299-9753

KFSN-TV (ABC)
1777 G St.
Fresno, CA 93706
209-442-1170

KFTV (Univision)
3239 W. Ashlan Ave.
Fresno, CA 93722
209-222-2121

KJEO (CBS)
4880 N. 1st St.
Fresno, CA 93726
209-222-2411

KMPH (Fox)
5111 E. McKinley Ave.
Fresno, CA 93727
209-255-2600

KSEE (NBC)
5035 E. McKinley Ave.
Fresno, CA 93727
209-454-2424

60. Richmond, VA

WRIC-TV (ABC)
Arboretum Place
Richmond, VA 23236
804-330-8888

WTVR-TV (CBS)
3301 W. Broad St.
Richmond, VA 23230
804-254-3600

WWBT (NBC)
5710 Midlothian Tpk.
Richmond, VA 23255
804-230-2793

61. Wichita/Hutchinson, KS

KLBY
990 S. Range St.
Colby, KS 67701
913-462-8644

KBSH-TV
2300 Hall St.
Hays, KS 67601
913-625-5277

KOOD (non-commercial)
Bunker Hill
Hays, KS 67626
913-483-6990

KAKE-TV (ABC)
1500 N. West St.
Wichita, KS 67203
316-943-4221

KSNW (NBC)
833 N. Main
Wichita, KS 67203
316-265-3333

KWCH-TV (CBS)
Box 12
Wichita, KS 67201
316-838-1212

62. Knoxville, TN

WINT-TV
Box 608
Crossville, TN 38555
615-484-1220

WATE-TV (ABC)
1306 N.E. Broadway
Knoxville, TN 37917
615-637-6666

WBIR-TV (NBC)
1513 Hutchison Ave.
Knoxville, TN 37917
615-637-1010

WKXT-TV (CBS)
Box 59088
Knoxville, TN 37950
615-689-8000

63. Mobile, AL/Pensacola, FL

WALA-TV (NBC)
210 Government St.
Mobile, AL 36602
205-434-1010

WEAR-TV (ABC)
Box 12278
Pensacola, FL 32581
904-456-3333

WKRG-TV (CBS)
555 Broadcast Dr.
Mobile, AL 36606
205-479-5555

64. Toledo, OH

WNWO-TV (ABC)
300 S. Byrne Rd.
Toledo, OH 43615
419-535-0024

WTOL-TV (CBS)
730 N. Summit St.
Toledo, OH 43695
419-248-1111

WTVG-TV (NBC)
4247 Dorr St.
Toledo, OH 43607
419-531-1313

65. Roanoke/Lynchburg, VA

WDBJ (CBS)
2001 Colonial Ave.
Roanoke, VA 24015
703-344-7000

WSET-TV (ABC)
2320 Langhorne Rd.
Lynchburg, VA 24501
804-528-1313

WSLS-TV (NBC)
Box 2161
Roanoke, WA 24009
703-981-9110

66. Syracuse, NY

WIXT-TV (ABC)
Box 9
E. Syracuse, NY 13057
315-446-4780

WSTM-TV (NBC)
1030 James St.
Syracuse, NY 13203
315-474-5000

WTVH-TV (CBS)
980 James St.
Syracuse, NY 13203
315-425-5555

67. Green Bay/Appleton, WI

WBAY-TV (CBS)
115 S. Jefferson
Green Bay, WI 54301
414-432-3331

WFRV-TV (ABC)
1181 E. Mason St.
Green Bay, WI 54307
414-437-5411

WLUK-TV (NBC)
787 Lombardi Ave.
Green Bay, WI 54307
414-494-8711

68. Austin, TX

KBVO (Fox)
10700 Metric Blvd.
Austin, TX 78758
512-835-0042

KTBC-TV (CBS)
119 E. 10th St.
Austin, TX 78701
512-476-7777

KVUE-TV (ABC)
3201 Steck Ave.
Austin, TX 78758
512-459-6521

KXAN-TV (NBC)
Box 490
Austin, TX 78767
512-476-3636

69. Portland/Poland Spring, ME

WCSH-TV (NBC)
One Congress Square
Portland, ME 04101
207-828-6666

WGME-TV (CBS)
Box 1731
Portland, ME 04104
207-797-9330

WMTW-TV (ABC)
99 Danville Cor Rd.
Auburn, ME 04210
207-775-1800

70. Des Moines, IA

KCCI-TV (CBS)
888 Ninth St.
Des Moines, IA 50309
515-247-8888

KDSM-TV (Fox)
4023 Fleur Dr.
Des Moines, IA 50321
515-287-1717

WHO-TV (NBC)
1801 Grand Ave.
Des Moines, IA 50309
515-242-3500

WOI-TV (ABC)
WOI Building
Ames, IA 50011
515-294-5555

71. Shreveport, LA/Texarkana, TX

KSLA-TV (CBS)
1812 Fairfield Ave.
Shreveport, LA 71104
318-222-1212

KTAL-TV (NBC)
3150 N. Market St.
Shreveport, LA 71007
318-425-2422

KTBS-TV (ABC)
312 E. Kings Hwy.
Shreveport, LA 71104
318-861-5800

73. Omaha, NE

KETV (ABC)
2665 Douglas St.
Omaha, NE 68131-2699
402-345-7777

KMTV (CBS)
10714 Mockingbird Dr.
Omaha, NE 68127
402-592-3333

KPTM (Fox)
4625 Farnam St.
Omaha, NE 68132
402-558-4200

WOWT (NBC)
3501 Farnam St.
Omaha, NE 68131
402-346-6666

74. Lexington, KY

WYMT-TV (CBS)
U.S. 15 Bypass
Hazard, KY 41702
606-436-5757

WKYT-TV (CBS)
2851 Winchester Rd.
Lexington, KY 40509
606-299-0411

WLEX-TV (NBC)
1065 Russell Cave Rd.
Lexington, KY 40505
606-255-4404

WTVQ-TV (ABC)
2940 Bryant Rd.
Lexington, KY 40509
606-233-3600

75. Paducah, KY/Cape Girardeau, MO/Harrisburg, IL

WPSD-TV (NBC)
100 Television Ln.
Paducah, KY 42003
502-442-8214

KFVS-TV (CBS)
310 Broadway
Cape Girardeau, MO 63701
314-335-1212

WSIL-TV (ABC)
21 Country Aire Rd.
Carterville, IL 62918
618-985-2333

75. Springfield/Decatur/Champaign, IL

WCIA (CBS)
509 S. Neil
Champaign, IL 61824
217-356-8333

WICD (NBC)
250 County Fair Dr.
Champaign, IL 61821
217-351-8500

WAND (ABC)
904 Southside Dr.
Decatur, IL 62521
217-424-2500

WFHL
2510 Parkway Ct.
Decatur, IL 62526
217-428-2323

WCEE
125 N. 11th St.
Mt. Vernon, IL 62864
618-822-6900

WICS (NBC)
2680 E. Cook St.
Springfield, IL 62703
217-753-5620

77. Springfield, MO

KOLR-TV (CBS)
2650 E. Division St.
Springfield, MO 65803
417-862-1010

KSPR (ABC)
1359 St. Louis St.
Springfield, MO 65802
417-831-1333

KYTV (NBC)
999 W. Sunshine
Springfield, MO 65807
417-868-3800

78. Tucson, AZ

KGUN (ABC)
7280 E. Rosewood St.
Tucson, AZ 85710
602-722-5486

KOLD-TV (CBS)
115 W. Drachman St.
Tucson, AZ 85705
602-624-2511

KUAT-TV (non-commercial)
Univ. of Arizona
Tucson, AZ 85721
602-621-5828

KVOA-TV (NBC)
209 W. Elm St.
Tucson, AZ 85705
602-792-2270

79. Las Vegas, NV

KLAS-TV (CBS)
3228 Channel 8 Dr.
Las Vegas, NV 89109
702-792-8888

KLVX (non-commercial)
4210 Channel 10 Dr.
Las Vegas, NV 89119
702-737-1010

KTNV (ABC)
3355 Valley View Blvd.
Las Vegas, NV 89102
702-876-1313

KVBC (NBC)
1500 Foremaster Ln.
Las Vegas, NV 89101
702-642-3333

80. Spokane, WA
KHQ-TV (NBC)
4202 S. Regal
Spokane, WA 99223
509-448-6000

KREM-TV (CBS)
4103 S. Regal
Spokane, WA 99203
509-448-2000

KXLY-TV (ABC)
West 500 Boone Ave.
Spokane, WA 99201
509-328-9084

81. Chattanooga, TN
WDEF-TV (CBS)
3300 Broad St.
Chattanooga, TN 37408
615-267-0009

WRCB-TV (NBC)
900 Whitehall Rd.
Chattanooga, TN 37405
615-267-5412

WTVC (ABC)
410 W. 6th St.
Chattanooga, TN 37402
615-756-5500

**82. Cedar Rapids/Waterloo/
Dubuque, IA**
KCRG-TV (ABC)
Box 816
Cedar Rapids, IA 52406
319-398-8422

KDUB-TV (ABC)
One Cycare Plaza
Dubuque, IA 52001
319-556-4040

KGAN (CBS)
Box 3131
Cedar Rapids, IA 52406
319-395-9060

KWWL (NBC)
500 E. 4th St.
Waterloo, IA 50703
319-291-1200

83. Johnstown/Altoona, PA
WATM-TV (ABC)
1450 Scalp Ave.
Johnstown, PA 15904
814-266-8088

WTAJ-TV (CBS)
Box 10, Commerce Park
Altoona, PA 16603
814-944-2031

WJAC-TV (NBC)
Hickory Lane
Johnstown, PA 15905
814-255-7600

WWCP-TV (Fox)
1450 Scalp Ave.
Johnstown, PA 15904
814-266-8088

**85. Bristol/Kingsport/
Johnson City, TN**
WJHL-TV (CBS)
Box 1130
Johnson City, TN 37601
615-926-2151

WKPT-TV (ABC)
222 Commerce St.
Kingsport, TN 37660
615-246-9578

WCYB-TV (NBC)
101 Lee St.
Bristol, VA 24203
703-669-4161

86. South Bend/Elkhart, IN

WNDU-TV (NBC)
Box 1616
South Bend, IN 46634
219-239-1616

WSBT-TV (CBS)
300 W. Jefferson Blvd.
South Bend, IN 46601
219-233-3141

WSJV (ABC)
Box 1646
South Bend, IN 46515
219-293-8616

87. Columbia, SC

WIS-TV (NBC)
1111 Bull St.
Columbia, SC 29201
803-799-1010

WLTX (CBS)
Drawer M
Columbia, SC 29250
803-776-3600

WOLO-TV (ABC)
5807 Shakespeare Rd.
Columbia, SC 29240
803-754-7525

WRLK-TV (non-commercial)
2712 Millwood Ave.
Columbia, SC 29205
803-737-3200

88. Huntsville/Decatur/ Florence, AL

WAAY-TV (ABC)
1000 Monte Sano Blvd.
Huntsville, AL 35801
205-533-3131

WAFF (NBC)
Box 2116
Huntsville, AL 35804
205-533-4848

WHNT-TV (CBS)
960 Monte Sano Blvd.
Huntsville, AL 35801
205-539-1919

WOWL-TV (NBC)
840 Cypress Mill Rd.
Florence, AL 35630
205-767-1515

89. Jackson, MS

WAPT (ABC)
One Channel 16 Way
Jackson, MS 39209
601-922-1607

WDBD (Fox)
7440 Channel 16 Way
Jackson, MS 39289
601-922-1234

WJTV (CBS)
1820 TV Rd.
Jackson, MS 39204
601-372-6311

WLBT (NBC)
715 S. Jefferson St.
Jackson, MS 39205
601-948-3333

WNTZ
625 Beltline Hwy.
Natchez, MS 39120
601-442-4800

90. Fort Myers/Naples, FL

WBBH-TV (NBC)
3719 Central Ave.
Fort Myers, FL 33911
813-939-2020

WEVU (ABC)
3451 Bonita Bay Blvd.
Bonita Springs, FL 33923
813-332-0076

WINK-TV (CBS)
2824 Palm Beach Blvd.
Fort Myers, FL 33916
813-334-1131

WNPL-TV
840 Goodlette Rd. N.
Naples, FL 33940
813-261-4600

91. Youngstown, OH

WFMJ-TV (NBC)
101 W. Boardman St.
Youngstown, OH 44503
216-744-8611

WKBN-TV (CBS)
3930 Sunset Blvd.
Youngstown, OH 44501
216-782-1144

WYTV (ABC)
3800 Shady Run Rd.
Youngstown, OH 44502
216-783-2930

92. Madison, WI

WISC-TV (CBS)
7025 Raymond Rd.
Madison, WI 53719
608-271-4321

WKOW-TV (ABC)
Box 100
Madison, WI 53701
608-274-1234

WMTV (NBC)
615 Forward Dr.
Madison, WI 53711
608-274-1515

93. Evansville, IN

WEHT (CBS)
800 Marywood Dr.
Henderson, KY 42420
812-424-9215

WFIE-TV (NBC)
1115 Mount Auburn Rd.
Evansville, IN 47712
812-426-1414

WTVW (ABC)
477 Carpenter St.
Evansville, IN 47708
812-422-1121

**94. Waco/Temple/
Bryan, TX**

KBTX-TV (CBS)
Drawer 3730
Bryan, TX 77805
409-846-7777

KCEN-TV (NBC)
4716 W. Waco Dr.
Waco, TX 76710
817-773-6868

KWTX-TV CBS)
6700 American Plaza
Waco, TX 76712
817-776-1330

KXXV (ABC)
1909 S. New Rd.
Waco, TX 76702
817-754-2525

95. Baton Rouge, LA

WAFB (CBS)
Box 2671
Baton Rouge, LA 70821
504-383-9999

WBRZ (ABC)
1650 Highland Rd.
Baton Rouge, LA 70802
504-387-2222

WVLA (NBC)
5220 Essen Ln.
Baton Rouge, LA 70809
504-766-3233

96. Springfield, MA

WGGB-TV (ABC)
1300 Liberty St.
Springfield, MA 01102
413-733-4040

WWLP (NBC)
Box 2210
Springfield, MA 01102
413-786-2200

**97. Burlington, VT/
Plattsburgh, NY**

WPTZ (NBC)
Old Moffitt Rd.
Plattsburgh, NY 12901
518-561-5555

WCAX-TV (CBS)
Box 608
Burlington, VT 05402
802-658-6300

WVNY (ABC)
100 Market Square
Burlington, VT 05401
802-658-8022

WNNE-TV (NBC)
Box 1310
White River Jct., VT 05001
802-295-3100

**98. Lincoln/Hastings/
Kearney, NE**

KHAS-TV (NBC)
Box 578
Hastings, NE 68901
402-463-1321

KHGI-TV (ABC)
Box 220
Kearney, NE 68848
308-743-2494

KOLN (CBS)
Box 30350
Lincoln, NE 68503
402-467-4321

KSNB-TV
Box 220
Superior, NE 68848
308-743-2494

**99. Colorado Springs/
Pueblo, CO**

KKTV (CBS)
3100 N. Nevada Ave.
Colorado Springs, CO 80907
719-634-2844

KOAA-TV (NBC)
530 Communications Circle
Colorado Springs, CO 80905
719-544-5781

KRDO-TV (ABC)
399 S. 8th St.
Colorado Springs, CO 80901
719-632-1515

100. El Paso, TX

KDBC-TV (CBS)
2201 Wyoming
El Paso, TX 79903
915-532-6551

KINT-TV (Univision)
5426 N. Mesa
El Paso, TX 79912
915-581-1126

KTSM-TV (NBC)
801 N. Oregon St.
El Paso, TX 79902
915-532-5421

KVIA-TV (ABC)
4140 Rio Bravo
El Paso, TX 79902
915-532-7777

XHIJ (Telemundo)
5925 Cromo
El Paso, TX 79912
915-833-0044

101. Savannah, GA

WJCL (ABC)
10001 Abercorn St.
Savannah, GA 31406
912-925-0022

WSAV-TV (NBC)
Box 2429
Savannah, GA 31402
912-651-0300

WTOC-TV (CBS)
Box 8086
Savannah, GA 31412
912-234-1111

102. Fort Wayne, IN

WANE-TV (CBS)
2915 W. State Blvd.
Fort Wayne, IN 46801
219-424-1515

WFFT-TV (Fox)
3707 Hillegas Rd.
Fort Wayne, IN 46808
219-424-5555

WKJG-TV (NBC)
2633 W. State Blvd.
Fort Wayne, IN 46808
219-422-7474

WPTA (ABC)
3401 Butler Rd.
Fort Wayne, IN 48604
219-483-0584

103. Lansing, MI

WLAJ-TV (ABC)
5815 S. Pennsylvania Ave.
Lansing, MI 48909
517-394-5300

WLNS-TV (CBS)
2820 E. Saginaw
Lansing, MI 48912
517-372-8282

WILX-TV (NBC)
500 American Rd.
Lansing, MI 48911
517-783-2621

104. Greenville/New Bern/ Washington, NC

WCTI (ABC)
400 Glenburnie Dr.
New Bern, NC 28561
919-638-1212

WITN-TV (NBC)
Highway 17 South
Greenville, NC 27889
919-946-3131

WNCT-TV (CBS)
3221 Evans St.
Greenville, NC 27835
919-355-8500

105. Charleston, SC

WCBD-TV (ABC)
210 W. Coleman Blvd.
Mount Pleasant, SC 29464
803-884-2222

WCIV (NBC)
1558 Highway 703
Mount Pleasant, SC 29464
803-881-4444

WCSC-TV (CBS)
485 E. Bay St.
Charleston, SC 29402
803-723-8371

106. Sioux Falls/Mitchell, SD

KDLT (NBC)
3600 S. Westport Ave.
Mitchell, SD 57116
605-361-5555

KELO-TV (CBS)
Phillips at 13th
Sioux Falls, SD 57102
605-336-1100

KSFY-TV (ABC)
300 N. Dakota
Sioux Falls, SD 57102
605-336-1300

107. Peoria/Bloomington, IL

WEEK-TV (NBC)
2907 Springfield Rd.
Peoria, IL 61611
309-698-2525

WHOI (ABC)
500 N. Stewart St.
Peoria, IL 61611
309-698-1919

WMBD-TV (CBS)
3131 N. University St.
Peoria, IL 61604
309-688-3131

108. Fargo, ND

KFME (non-commercial)
207 N. 5th St.
Fargo, ND 58108
701-241-6900

KTHI-TV (NBC)
Box 1878
Fargo, ND 58107
701-237-5211

KXJB-TV (CBS)
4302 13th Ave. S.
Fargo, ND 58103
701-282-0444

WDAY-TV (ABC)
301 S. 8th St.
Fargo, ND 58107
701-237-6500

**109. Santa Barbara/Santa Maria/
San Luis Obispo, CA**

KCOY-TV (CBS)
1211 W. McCay Ln.
Santa Maria, CA 93455
805-925-1200

KSBY-TV (NBC)
467 Hill St.
San Luis Obispo, CA 93401
805-541-6666

KEYT-TV (ABC)
Miramonte Dr.
Santa Barbara, CA 93109
805-965-8533

110. Montgomery/Selma, AL

WHOA-TV (ABC)
3251 Harrison Rd.
Montgomery, AL 36109
205-272-5331

WSFA (NBC)
10 East Delano Ave.
Montgomery, AL 36105
205-281-2900

WAKA (CBS)
3020 East Blvd.
Selma, AL 36116
205-279-8787

111. Salinas/Monterey, CA

KCBA (Fox)
1550 Moffett St.
Salinas, CA 93905
408-422-3500

KMST (CBS)
2200 Garden Rd.
Monterey, CA 93940
408-649-0460

KSBW (NBC)
238 John St.
Salinas, CA 93901
408-758-8888

KSMS-TV (Univision)
67 Garden Ct.
Monterey, CA 93940
408-373-6767

112. Augusta, GA

WAGT (NBC)
905 Broad St.
Augusta, GA 30901
404-826-0026

WJBF (ABC)
10th & Reynolds St.
Augusta, GA 30901
404-722-6664

WRDW-TV (CBS)
1301 Georgia Ave.
North Augusta, SC 29841
803-278-1212

**113. Tyler/Longview/
Jacksonville, TX**

KETK-TV (NBC)
4300 Richmond Rd.
Tyler, TX 75703
903-581-5656

KLTV (ABC)
2609 E. Irwin
Tyler, TX 75702
903-597-5588

KTRE-TV (CBS)
Box 729
Lufkin, TX 75901
409-853-5873

114. McAllen/Brownsville, TX

KGBT-TV (CBS)
9201 W. Expressway 83
Harlingen, TX 78552
512-421-4444

KRGV-TV (ABC)
Box 5
Weslaco, TX 78596
512-968-5555

KVEO-TV (NBC)
394 N. Expressway
Brownsville, TX 78521
512-544-2323

115. Tallahassee, FL

WCTV (CBS)
Box 3048
Tallahassee, FL 32315
904-893-6666

WTWC (NBC)
8440 Deerlake Rd.
Tallahassee, FL 32312
904-893-4140

WTXL-TV (ABC)
8927 Thomasville Rd.
Tallahassee, FL 32312
904-893-3127

116. Reno, NV

KOLO-TV (ABC)
4850 Ampere Dr.
Reno, NV 89502
702-786-8880

KRNV (NBC)
1790 Vassar St.
Reno, NV 89510
702-322-4444

KTVN (CBS)
4925 Energy Way
Reno, NV 89502
702-786-2212

117. Eugene, OR

KCBY-TV (CBS)
611 Coalbank Slough Rd.
Coos Bay, OR 97420
503-269-1111

KEZI (ABC)
2225 Coburg Rd.
Eugene, OR 97401
503-485-5611

KMTR-TV (NBC)
3825 International Ct.
Springfield, OR 97477
503-746-1600

KVAL-TV (CBS)
Box 1313
Eugene, OR 97440
503-342-4961

118. Fort Smith, AR
KHOG-TV (ABC)
15 N. Church St.
Fayetteville, AR 72702
501-521-1010

KFSM-TV (CBS)
Box 369
Fort Smith, AR 72902
501-783-3131

KHBS (ABC)
2415 N. Albert Pike
Fort Smith, AR 72904
501-783-4040

KPOM-TV (NBC)
Box 4610
Fort Smith, AR 72914
501-785-2400

119. Lafayette, LA
KADN (Fox, ABC)
1500 Eraste Landry Rd.
Lafayette, LA 70506
318-237-1500

KATC (ABC)
Box 93133
Lafayette, LA 70509
318-235-3333

KLFY-TV (CBS)
Box 90665
Lafayette, LA 70509
318-981-4823

120. Macon, GA
WGXA (ABC)
Box 340
Macon, GA 31297
912-745-2424

WMAZ-TV (CBS)
Box 5008
Macon, GA 31213
912-752-1313

WMGT (NBC)
6525 Ocmulgee E. Blvd.
Macon, GA 31213
912-745-4141

121. Columbus, GA
WLTZ (NBC)
6140 Buena Vista Rd.
Columbus, GA 31995
404-561-3838

WRBL (CBS)
1350 13th Ave.
Columbus, GA 31994
404-323-3333

WTVM (ABC)
Box 1848
Columbus, GA 31902
404-324-6471

122. Traverse City/Cadillac, MI
WWTV (CBS)
10360 N. 130th Ave.
Cadillac, MI 49601
616-775-3478

WPBN-TV (NBC)
Box 546
Traverse City, MI 49684
616-947-7770

WGTU (ABC)
201 E. Front St.
Traverse City, MI 49684
616-946-2900

WWUP-TV (CBS)
601 Osborne
Sault Ste. Marie, MI 49783
906-635-6225

123. La Crosse/Eau Claire, WI

WEAU-TV (NBC)
1907 S. Hastings Way
Eau Claire, WI 54702
715-835-1313

WQOW-TV (ABC)
2881 S. Hastings Way
Eau Claire, WI 54701
715-835-1881

WKBT (CBS)
141 S. 6th St.
La Crosse, WI 54601
608-782-4678

WXOW-TV
3705 County Hwy. 25
La Crescent, MN 55947
507-895-9969

124. Columbus/Tupelo, MS

WCBI-TV (CBS)
Box 271
Columbus, MS 39703
601-327-4444

WTVA (NBC)
Box 350
Tupelo, MS 38801
601-842-7620

WLOV-TV (ABC)
Box 777
West Point, MS 39773
601-494-8327

125. Corpus Christi, TX

KEDT (non-commercial)
4455 W. Padre Island Dr.
Corpus Christi, TX 78411
512-855-2213

KIII (ABC)
Box 6669
Corpus Christi, TX 78411
512-854-4733

KORO (Univision)
102 N. Mesquite
Corpus Christi, TX 78403
512-883-2823

KRIS-TV (NBC, Fox)
409 S. Staples St.
Corpus Christi, TX 78401
512-886-6100

KZTV (CBS)
301 Artesian
Corpus Christi, TX 78403
512-883-7070

126. Duluth/Superior, MN

KBJR-TV (NBC)
230 E. Superior St.
Duluth, MN 55802
218-727-8484

KDLH (CBS)
425 W. Superior St.
Dultuh, MN 55802
218-727-8911

WDIO-TV (ABC)
10 Observation Rd.
Duluth, MN 55816
218-727-6864

127. Amarillo, TX

KAMR-TV (NBC)
Box 751
Amarillo, TX 79189
806-383-3321

KFDA-TV (CBS)
Broadway & Cherry
Amarillo, TX 79189
806-383-2226

KVII-TV (ABC)
One Broadcast Center
Amarillo, TX 79101
806-373-1787

**128. Monroe, LA/
El Dorado, AR**

KNOE-TV (CBS)
Box 4067
Monroe, LA 71211
318-388-8888

KARD (ABC)
102 Thomas Rd., Suite 22
W. Monroe, LA 71291
318-323-1972

KTVE (NBC)
400 W. Main
El Dorado, AR 71730
501-862-6651

**129. Yakima/Pasco/
Richland/Kennewick, WA**

KEPR-TV (CBS)
2807 W. Lewis
Pasco, WA 99301
509-547-0547

KNDU (NBC)
3312 W. Kennewick Ave.
Kennewick, WA 99336
509-783-6151

KAPP (ABC)
1610 S. 24th Ave.
Yakima, WA 98902
509-453-0351

KIMA-TV (CBS)
2801 Terrace Heights Dr.
Yakima, WA 98901
509-575-0029

KNDO (NBC)
1608 S. 24th Ave.
Yakima, WA 98902
509-248-2300

KVEW
601 N. Edison
Kennewick, WA 99336
509-735-8369

130. Chico/Redding, CA

KCPM (NBC)
180 E. 4th St.
Chico, CA 95928
916-893-2424

KHSL-TV (CBS)
Box 489
Chico, CA 95927
916-342-0141

KRCR-TV (ABC)
755 Auditorium Dr.
Redding, CA 96001
510-768-6731

131. Wausau/Rhinelander, WI

WJFW-TV (NBC)
South Oneida Ave.
Rhinelander, WI 54501
715-369-4700

WAOW-TV (ABC)
1908 Grand Ave.
Wausau, WI 54401
715-842-2251

WSAW-TV (CBS)
1114 Grand Ave.
Wausau, WI 54401
715-845-4211

132. Bakersfield, CA

KBAK-TV (ABC)
Box 2929
Bakersfield, CA 93303
805-327-7955

KERO-TV (CBS)
321 21st St.
Bakersfield, CA 93301
805-327-1441

KGET (NBC)
2831 Eye St.
Bakersfield, CA 93301
805-327-7511

133. Binghamton, NY

WBNG-TV (CBS)
50 Front St.
Binghamton, NY 13902
607-723-7311

WICZ-TV (NBC)
4600 Vestal Pkwy. E.
Vestal, NY 13850
607-770-4040

WMGC-TV (ABC)
Ingraham Hill Rd.
Binghamton, NY 13902
607-723-7464

WSKG (non-commercial)
Willow Point Broadcast Ctr.
Binghamton, NY 13902
607-729-0100

134. Beaumont/Port Arthur, TX

KBMT (ABC)
525 I-10 South
Beaumont, TX 77701
409-833-7512

KFDM-TV (CBS)
Box 7128
Beaumont, TX 77726
409-892-6622

KJAC-TV (NBC)
2900 17th St.
Beaumont, TX 77642
409-985-5557

135. Rockford, IL

WIFR-TV (CBS)
2523 N. Meridian Rd.
Rockford, IL 61103
815-987-5300

WREX-TV (ABC)
10322 W. Auburn Rd.
Rockford, IL 61103
815-968-1813

WTVO (NBC)
1917 N. Meridian Rd.
Rockford, IL 61105
815-963-5413

136. Terre Haute, IN

WBAK-TV (ABC)
Box 719
Terre Haute, IN 47808
812-238-1515

WTHI-TV (CBS)
918 Ohio St.
Terre Haute, IN 47808
812-232-9481

WTWO (NBC)
Box 299
Terre Haute, IN 47808
812-696-2121

137. Sioux City, IA

KCAU-TV (ABC)
7th & Douglas St.
Sioux City, IA 51101
712-277-2345

KMEG (CBS)
Box 657
Sioux City, IA 51102
712-277-3554

KTIV (NBC)
3135 Floyd Blvd.
Sioux City, IA 51105
712-239-4100

138. Florence/Myrtle Beach, SC

WBTW (CBS)
3430 TV Rd.
Florence, SC 29501
803-662-1565

WPDE-TV (ABC)
Box F-15
Florence, SC 29501
803-665-1515

WGSE
Box 1243
Myrtle Beach, SC 29577
803-626-4300

**139. Wichita Falls, TX/
Lawton, OK**
KSWO-TV (ABC)
Box 708, Highway 7
Lawton, OK 73502
405-355-7000

KAUZ-TV (CBS)
Box 2130
Wichita Falls, TX 76307
817-322-6957

KFDX-TV (NBC)
4500 Seymour Hwy.
Wichita Falls, TX 76309
817-692-4530

140. Erie, PA
WICU-TV (NBC)
3514 State St.
Erie, PA 16508
814-454-5201

WJET-TV (ABC)
8455 Peach St.
Erie, PA 16509
814-864-2400

WSEE-TV (CBS)
1220 Peach St.
Erie, PA 16501
814-455-7575

141. Topeka, KS
KSNT (NBC)
Box 2700
Topeka, KS 66601
913-582-4000

KTKA-TV (ABC)
101 S.E. Monroe
Topeka, KS 66603
913-234-4949

WIBW-TV (CBS)
5600 W. 6th St.
Topeka, KS 66606
913-272-3456

142. Boise, ID
KAID (non-commercial)
1910 University Dr.
Boise, ID 83725
208-385-3727

KBCI-TV (CBS)
1007 W. Jefferson
Boise, ID 83707
208-336-5222

KIVI (ABC)
1866 E. Chisholm Dr.
Nampa, ID 83687
208-336-0500

KTVB (NBC)
Box 7
Boise, ID 83707
208-375-7277

KTRV (Fox)
679 6th St. N. Ext.
Nampa, ID 83652
208-466-1200

143. Wilmington, NC
WECT (NBC)
Box 4029
Wilmington, NC 28406
919-791-8070

WJKA (CBS)
1926 Oleander Dr.
Wilmington, NC 28403
919-343-8826

WWAY (ABC)
Box 2068
Wilmington, NC 28402
919-762-8581

**144. Wheeling, WV/
Steubenville, OH**
WTRF-TV (CBS, ABC)
96 16th St.
Wheeling, WV 26003
304-232-7777

WTOV-TV (NBC)
Altamont Hill
Steubenville, OH 43952
614-282-0911

145. Joplin, MO/Pittsburg, KS
KODE-TV (ABC)
1928 W. 13th St.
Joplin, MO 64801
417-623-7260

KSNF-TV (NBC)
Box 1393
Joplin, MO 64802
417-781-2345

KOAM-TV (CBS)
Highway 69 & Lawton Rd.
Pittsburg, KS 66762
417-624-0233

**146. Bluefield/Beckley/
Oak Hill, WV**
WVVA (NBC)
Route 460 By-Pass
Bluefield, WV 24701
304-325-5487

WOAY-TV (ABC)
Box 251
Oak Hill, WV 25901
304-469-3361

147. Lubbock, TX
KAMC (ABC)
1201 84th St.
Lubbock, TX 79423
806-745-2828

KCBD-TV (NBC)
Box 2190
Lubbock, TX 79408
806-744-1414

KLBK-TV (CBS)
7400 S. University Ave.
Lubbock, TX 79408
806-745-2345

**148. Rochester, MN/Mason
City, IA/Austin, MN**
KAAL (ABC)
Box 577
Austin, MN 55912
507-433-8836

KIMT (CBS)
112 N. Pennsylvania Ave.
Mason City, IA 50401
515-423-2540

KTTC (NBC)
601 1st Ave. S.W.
Rochester, MN 55902
507-288-4444

149. Medford, OR
KDRV (ABC)
1090 Knutson Ave.
Medford, OR 97504
503-773-1212

KOBI (NBC)
125 S. Fir St.
Medford, OR 97501
503-779-5555

KTVL (CBS)
1440 Rossanley Dr.
Medford, OR 97501
503-773-7373

**149. Minot/Bismarck/
Dickinson/Glendive**

KFYR-TV (NBC)
200 N. 4th St.
Bismarck, ND 58501
701-255-5757

KXMB-TV (CBS)
1811 N. 15th St.
Bismarck, ND 53501
701-223-9197

KMCY (ABC)
Box 2276
Minot, ND 58702
701-838-6614

KMOT (NBC)
1800 S.W. 16th St.
Minot, ND 58702
701-852-4101

KXMC-TV (CBS)
Box 1686
Minot, ND 58701
701-852-2104

KXGN-TV (CBS)
201 S. Douglas St.
Glendive, MT 59330
406-365-3377

151. Odessa/Midland, TX

KMID-TV (ABC)
3200 Laforce Blvd.
Midland, TX 79711
915-563-2222

KOSA-TV (CBS)
1211 N. Whitaker St.
Odessa, TX 79763
915-337-8301

KTPX (NBC)
Box 60150
Midland, TX 79711
915-563-4210

152. Columbia/Jefferson City, MO

KMIZ (ABC)
501 Business Loop 70 East
Columbia, MO 65201
314-449-0917

KOMU-TV (NBC)
Highway 63 S.
Columbia, MO 65201
314-442-1122

KRCG (CBS)
Old Highway 54
Holts Summit, MO 65043
314-896-5144

153. Albany, GA

WALB-TV (NBC)
1709 Stuart Ave.
Albany, GA 31708
912-883-0154

WFXL (Fox)
Box 4050
Albany, GA 31708
912-435-3100

WVGA (ABC)
275 Norman Dr.
Valdosta, GA 31603
912-242-4444

154. Sarasota, FL

WWSB (ABC)
5725 Lawton Dr.
Sarasota, FL 34233
813-923-8840

155. Bangor, ME

WABI-TV (CBS)
35 Hildreth St.
Bangor, ME 04401
207-947-8321

WLBZ-TV (NBC)
Mt. Hope Ave.
Bangor, ME 04401
207-942-4822

WVII-TV (ABC)
371 Target Industrial Circle
Bangor, ME 04401
207-945-6457

WMEB-TV (non-commerical)
65 Texas Ave.
Bangor, ME 04401
207-941-1010

156. Quincy, IL/Hannibal, MO

KHQA-TV (CBS)
510 Main St.
Quincy, IL 62301
217-222-6200

WGEM-TV (NBC)
513 Hampshire St.
Quincy, IL 62306
217-228-6600

WTJR
Old Cannonball Rd.
Quincy, IL 62305
217-228-1275

157. Abilene/Sweetwater, TX

KRBC-TV (NBC)
Box 178
Abilene, TX 79604
915-692-4242

KTAB-TV (CBS)
5401 S. 14th St.
Abilene, TX 79608
915-695-2777

KTXS-TV (ABC)
Box 2997
Abilene, TX 79604
915-677-2281

**158. Biloxi/Gulfport/
Pascagoula, MS**

WLOX-TV (ABC)
208 De Buys Rd.
Biloxi, MS 39535
601-896-1313

159. Clarksburg/Weston, WV

WBOY-TV (NBC)
912 West Pike St.
Clarksburg, WV 26302
304-623-3311

WDTV (CBS)
5 Televison Dr.
Bridgeport, WV 26330
304-623-5555

160. Idaho Falls/Pocatello, ID

KIDK (CBS)
1255 E. 17th St.
Idaho Falls, ID 83404
208-522-5100

KIFI-TV (NBC)
1915 N. Yellowstone Hwy.
Idaho Falls, ID 83401
208-525-8888

KPVI (ABC)
Box 667
Pocatello, ID 83204
208-232-6666

KISU-TV (non-commerical)
Box 8111/Idaho State U.
Pocatello, ID 83209
208-236-2857

161. Utica, NY

WKTV (NBC)
Box 2
Utica, NY 13503
315-733-0404

WUTR (ABC)
Box 20
Utica, NY 13503
315-797-5220

162. Panama City, FL

WJHG-TV (NBC)
8195 Front Beach Rd.
Panama City Beach, FL 32407
904-234-2125

WMBB (ABC)
613 Harrison Ave.
Panama City, FL 32402
904-769-2313

WPGX (Fox)
700 W. 23rd St., Suite 28
Panama City, FL 32405
904-784-0028

163. Salisbury, MD

WBOC-TV (CBS)
Radio TV Park
Salisbury, MD 21801
301-749-1111

WMDT (ABC-NBC)
202 Downtown Plaza
Salisbury, MD 21801
301-742-4747

164. Laurel/Hattiesburg, MS

WDAM-TV (NBC)
Box 16269
Hattiesburg, MS 39402
601-544-4730

WHLT (CBS)
990 Hardy St.
Hattiesburg, MS 39401
601-545-2077

165. Gainesville, FL

WCJB-TV (ABC)
6220 N.W. 43rd St.
Gainesville, FL 32614
904-377-2020

166. Dothan, AL

WDHN (ABC)
Highway 52 East
Dothan, AL 36302
205-793-1818

WTVY (CBS)
Box 1089
Dothan, AL 36301
205-792-3195

167. Harrisonburg, VA

WHSV-TV (ABC)
Highway 33 West
Harrisonburg, VA 22801
703-433-9191

168. Watertown/Carthage, NY

WNPE-TV (non-commerical)
Arsenal St.
Watertown, NY 13601
315-782-3142

WWNY-TV (CBS, NBC)
120 Arcade St.
Watertown, NY 13601
315-788-3800

WWTI (ABC)
Box 6250
Watertown, NY 13601
315-785-8850

169. Elmira, NY

WENY-TV (ABC)
Box 208
Elmira, NY 14902
607-739-3636

WETM-TV (NBC)
One Broadcast Center
Elmira, NY 14901
607-733-5518

170. Palm Springs, CA

KESQ-TV (ABC)
42-650 Melanie Pl.
Palm Desert, CA 92260
619-773-0342

KMIR-TV (NBC)
72920 Parkview Dr.
Palm Desert, CA 92260
619-568-3636

171. Rapid City, SD

KCLO-TV (CBS)
2497 W. Chicago St.
Rapid City, SD 57702
605-341-1500

KEVN-TV (NBC)
Box 677
Rapid City, SD 57709
605-394-7777

KOTA-TV (ABC)
Box 1760
Rapid City, SD 57709
605-342-2000

172. Billings/Hardin, MT

KTVQ (CBS)
Box 2557
Billings, MT 59103
406-252-5611

KULR-TV (NBC)
2045 Overland Ave.
Billings, MT 59102
406-656-8000

KOUS-TV (ABC)
445 S. 24th St., W.
Billings, MT 59104
406-652-4743

173. Alexandria, LA

KALB-TV (NBC)
605-11 Washington St.
Alexandria, LA 71301
318-445-2456

KLAX-TV (ABC)
1811 England Dr.
Alexandria, LA 71306
318-473-0031

174. Lake Charles, LA

KPLC-TV (NBC)
320 Division St.
Lake Charles, LA 70601
318-439-9071

KVHP (Fox)
129 W. Prien Lake Rd.
Lake Charles, LA 70602
318-474-1316

175. Greenwood/Greenville, MS

WABG-TV (ABC)
849 Washington Ave.
Greenville, MS 38701
601-332-0949

WXVT (CBS)
3015 E. Reed Rd.
Greenville, MS 38703
601-334-1500

176. Jonesboro, AR

KAIT-TV (ABC)
Highway 41 N.
Jonesboro, AR 72401
501-931-8888

177. Missoula, MT

KECI-TV (NBC)
340 W. Main
Missoula, MT 59802
406-721-2063

KPAX-TV (CBS)
2204 Regent St.
Missoula, MT 59801
406-543-7106

178. Ardmore/Ada, OK

KTEN (ABC, NBC)
101 E. Main
Denison, TX 75020
214-465-5836

KXII (CBS, NBC)
4201 Texoma Pkwy.
Sherman, TX 75090
903-892-8123

179. Grand Junction/Durango, CO

KJCT (ABC)
Box 3788
Grand Junction, CO 81502
303-245-8880

KREX-TV (CBS)
Box 789
Grand Junction, CO 81502
303-242-5000

180. El Centro, CA/Yuma, AZ

KECY-TV (CBS)
646 Main St.
El Centro, CA 92243
619-353-9990

KSWT (ABC)
1301 3rd Ave.
Yuma, AZ 85364
602-782-5113

KYMA (ABC)
1385 S. Pacific Ave.
Yuma, AZ 85365
602-782-1111

181. Meridian, MS

WTOK-TV (ABC)
Box 2988
Meridian, MS 39302
601-693-1441

WTZH (CBS)
Box 5185
Meridian, MS 39301
601-693-2933

182. Great Falls, MT

KFBB-TV (ABC)
Havre Highway
Great Falls, MT 59403
406-453-4377

KRTV (CBS)
Box 1331
Great Falls, MT 59403
406-453-2431

KTGF (NBC)
118 Sixth St. South
Great Falls, MT 59405
406-761-8816

183. Jackson, TN

WBBJ-TV (ABC)
346 Muse St.
Jackson, TN 38301
901-424-4515

184. Parkersburg, WV

WTAP-TV (NBC)
One Television Plaza
Parkersburg, WV 26101
304-485-4588

185. Tuscaloosa, AL

WCFT-TV (CBS)
4000 37th St. E.
Tuscaloosa, AL 35405
205-553-1333

186. Marquette, MI

WLUC-TV (CBS, NBC)
177 U.S. Highway 41
Negaunee, MI 49866
906-475-4161

187. Eureka, CA

KIEM-TV (NBC)
5650 S. Broadway
Eureka, CA 95501
707-443-3123

KVIQ (CBS)
1800 Broadway
Eureka, CA 95501
707-443-3061

188. San Angelo, TX

KLST (CBS)
2800 Armstrong
San Angelo, TX 76903
915-949-8800

189. St. Joseph, MO

KQTV (ABC)
40th & Faron St.
St. Joseph, MO 64506
816-364-2222

190. Butte, MT

KTVM (NBC)
750 Dewey Blvd., Suite 1
Butte, MT 59701
406-494-7603

KXLF-TV (CBS)
1003 S. Montana
Butte, MT 59701
406-782-0444

191. Bowling Green, KY

WBKO (ABC)
2727 Russellville Rd.
Bowling Green, KY 42101
502-781-1313

192. Hagerstown, MD

WHAG-TV (NBC)
13 E. Washington St.
Hagerstown, MD 21740
301-797-4400

193. Lafayette, IN

WLFI-TV (CBS)
2605 Yeager Rd.
West Lafayette, IN 47906
317-463-1800

194. Anniston, AL

WJSU-TV (CBS)
1330 Noble St.
Anniston, AL 36202
205-237-8651

**195. Cheyenne, WY/
Scottsbluff, NE**

KGWN-TV (CBS, ABC)
2923 E. Lincolnway
Cheyenne, WY 82001
307-634-7755

KKTU (NBC)
4200 E. 2nd St.
Cheyenne, WY 82069
307-237-3711

KDUH-TV (ABC)
Box 1529
Scottsbluff, NE 69363
308-632-3071

KSTF (CBS, Fox)
3385 N. 10th Ave.
Gering, NE 69341
308-632-6107

196. Charlottesville, VA

WVIR-TV (NBC)
503 E. Market St.
Charlottesville, VA 22902
804-977-7082

197. Casper/Riverton, WY

KGWC-TV (CBS, Fox)
304 N. Center
Casper, WY 82601
307-234-1111

KTWO-TV (NBC)
4200 E. 2nd St.
Casper, WY 82602
307-237-3711

KFNE (ABC, CBS)
7075 Salt Creek Rd.
Casper, WY 82601
307-237-2020

KGWR-TV (CBS)
Box 170
Casper, WY 82602
307-234-1111

198. Lima, OH

WLIO (NBC)
1424 Rice Ave.
Lima, OH 48505
419-228-8835

199. Laredo, TX

KGNS-TV (NBC)
102 W. Del Mar Blvd.
Laredo, TX 78044
512-727-8888

200. Twin Falls, ID

KMVT (CBS)
1100 Blue Lakes Blvd., N.
Twin Falls, ID 83301
208-733-1100

**201. Ottumwa, IA/
Kirksville, MO**

KOIA-TV (Fox)
820 W. 2nd St.
Ottumwa, IA 52501
515-684-5415

KTVO (ABC)
Box 949
Kirksville, MO 63501
816-627-3333

202. Presque Isle, ME

WAGM-TV (CBS, ABC, NBC)
Box 1149
Presque Isle, ME 04769
207-764-4461

203. Zanesville, OH

WHIZ-TV (NBC)
629 Downard Rd.
Zanesville, OH 43701
614-452-5431

204. Mankato, MN

KEYC-TV (CBS)
1570 Lookout Dr.
N. Mankato, MN 56001
507-625-7905

205. Flagstaff, AZ

KNAZ-TV (NBC)
Box 3360
Flagstaff, AZ 86004
602-526-2232

206. Bend, OR

KTVZ (NBC)
62990 O.B. Riley Rd.
Bend, OR 97701
503-383-2121

207. Victoria, TX

KAVU-TV (ABC, NBC)
3808 N. Navarro
Victoria, TX 77903
512-575-2500

208. Helena, MT

KTVH (NBC)
2433 N. Montana Ave.
Helena, MT 59601
406-443-5050

209. North Platte, NE

KNOP-TV (NBC)
Box 749
North Platte, NE 69103
308-532-2222

KPNE-TV (PBS)
Box 83111
Lincoln, NE 68501
402-472-3611

210. Alpena, MI

WBKB-TV (CBS)
1390 Bagley St.
Alpena, MI 49707
517-356-3434

Stations in Areas
Not Covered by ADI Rankings

Alaska

KIMO (ABC)
2700 East Tudor Rd.
Anchorage, AK 99507
907-561-1313

KTUU-TV (NBC)
Box 102880
Anchorage, AK 99510
907-257-0202

KTVA (CBS)
1007 West 32nd Ave.
Anchorage, AK 99503
907-562-3456

KATN (ABC, NBC)
Box 74730
Fairbanks, AK 99707
907-452-2125

KTVF (CBS, NBC)
3528 International
Fairbanks, AK 99701
907-452-5121

KJUD (ABC, NBC)
1107 West 8th St.
Juneau, AK 99801
907-586-3145

KTNL (ABC, CBS, NBC)
520 Lake St.
Sitka, AK 99835
907-747-8488

American Somoa

KVZK-TV
Pago Pago, Somoa 96799
684-633-4191

Guam

KUAM-TV (CBS, NBC)
Box 368
Agana, Guam 96910
671-477-9861

Hawaii

KGMB (CBS)
1534 Kapiolani Blvd.
Honolulu, HI 96814
808-944-5200

KHON-TV (NBC)
1116 Auahi St.
Honolulu, HI 96814
808-531-8585

KITV (ABC)
1290 Ala Moana Blvd.
Honolulu, HI 96814
808-545-4444

Puerto Rico

WOLE-TV
Box 1200
Mayaguez, PR 00709
809-833-1200

WCCV-TV
Box A
Arecibo, PR 00613
809-879-0054

WLII (NBC)
Ave. Condado #657
Santurce, PR 00907
809-724-1111

WPRV-TV (Fox)
Box 31313
Rio Pedras, PR 00929
809-758-0013

WECN
Box 310
Bayamon, PR 00621
809-797-3447

WSTE
Box A, Old San Juan Sta.
San Juan, PR 00902
809-724-7575

WAPA-TV
State Road 19
San Juan, PR 00657
809-792-4444

WKAQ-TV
383 Roosevelt Ave.
Hato Rey, PR 00918
809-758-2222

U.S. Virgin Islands

WBNB-TV (CBS)
Box 1947
St. Thomas, VI 00801
809-744-0300

U.S. Networks & Their Bureaus

ABC-TV
47 West 66th St.
New York, NY 10023
212-456-1000

Bureaus: Atlanta, Boston, Denver, Los Angeles, Miami, Philadelphia, San Francisco, Washington D.C.

CBS-TV
524 West 57th St.
New York, NY 10019
212-975-4321

Bureaus: Los Angeles, Miami, Washington D.C.

CNN
1 CNN Center
Atlanta, GA 30348
404-827-1500

Bureaus: Chicago, Dallas, Detroit, Los Angeles, Miami, New York, San Francisco, Washington D.C.

NBC-TV
30 Rockefeller Plaza
New York, NY 10112
212-664-4444

Bureaus: Atlanta, Boston, Burbank, Chicago, Dallas, Denver, Washington D.C.

Canadian Stations with News Programs

Alberta

CFCN-TV (CTV)
Postal Station E
Calgary, AL T3C 3L9
403-246-7111

CKKX-TV
222 23rd St. N.E.
Calgary, AL T2E 7N2
403-235-7727

CBXT (CBC)
Box 555
Edmonton, AL T5J 2P4
403-468-7500

CITV-TV
5325 104th St.
Edmonton, AL T6H 5B8
403-436-1250

CISA-TV
1401 28th St. North
Lethbridge, AL T1J 4A4
403-327-1521

CITL-TV (CTV)
5026 50th St.
Lloydminster, AL T9V 1P3
403-875-3321

CHAT-TV (CBC)
Box 1270
Medicine Hat, AL T1A 7H5
403-529-1270

CKRD-TV (CBC)
2840 Bremner Ave.
Red Deer, AL T4R 1M9
403-346-2573

British Columbia

CJDC-TV (CBC)
901 102nd Ave.
Dawson Creek, BC V1G 2B6
604-782-3341

CFJC-TV (CBC)
460 Pemberton Terr.
Kamloops, BC V2C 1T5
604-372-3322

CHBC-TV (CBC)
342 Leon Ave.
Kelowna, BC V1Y 6J2
604-762-4535

CKPG-TV (CBC)
1220 6th Ave.
Prince George, BC V2L 3M8
604-564-8861

CFTK-TV (CBC)
4625 Lazelle Ave.
Terrace, BC V8G 1S4
604-635-6316

CBUT (CBC)
700 Hamilton St.
Vancouver, BC V6B 2R5
604-662-6000

CHAN-TV (CTV)
Box 4700
Vancouver, BC V6B 4A3
604-420-2288

CKVU-TV
180 West 2nd Ave.
Vancouver, BC V5Y 3T9
604-876-1334

Manitoba

CKX-TV (CBC)
2940 Victoria Ave.
Brandon, MN R7A 6A5
204-728-1150

CKY-TV
Polo Park
Winnipeg, MN R3G 0L7
204-775-0371

CHMI-TV
350 River Rd.
Winnipeg, MN R1N 3V3
204-775-8351

CKND-TV
603 St. Mary's Rd.
Winnipeg, MN R2M 4A5
204-233-3304

New Brunswick

CBAFT (CBC)
250 Archibald St.
Moncton, NB E1C 8N8
506-853-6725

CKCW-TV (CTV)
Box 5004
Moncton, NB E1C 8R6
506-857-2600

CHSJ-TV (CBC)
335 Union St.
St. John, NB E2L 3T4
506-632-2222

Newfoundland

CBYT (CBC)
Box 610
Corner Brook, NF A2H 6G1
709-634-3141

CFLA-TV (CBC)
Box 3015, Sta. B
Happy Valley, NF A1C 5S2
709-896-2911

CBNLT
Box 576
Labrador City, NF A2V 2L3
709-944-3616

CBNT
Box 12010, Sta. A
St. John's, NF A1B 3T8
709-737-4140

CJON-TV (CTV)
446 Logy Bay Rd.
St. John's, NF A1C 5S2
709-722-5015

Nova Scotia

CIHF-TV
14 Akerley Blvd.
Dartmouth, NS B3B 1J3
902-494-5200

CJCH-TV (CTV)
2885 Robie St.
Halifax, NS B3J 2Z4
902-453-4000

CBIT (CBC)
285 Alexandra St.
Sydney, NS B1P 6H7
902-539-5050

CJCB-TV (CTV)
Box 469
Sydney, NS B1P 6H5
902-562-5511

Ontario

CKVR-TV (CBC)
33 Beacon Rd.
Barrie, ON L4M 4T9
705-734-3300

CHCH-TV
163 Jackson St. W.
Hamilton, ON L8N 3A6
416-522-1101

CJBN-TV (CTV)
104 10th St.
Keewatin, ON P0X 1C0
807-547-2852

CFPL-TV
Box 2880
London, ON N6A 4H9
519-686-8810

CKNY-TV (CTV)
Box 3220
North Bay, ON P1B 8P8
705-476-3111

CBOT (CBC)
250 Lanark Ave.
Ottawa, ON K1Y 1E4
613-725-3511

CHEX-TV (CBC)
1925 Television Rd.
Peterborough, ON K9J 6Z9
705-742-0451

CICI-TV (CTV)
699 Frood Rd.
Sudbury, ON P3C 5A3
705-674-8301

CKPR-TV (CBC)
87 N. Hill St.
Thunder Bay, ON P7A 5V6
807-344-9685

CITO-TV (CTV)
681 Pine St. N.
Timmins, ON P4N 7G3
705-264-4211

CFMT-TV
545 Lakeshore Blvd. W.
Toronto, ON M5V 1A3
416-593-4747

CIII-TV (Global)
81 Barber Greene Rd.
Don Mills, ON M3C 2A2
416-446-5311

CITY-TV
299 Queen St. W.
Toronto, ON M5V 2Z5
416-591-5757

CKNX-TV
215 Carling Terrace
Wingham, ON N0G 2W0
519-357-1310

Quebec

CHAU-TV (TVA)
141 Rt. de LaMontagne
Carleton, QB G0C 1J0
418-364-3344

CFAP-TV (Quatre Saisons)
500 Bouvier St.
Quebec City, QB G1K 7X2
418-624-2222

CFKS-TV (Quatre Saisons)
3720 Boul. Industriel
Sherbrooke, QB J1L 1Z9
819-565-9999

Saskatchewan

CIPA-TV (CTV)
22 10th St. West
Prince Albert, SK S6V 3A5
306-922-6066

CBKT
2440 Broad St.
Regina, SK S4P 4A1
306-347-9540

CFRE-TV
370 Hoffer Dr.
Regina, SK S4N 7A4
306-721-2211

CKCK-TV (CTV)
Box 2000
Regina, SK S4P 3E5
306-569-2000

CFQC-TV (CTV)
216 1st Ave. North
Saskatoon, SK S7K 3W3
306-665-8600

CFSK-TV
218 Robin Crescent
Saskatoon, SK S7L 7C3
306-665-6969

CICC-TV (CTV)
95 E. Broadway
Yorkton, SK S3N 0L1
306-783-3685

About the Authors

Carl Filoreto, a photojournalist who has worked in local T.V. news since 1980, is currently at KMGH, the CBS-affiliate in Denver, where he has won five Emmy Awards and two NPPA national awards. He has covered Super Bowls, political conventions, various local disasters, and the 1992 Winter Olympics in Albertville, France. He also worked at WTNH in New Haven, CT and WGGB in Springfield, MA. He taught television production courses at Mt. Wachusett Community College in Gardner, MA.

Filoreto received a Master's Degree from the University of Massachusetts at Amherst and graduated *magna cum laude* from the S.I. Newhouse School of Public Communications at Syracuse University.

Lynn Setzer Filoreto, a reporter and anchor with KMGH in Denver, has worked in radio and televison since 1977. She has covered national political conventions, local politics, and a vast array of stories over the years and has won two Emmy awards for reporting. She graduated from Wilson College in Chambersburg, PA.

Lynn and Carl met while working at WTNH in New Haven. They moved to Denver together and were married 'neath the Aspen trees in 1987. Currently, they live in the foothills west of Denver with their two best friends—their golden retrievers, Gansett and Remington.

Att: Job Applicants!
Résumé Tape Critique

Vista Visions, a company created by the authors of this book, is now offering a professional appraisal of your cover letter, résumé, and résumé tape. We will review all aspects of your application package and tell you how to improve it. Our team of seasoned reporters and photographers will examine your tape and offer realistic, practical suggestions to make it better—and get you a job!

To order this service, send a copy of your résumé tape (either Beta or ¾" format), your résumé, your basic cover letter, and a check or money order for $50 to

Vista Visions
1069 Genesee Vista Rd.
Golden, CO 80401

Please allow four weeks for your critique to be prepared.

We'd also like to hear about your experiences in the job market. If something worked or flopped for you, please let us know so we can share it with future job hunters when we update this book. Plus, if you know of additional job sources and advice that we failed to include, please drop us a line at the above address. Thanks!

More Great Books
from Mustang Publishing

Speedy Greens Organic Restaurant

Megan,
Happy Cooking!
Cathleen M. Kelly

Recipes for Healthier Living

Cathleen Kelly RN, BSN, HN-BC

BALBOA
PRESS

A DIVISION OF HAY HOUSE

Balboa Press books may be ordered through booksellers or by contacting:

Balboa Press
A Division of Hay House
1663 Liberty Drive
Bloomington, IN 47403
www.balboapress.com
1-(877) 407-4847

Because of the dynamic nature of the Internet, any Web addresses or links contained in this book may have changed since publication and may no longer be valid. The views expressed in this work are solely those of the author and do not necessarily reflect the views of the publisher, and the publisher hereby disclaims any responsibility for them.

ISBN: 978-1-4525-3206-6 (sc)
ISBN: 978-1-4525-3207-3 (e)

The author of this book does not dispense medical advice or prescribe the use of any technique as a form of treatment for physical, emotional, or medical problems without the advice of a physician, either directly or indirectly. The intent of the author is only to offer information of a general nature to help you in your quest for emotional and spiritual well-being. In the event you use any of the information in this book for yourself, which is your constitutional right, the author and the publisher assume no responsibility for your actions.

Printed in the United States of America

Balboa Press rev. date: 4/18/2011

Dedication

For the Plants, Animals, and Our Earth

that Nourish and Heal Us

May We Honor Them

Table of Contents

Dedication. v

Introduction 1

Ingredient Key 11

Appetizers and Beverages. 13

Raw and Juices. 19

Salads and Side Dishes 29

Soups 45

Sandwiches and Wraps. 61

Entrées 69

Treats. 81

Desserts 91

Brunch Favorites 101

Glossary 109

Afterword 111

Appendix. 113

Recommended Resources. 117

Acknowledgements. 119

Notes. 121

Pay attention to your body. The point is everybody is different. You have to figure out what works for you.

— Andrew Weil

Introduction

My healing journey

When I am asked how and why I began Holistic Horizons, and subsequently, Speedy Greens Organic Restaurant, many thoughts run through my mind. My passion for wellness and the belief in the inherent healing powers of the body underlies the motivation from friends, personal experience, and professional apathy. As a nurse, I have been trained to "do it this way and for this reason". Beginning one's own practice, especially in the volatile field of complementary care, resembled nothing of this solid structure.

My first "toe-over-the-line" experience in 1990 was chiropractic. I had migratory arthritis with swollen, immobile joints difficult to walk on, and a perforated bowel from taking ibuprofen. I was next led, kicking and screaming, to homeopathy and to a life-saving aloe drink.

With a paltry understanding of energy medicine, I was intrigued by Reiki and received training in the Usui method. In 1997, when I was asked to leave the supervisory nursing position I had been in for six years, I was devastated. My right arm became frozen. I dragged myself to a healer who helped me realize how powerful "stuck" emotions can be and I slowly began to unearth my buried heart.

In a new part-time position, I was introduced to such modalities as intravenous chelation therapy, acupuncture, massage, colonic irrigation and food antibody testing. I discovered I had severe allergies to eggs and yeast, which contributed to my ulcerated bowel and asthma. When I left these foods out of my diet and addressed the underlying emotions, I became symptom free!

The American Holistic Nurses Association provided the missing professional link. I had been searching for a philosophy that considers our interconnectedness with the Universe; that body, mind, and spirit cannot be separated; *and* that we have control of our bodies.

The Restaurant

Speedy Greens Organic Restaurant was established in October 2007, consistent with the vision of its parent company, Holistic Horizons. The time had come to include food as part of healing in the motto "Nurture Yourself and Our Earth". Since 1998, clients were becoming healthier and began requesting healthier food. Three major tenets provided the foundation: Green Salad (no white iceberg), Green Containers (no Styrofoam), and Green Operation (Environmental Stewardship). Speedy Greens Organic Restaurant is represented by Dexter Rabbit holding a rather large carrot in his mouth while riding a bicycle and delivering organic vegetables in a cart.

The first request was from a client to "cook healthy food" for her. Soon after, it became a quest to create familiar food in healthier ways while maintaining great taste and quality. As a "healing artist", I found myself enthralled with the colors, aromas, and presentation of food. My "pièce de résistance" is the expression of joy, relief, and calm on a customer's face when united with a dish they know can be consumed without worry or "side effects".

This book

The "diet" most readily available to us is primarily white and devoid of minerals. Many find it difficult to incorporate green into their diet. Although I may reiterate what other authors of healthy cooking have stated prior, I present a practical approach to introducing, and keeping, more green in your diet. You may have heard cautions about combining foods like fruit and carbohydrate, or that certain blood types digest certain foods more easily. Not everyone fits the same mold. There are many tools available to help guide our food choices.

Do what feels right for you. This is not a book about becoming vegetarian, vegan, lactose-free or gluten-free. It's about learning the combination of food that helps you feel your best while providing optimum nutrition. It is a compilation of what I have read, combining techniques and recommendations from multiple authors and sources, including my experience in preparing and serving food at Speedy Greens Organic Restaurant.

Since I have witnessed the major culprits (wheat and gluten, meat and poultry, cow's milk products, eggs, salt, and sugar) repeatedly demonstrate stresses upon the body, you will find this a collection of recipes that use little or none of these ingredients. I am proud to say that making these changes has not only maintained excellent taste, vibrancy, texture, and satiety, but even improved it.

The recipes are divided into the traditional categories as served at Speedy Greens Organic Restaurant, although I believe food can be eaten in any order according to what feels appropriate to your body, e.g. one morning I might choose celery with peanut butter, another morning Sloppy Lentil. Certainly doubling the amount of a "Side Dish" to make it an "Entrée" is not a culinary crime, either.

By popular demand, a key has been included, to quickly identify which recipes are raw, vegan, vegetarian, lactose-free, gluten-free, soy-free, or sugar-free. The glossary provides their definitions.

About Being (Inner) Green

The Plant Connection

Chlorophyll is the basic building block for growth and efficient cell synthesis. It's green. So must food be green in order to provide this life-sustaining wonder.

Chlorophyll is so similar to human blood that chlorophyll has the ability to release magnesium from its center and absorb iron. More iron in the blood means more ability to deliver oxygen to the cells. Chlorophyll also releases carbon dioxide, which helps protect our cells from damage and prevent disease.

Fit for Humans

Dark green leafy vegetables are not only a great source of chlorophyll, they are the most concentrated source of nutrition of any food. Greens contain minerals (iron, calcium, potassium, and magnesium) and vitamins K, C, E, and many of the B vitamins. They are low in carbohydrate, high in fiber, with little impact on blood glucose. The phytonutrients in greens protect our cells from damage and our eyes from age-related problems. The Vitamin K regulates blood clotting, helps protect bones from osteoporosis, decreases inflammation and may help prevent diabetes.

Eat with Feeling

- Where were you when you ate last? Standing at the counter, running the "to do" list through your head, or sitting at the table, present in the moment, smelling, tasting, and giving thanks for your food?

- Where does your food come from? Conscious eaters can turn into conscious consumers, and vice versa.

- Think about it. What were you thinking last time you ate? Thoughts are things and exert a profound effect on body chemistry. Honor the body by offering positive, encouraging thoughts. Consider "This food nourishes and protects me," instead of "I shouldn't be eating this."

- Eat in moderate amounts. Any food in excess accumulates its effects on the body and creates more work for the body.

Learn the "Body Language"

How do you figure out what resonates with your body? Some cues that certain foods are "disagreeing" may include gastric upset, wheezing, phlegm in the throat, cough, intestinal issues including ulcers, joint pain and swelling, skin rash, mouth blisters, and fatigue after eating. Food is fuel for the body and energy is the outcome, not fatigue. Check your eyes for brightness, color, and vibrancy, your skin for color and elasticity, and your elimination for regularity. It is a normal function of the bladder to empty four or five times a day and the bowels to evacuate at least twice daily.

Chug, Chug, Chug!

Water is a human body's main "ingredient" (70%). Fresh fruits and vegetables are excellent sources of water. Consuming enough water to maintain bodily functions and not cause the "radiator to run dry" seems to be a great challenge. Well, consider this. The brain comprises 2% of our body weight yet demands 20% of our circulation. That leaves only 80% of the circulation to supply the remaining 98% of the body. Without adequate water, the body must ration distribution to the organs. One of the first signs of dehydration is impaired cognition (brain, remember) and although our bodies adapt, the long-term effects of lack of water surface as problems in lung, kidney, liver, and bowel function.

Not all drinks are created equal. Water as a main "ingredient" is not as healthful as pure water. Some beverages, like tea, coffee, and soda, actually drain water from the body. Our goal is to replenish half our body weight in ounces of water daily, e.g., a person who weighs 100 pounds needs 50 ounces, or 1.5 quarts of water per day. We need even more when perspiring, taking diuretics, or ingesting caffeine and alcohol.

pH Problem

Caffeine, coffee, alcohol, and soda not only dehydrate the body, they also cause more acidity in the bloodstream. pH is measured on a scale from 0 (acid) to 14 (base), with 7 being neutral. The pH level of our bloodstream determines how our bodies' chemical reactions occur. Acid pH encourages "hot and fast" reactions, while alkaline pH promotes reactions that are "slow and cool".

Coffee and soda average a pH of 3 and rarely have a pH above 5. Caffeine and alcohol pH ranges from 5-7, making them acidic on average. When consuming large amounts of acidic foods, we are not only running "hot and fast" but we also provide a breeding ground for unhealthy conditions like candida (yeast), fungus, bacterial infections, cancer, arthritis, chronic fatigue, obesity, or allergies.

Alkaline environments, with a pH between 7 and 8, promote health by neutralizing harmful acids, and regenerating unhealthy cells. The body responds with increased mental clarity, reduced allergies, clearer skin, and more energy. "Eating green" (vegetables, sprouts, grasses, greens, and seeds) provides a healthy, alkaline environment in the body.

So many choices! Eating Whole and "Clean"

Isn't All Food "Whole"?

Whole foods are considered to be any food that exists in its natural form or as close to it as possible. The more you process food, the less nutrition remains. Whole foods contain essential vitamins and minerals that are needed to insure a healthy immune system and a greater quality of life.

Anything that grows from the earth on a plant or tree (grains, nuts, seeds, beans, fresh fruits and vegetables) is considered "whole". Something created from "ingredients" is considered processed and not a whole food (bread, crackers, cereal, cakes, cookies, soup mixes, chips, pasta, frozen meals, prepackaged meals, breakfast bars or toaster pastries, white flour, white rice, sodas, margarine, mayonnaise, etc.). Basically, if you are reading a "label" it's not a whole food. When was the last time you saw an ingredient label on a head of broccoli?

- Fresh fruits and vegetables are best. Your next best choice is frozen. Canned is your third choice. The freezing and canning process usually involves the addition of salts, sugars, or preservatives, and the nutritional value of the fruit or vegetable is decreased.

- Juices are always best fresh-squeezed or "juiced". Bottled juices are a second choice when they are organic and 100%, "**not** from concentrate".

- Look for whole grains. Otherwise, important parts of the grain have been removed. Whole grain foods naturally contain essential antioxidants, minerals, and fiber.

- Protein is found in legumes (beans), nuts, seeds, and grains. When choosing meat, poultry, or fish as a protein source, consider local (as close as possible), organically fed, free-range, or wild-caught versus farm-raised.

- Be aware of the term "healthy". When you cannot avoid the "no labels rule", check for additives or preservatives (they can act as toxins in the body), as well as added fat, sugar, or sodium.

- Be package-free, or at least "package-picky". Eating clean includes being conscious of packaging food comes in. Plastic and styrofoam leach harmful substances into food, especially when heated. Vegetables and fruit like to breathe, so a mesh, cloth, or paper bag is fine.

- Find some reusable grocery bags or boxes, and "say no" to the plastic. For those who still can't resist, be mindful of the number of bags you use and recycle them when you are finished with them.

- Pots and pans are another source of potential harm for our food. When scratched, "non-stick" materials (Perfluorooctanoic acid or PFOA),can get into food and cause harm in the body and in the environment. Stainless steel, cast iron, and some ceramic cookware are healthier options.

Eating "Clean"

Organic farming promotes practices that encourage ecological harmony and environmental responsibility. Food raised with organic methods is not only "cleaner", it tastes better, and is better for your body and family because it has less pesticides, chemicals, hormones, antibiotics, and health hazards, and actually MORE vitamins, minerals and health benefits!

Making the Transition

"Empowering myself to Empower the world!"

Start small

1. Do a diet review. Write down everything you eat for one week.
2. Decide one thing you want to change (e.g. stop drinking soda)
3. Change it for one week
4. Reward yourself with...make a list of rewards
5. Continue the change for a second week
6. Another reward!
7. Appreciate!!! Listen to what you tell your body. Be aware of guilt feelings.
8. Record any differences in how you feel since making the change
9. Continue the change for a third and fourth week
10. Once you've incorporated the first change, begin on another
11. Have some whole-food snacks on hand for when you're in a hurry or traveling: organic granola, raw bars, nuts, fresh or dried fruit.

About Being (Outer) Green

Green Operation

Consistent with Green Restaurant Association Standards for Certification, Speedy Greens Organic Restaurant adheres to environmentally sound practices that are not only great for us and the environment, but also contribute to the charm and comfort of the unique dining experience our customers love.

Containers for take-out are biodegradable and compostable, made from coated paper or corn. Take-out napkins are recycled paper, flatware is biodegradable corn, and bags are reusable and recyclable brown paper. Paper and corn are annually-renewable resources and when composted, they turn back into dirt in 45-60 days.

In the dining room, reusable tableware, glassware, napkins, and flatware are used. In the kitchen, minimal grease is produced, food scraps are composted for gardening, paper towels are made from recycled paper, and all paper, glass, plastic, and metal is recycled at a local recycling facility, making trash minimal (one 10-pound bag/week).

Fluorescent bulbs operate in all lighting fixtures, green wind power is the utility of choice, and non-toxic, biodegradable, no-phosphate dishwashing and cleaning products are used.

Supplies are purchased in bulk from a national warehouse to minimize number of deliveries and use of oil-based transportation. Produce, eggs, and cheeses are purchased locally. The owner drives a hybrid vehicle, reducing emissions and decreasing dependence on oil-based transportation.

Environmental Justice

Remember the Environment. It's green, too. It can stay green if we use less disposable items and more reusable, recyclable, or compostable containers. Plastic wrap, bags, containers, cups, and utensils harm the environment and our food. Aluminum foil and containers do more harm than help and don't degrade. Household cleaners, health and beauty products, paper products, and "air fresheners" contain perfumes, dyes, and chemicals detrimental to our bodies and the environment. Use of excess paper (printer, towels, napkins, tissues, diapers, plates) wastes trees. Consider a vegetable-scrap compost pile in your yard to reduce landfill.

Ingredient Key

DF	**Dairy-Free**
GF	**Gluten-Free**
LF	**Lactose-Free**
R	**Raw Food**
SF	**Sugar-Free**
SYF	**Soy-Free**
VG	**Vegetarian**
VGN	**Vegan**

Appetizers and Beverages

Spicy Sunflower Seeds

GF, DF, LF, R, SYF, SF, VG, VGN

2 tsp fresh squeezed lime juice
1 tsp chili powder
1 tsp ground cumin
½ tsp cayenne pepper
2 cups raw organic sunflower seeds

Mix lime juice and spices in medium size bowl. Add seeds and stir to coat evenly. Spread on dehydrator tray in single layer. Dry at 140° for 8 hours (raw version), OR spread on cookie sheet in single layer and toast in 400° oven for 6 minutes, stirring halfway through.

Hot Cocoa

GF, DF, LF, SYF, VG, VGN

¼ cup cocoa powder
¼ cup sugar
1 tsp arrowroot powder
4 cups rice, almond or other nut milk

In medium saucepan, combine sugar, cocoa, arrowroot and ½ cup milk. Cook and stir over medium heat until steaming. Stir in remaining milk. Heat through but do not boil.

Makes four servings.

ChickPea Pita Bread

GF, DF, LF, SYF, SF, VG, VGN

2 ¼ cups garbanzo bean flour
1 tsp salt
2 tsp baking soda
2 tsp lemon juice
2 tsp olive oil

In mixing bowl, combine dry ingredients. Stir in lemon juice and oil until mixture forms a ball. Cover bowl with a clean towel and allow it to rest for 30 minutes. Transfer dough to a floured surface and divide it into 6 pieces. Form the pieces into balls, then flatten with hands or a rolling pin into rounds or ovals about ¼ inch thick. Place on ungreased baking sheets in a preheated 450° oven. Bake until the bread is puffed up, 5- 6 minutes. The pita will be barely browned. Cool 5 minutes.

Makes 6.

Yeast-Free!

Fresh Garbanzo Hummus
GF, DF, LF, SYF, SF, VG, VGN

1 ½ pounds dried garbanzos beans
¼ cup water
Juice of 2 lemons
2 garlic cloves
Dash cayenne
1 tsp ground cumin
¼ cup extra-virgin olive oil
Salt to taste
Additional olive oil and pita bread, to serve.

Place garbanzos in large bowl, cover with water and soak overnight. Once soaked, drain and place in saucepan . Cover with fresh water and cook for 2 hours, until tender but not mushy.

Cool for 5 minutes. Place the garbanzos in a food processor with ¼ cup water, lemon juice, garlic, cayenne, cumin, and olive oil. Blend until smooth.

To serve, accompany with pita.

Makes about 3 cups.

Raw and Juices

Kale Salad

GF, DF, LF, R, SYF, SF, VG, VGN

It's amazing how tender the kale is once "massaged"!

1 large bunch kale, washed well, stemmed, and cut in 3-inch pieces
Drizzle of olive oil
1 avocado
Juice of 1 lemon
Salt to taste
½ cup diced tomato
½ cup diced apple
¼ cup raisins
¼ cup raw sunflower seeds

Place prepared kale in large bowl. Drizzle olive oil over kale and massage oil into greens, using hands. Scoop avocado from shell. Massage into kale, leaving some larger pieces of avocado remaining. Sprinkle with lemon juice and salt. Add tomato, apple, raisins, and sunflower seeds.

Makes 2 servings.

Easy Mock Turkey
GF, DF, LF, R, SYF, SF, VG, VGN

1 bunch celery
1 green onion
Parsley to taste
1 cup almonds
1 avocado
Sage to taste

In food processor, purée celery, onion, and parsley. Drain, reserving juice. Grind almonds in nut grinder or coffee grinder until fine. In medium bowl, mash avocado with fork. Combine celery mixture and ground nuts with avocado. Mix well. Form into four patties. Serve each patty on a leaf of lettuce with Cranberry Relish.

Cranberry Relish
GF, DF, LF, R, SYF, SF, VG, VGN

1 cup fresh cranberries
1 date
1 orange, juiced

Process all ingredients in food processor. Serve immediately.

Summer Squash with Cashew-Basil Dressing

GF, DF, LF, R, SYF, SF, VG, VGN

2 medium yellow summer squash
1 cup raw cashews
1 tsp fresh garlic, minced
¼- ½ cup water
1 TBS fresh basil leaves, minced
½ tsp ground cumin
Salt to taste
¼ cup dice tomato

Cut squash into "noodles" on spiral slicer, or grate them. Place in medium mixing bowl. In food processor, grind cashews until fine. Add garlic and water until mixture is thick and creamy. Adjust water to reach desired consistency. Add basil, cumin, and salt to taste. Mix in tomatoes.

Makes 2 servings.

Cashew Bars

GF, DF, LF, R, SYF, SF, VG, VGN

2 cups cashews, processed into fine crumbs
5 dates, soaked 20 minutes
4 apricots, soaked
3 TBS date water
1 TBS agave nectar
1 tsp vanilla

Add dates and apricots to cashew crumbs in processor. Run one minute or until well chopped and combined. Add liquids and process until ball forms. Spread onto drying sheet, score with knife. Dehydrate at 150° for 3 hours. Transfer to mesh and dry at 140° 6-8 hours or overnight.

Makes 8 bars 2"x4".

Tanja's Cocoa Balls
GF, DF, LF, R, SYF, SF, VG, VGN

1 cup walnuts, finely processed
4 dates, soaked 20 minutes
¼ cup cocoa powder
Chopped walnuts for rolling (optional)

Cut dates into small pieces and add to walnuts in food processor with cocoa powder. Blend until mixture forms a ball. With hands, form mixture into 1-inch balls, roll in chopped nuts if desired. Place on serving plate. Refrigerate until ready to serve.

Makes 1 dozen.

Gingered Carrot and Beet Salad

GF, DF, LF, R, SYF, SF, VG, VGN

2 medium carrots
1 medium beet
1 tsp ginger, minced

Shred carrot and beet, place in mixing bowl. Add ginger. Stir to combine.

Makes 2 servings.

Apple Slaw
GF, DF, LF, R, SYF, SF, VG, VGN

1 large tart apple, grated
1 medium carrot, grated
¼ tsp garam marsala
½ cup walnuts, chopped
¼ cup raisins

Mix all ingredients together and enjoy immediately!

Carrot Juice

GF, DF, LF, R, SYF, SF, VG, VGN

5 or 6 medium carrots, washed and stemmed
½ apple

Juice carrots and apple in juicer or high-powered blender. Pour and enjoy! Best served immediately.

Salads and Side Dishes

Speedy Greens Signature Salad

GF, DF, LF, R, SYF, SF, VG, VGN

Get the most for "your chew"- use the greenest leafys you can find!

1 head green leaf lettuce
4 ounces mescaline mix OR field greens
½ cup shredded carrot
2 TBS diced celery
4 grape or cherry tomatoes, halved

Cut lettuce into 3-inch segments, discarding stem end. Wash thoroughly and spin in salad spinner to remove excess water. Place lettuce in serving bowl. Add greens, toss with lettuce. Distribute shredded carrot over top, add celery and tomato. Add other vegetables and dressing as desired.

Makes two servings.

Lentil Salad

GF, DF, LF,SYF, SF, VG, VGN

2 cups water
1 cup lentils, sorted and rinsed
1 TBS olive oil
¼ cup minced celery
¼ cup minced carrot
Dressing:
2 TBS apple cider vinegar
1 TBS lemon juice
1 tsp chives (1 TBS chopped fresh)
1 tsp parsley (1 TBS chopped fresh)
3 green onions, minced
Salt and pepper to taste

In medium saucepan, bring water to boil. Add lentils, cover and reduce heat to simmer 15 minutes. Heat oil in skillet, sauté celery and carrot until soft. In small bowl, combine dressing ingredients. Add sautéed vegetables to lentils. Stir in dressing. Serve warm.

Makes 4 servings.

Sautéed Greens

GF, DF, LF, SYF, SF, VG, VGN

1 bunch greens (chard, kale and/or spinach), washed thoroughly
¼ cup chopped onions
2 tablespoons sunflower seeds
1 tablespoon olive oil

Heat oil over medium heat. Sauté seeds and onions for 1 to 2 minutes. Add greens, cover. Cook 2 to 3 minutes. Lift lid and stir. When the greens are wilted to your liking, take them off the heat and serve.

Makes two servings.

Rice Quinoa Pilaf

GF, DF, LF, SYF, SF, VG, VGN

1 TBS olive oil
¼ cup celery, diced
¼ cup carrot, diced
2 TBS onion, diced
¼ cup shelled edamame
½ cup cooked brown rice
½ cup cooked quinoa

Heat oil in skillet. Sauté vegetables 5 minutes, until fork tender. Add rice and quinoa with one TBS water if needed. Cook until heated through. Add your favorite spice or hot pepper sauce.

Makes two servings.

Curried Rice and Lentils

GF, DF, LF, SYF, SF, VG, VGN

1 TBS olive oil
½ cup onion, diced
1 tsp fresh garlic, minced
1 TBS curry powder
¼ tsp pepper
½ tsp salt
5 cups water
1 cup brown rice (uncooked)
½ cup lentils, rinsed (uncooked)

Heat oil in medium saucepan. Sauté onion and garlic for 5 minutes. Add spices, stirring to coat onion and garlic. Add water, bring to boil. Add rice and lentils. Reduce heat to low and cook, covered 2 hours or until water is absorbed.

Makes 4 servings.

Baked Squash

GF, DF, LF, SYF, SF, VG, VGN

1 winter squash (butternut, buttercup, acorn, or delicata) washed, cut in half, and seeded
3 cups water
Pinch of cinnamon

Place prepared squash face-down in 9x13 baking pan. Fill pan with water to 1-inch from bottom. Bake in 350° oven for 30-45 minutes, until fork pierces through skin easily. Remove from oven, drain off water and turn squash over in pan. Allow to cool 10 minutes. Scoop squash into bowl, sprinkle with cinnamon, and serve.

Makes 2 servings.

Quinoa Salad
GF, DF, LF, SYF, SF, VG, VGN

2 cups water
1 cup quinoa, rinsed and agitated
¼ cup carrot, diced
¼ cup celery, diced
10 ounces Italian-style salad dressing (soy and lactose-free)

In small saucepan, bring water to boiling. Add quinoa, cover and turn heat to low. Cook 20 minutes. Remove from heat and allow to cool 20 minutes. Add veggies and salad dressing. Chill in refrigerator one hour.

Makes four servings.

Sweet Potato-Carrot Tsimmes

GF, DF, LF, SYF, VG, VGN

"To mix up" or "To cause trouble"

2 large sweet potatoes
8 carrots, peeled
Juice and zest of one lemon
½ tsp salt
¼ tsp pepper
¼ cup maple syrup
¼ tsp nutmeg

Cut sweet potatoes and carrots into 3-inch chunks. Put in steamer, cook until soft, about 20 minutes. Remove from steamer and peel potatoes. Mash or process potatoes and carrots until smooth. Add remaining ingredients. Mix well. Pour into greased casserole. Bake 20 minutes in 350° oven.

Makes 2 servings.

Potato Pancakes

GF, DF, LF, SYF, SF, VG, VGN

That's what we called them. No doubt a German version of "latke" from my Webert heritage.

4 medium potatoes, peeled and shredded
1 onion, shredded
1 carrot, shredded
1 TBS arrowroot powder OR gluten-free flour
Olive oil

Preheat cast iron skillet with 2 TBS oil on medium-high heat. Combine shredded potato, carrot, and onion in medium mixing bowl. Stir in arrowroot. Scoop mixture by ¼ cup (metal) measure or ice cream scoop onto skillet. Flatten with scoop to ¼-inch thickness. Brown one minute, then flip to brown other side one minute. Add oil to pan as needed for remaining "pancakes". Serve immediately. Top with your favorite butter alternative, sprinkle with salt. Accompany with maple syrup or applesauce.

Makes 10.

Roasted Red Potatoes

GF, DF, LF, SYF, SF, VG, VGN

8 red potatoes, washed and cut into quarters
Drizzle of olive oil
½ tsp oregano
½ tsp basil
½ tsp thyme

Place potatoes in 9x13 baking pan. Drizzle oil over potatoes, stirring to coat. Sprinkle spices over potatoes and stir until evenly coated. Bake in 350° oven for 40 minutes, stirring every 10 minutes, until potatoes are fork-tender and edges are crispy.

Stuffed Acorn Squash

GF, DF, LF, SYF, SF, VG, VGN

1 acorn squash, washed, halved, and seeded
Rice Stuffing (as below)

Place prepared squash in baking pan, face down with 1" of water in bottom of pan. Bake in 350° oven until fork pierces skin easily, 30 minutes. Remove from oven, flip squash over and transfer to serving plate. Fill with Rice Stuffing.

Makes 2 servings.

Rice "Stuffing"

GF, DF, LF, SYF, SF, VG, VGN

2 cups cooked brown rice
1 TBS sunflower oil
½ cup diced onion
½ cup diced celery
1 tsp sage
½ tsp thyme
½ cup diced apple
¼ cup chopped walnuts

While rice is cooking, heat oil in small skillet, and sauté onion and celery until tender. Add spices, stirring to coat vegetables. Remove from heat. Combine cooked vegetables, rice, apples, and walnuts. Serve as a side or use as "stuffing".

Makes 4 servings.

Steamed Vegetable Medley

GF, DF, LF, SYF, SF, VG, VGN

Deliciously edible without any condiment at all!

2 carrots, peeled, and sliced ¼" thick on diagonal
½ small head broccoli, washed and cut with 2" stems
1 small summer squash, washed and cut into ½ " slices

Place prepared vegetables in steamer basket or in saucepan with ½ inch of water covering bottom of pan. Cover and bring to boil. Steam until fork-tender and bright-colored, 7 minutes.

Makes 2 servings.

Stuffed Tomatoes

GF, DF, LF, SYF, SF, VG, VGN

Red, ripe tomatoes surround a long-grain brown rice, onion, garlic, and walnut medley

2 large, ripe tomatoes
1 TBS olive oil
1 tsp minced garlic
½ cup diced onion
1 cup cooked brown rice
¼ cup chopped walnuts

Wash and core tomatoes, place in baking pan. Heat oil in small skillet and sauté garlic and onion until soft. Remove from heat. Add rice and walnuts to onion mixture, stir to combine. Stuff into tomato cavities. Bake in 350° oven for 15 minutes.

Makes 2 servings.

Asparagus with Sun-dried Tomato Dressing
GF, DF, LF,SYF, SF, VG, VGN

¼ cup dry-packed sun-dried tomatoes, soaked in hot water 30 minutes
1 tsp minced garlic
1 shallot, peeled and chopped
2 TBS apple cider vinegar
2 tsp fresh-squeezed lemon juice
1 TBS fresh basil, finely chopped
¼ cup olive oil
1 bunch asparagus, washed and trimmed

Cut sun-dried tomatoes into thin strips. In food processor, combine garlic, shallot, and tomatoes. Process until minced. Add vinegar, lemon juice, and basil. Process until combined. With motor running, slowly add olive oil in steady stream.

Steam asparagus in vegetable steamer or in saucepan with ½" water covering bottom of pan. Bring to boil. Steam until asparagus is just fork-tender. Top with Sun-Dried Tomato Dressing.

Makes 4 servings.

Soups

Veggie Lentil Soup

GF, DF, LF, SF, VG, VGN

1 TBS olive oil
½ cup diced onion
¼ cup diced celery
½ cup diced carrot
1 clove garlic, minced
1 ¼ cup lentils, rinsed and sorted
6 cups water
1 TBS Braggs Liquid Aminos
Salt and pepper to taste

Heat oil in large saucepan over medium heat. Add onion, celery, carrot, and garlic. Cook unto softened, 10 minutes. Add water, lentils, and Braggs. Bring to boil, turn heat to low, cover and cook until lentils are soft, 4 hours. Add salt and pepper to taste.

Makes 4 servings.

Smashin' Split Pea Soup

GF, DF, LF, SF, VG, VGN

2 TBS olive oil
½ cup diced carrots
½ cup diced celery
¼ cup diced onion
1 tsp basil
½ tsp black pepper
1 tsp cumin
1 tsp salt
2 cups split peas
1 TBS lemon juice
7 cups *boiling* water
1 TBS Braggs Liquid Aminos

Heat oil in large saucepan. Sauté carrots, celery, and onions 5 minutes. Add spices, stirring to coat vegetables. Add boling water, split peas, and lemon juice. Bring to boil. Reduce heat to low, add Braggs, and simmer two hours, until peas are consistently smooth. Soup will be thick, especially after sitting overnight.

Makes 4 servings.

Roasted Squash and Apple Soup

Inspired by Dr. Andrew Weil
GF, DF, LF, SYF, SF, VG, VGN

1 large butternut squash (2 pounds) peeled, cut into 2-inch pieces
2 medium onions, peeled and quartered
2 cloves garlic, peeled
2 tart, firm apples, peeled and quartered
2 TBS olive oil
2 tsp coarse salt
2 tsp chili powder
4 cups water

Preheat oven to 400°. In large roasting pan, combine squash, onions, garlic, apples, and oil. Toss to coat. Season with salt and chili powder, stirring to distribute spices evenly. Roast for 45-60 minutes, stirring every 10 minutes, until squash is tender. In food processor, combine half the vegetables and half the water. Purée until smooth , then remove to clean saucepan. Repeat with remaining vegetables and water. Heat over medium-low, stirring occasionally, until heated through.

Makes 4 servings.

Potato Broccoli Soup

GF, DF, LF, SYF, SF, VG, VGN

1 TBS olive oil
½ cup diced onion
1 tsp minced garlic
1 cup chopped broccoli
½ tsp Thyme
½ tsp salt
5 medium potatoes, washed, peeled, and cubed
5 cups water
1 cup rice milk

Heat oil in large saucepan. Sauté onion and garlic 5 minutes. Add broccoli, thyme, and salt. Cook 5 minutes. Add water and potatoes. Bring to boil and cook until potatoes and broccoli are tender, 20 minutes. Purée in small batches using food processor, adding rice milk ⅓ cup at a time. Return to pan and heat on medium before serving.

Makes 4 servings.

Cream of Carrot Soup

GF, DF, LF, SYF, VG, VGN

1 TBS olive oil
¼ cup diced celery
¼ cup diced onion
½ tsp salt
⅛ tsp black pepper
4 cups carrots, chopped
3 cups water
1 cup rice milk
1 tsp honey or alternative (vegan) sweetener

Heat oil in medium saucepan. Add onion, and celery and sauté 5 minutes. Add salt and pepper, stirring to coat vegetables. Add carrots, sauté 5 minutes. Add water and bring to boil. Cook until carrots are tender, 10 minutes. Purée in small amounts in food processor until smooth, adding rice milk ⅓ cup at a time. Add sweetener. Return to pan and heat on medium before serving.

Makes 4 servings.

Winter Squash and Sweet Potato Soup
GF, DF, LF, SYF, SF, VG, VGN

1 TBS olive oil
¼ cup diced onion
¼ cup diced celery
1 tsp thyme
½ tsp sage
Salt and pepper to taste
4 cups water
2 medium sweet potatoes, peeled and cubed
1 small squash (butternut, acorn, or buttercup), peeled, seeded, and cubed

Heat oil in medium saucepan, add onion and celery. Cook until softened, 5 minutes. Stir in spices to coat vegetables. Add water, sweet potatoes, and squash. Bring to boil, cook until potatoes and squash are fork-tender, about 30 minutes. Purée small amounts at a time in food processor. Return to pan to heat over medium-low, stirring occasionally, until heated through.

Makes 4 servings.

Butternut Ginger Soup

GF, DF, LF, SYF, SF, VG, VGN

1 TBS olive oil
½ cup diced carrots
½ cup diced celery
¼ cup diced onion
1 TGBS grated ginger
⅛ tsp garam marsala
4 cups water
1 small butternut squash, peeled, seeded, and cubed

Heat oil in medium saucepan. Sauté carrots, celery, and onion until soft, 5 minutes. Add ginger and garam marsala, stirring to coat vegetables. Add water and squash. Bring to boil, cook until squash is fork-tender, 20 minutes. Purée small amounts at a time in food processor. Return to pan. Heat over medium-low, stirring occasionally, until heated through.

Makes 4 servings.

Vegetable Barley Soup

DF, LF, SYF, SF, VG, VGN

1 TBS olive oil
½ cup diced carrots
¼ cup diced celery
¼ cup diced onion
1 TBS parsley
½ tsp thyme
1 bay leaf
Dash nutmeg
½ cup uncooked barley
6 cups water
2" kombu seaweed **OR** ½ tsp salt

Sauté vegetables in oil 5 minutes. Add spices, stir to coat vegetables. Add water, barley, and kombu. Bring to boil. Reduce heat to low, cover, and cook 45 minutes, until barley is tender and broth is thickened.

Makes 4 servings.

Creamy Asparagus Soup
GF, DF, LF, SYF, SF, VG, VGN

2 bunches asparagus, trimmed, and cut into 1" pieces, separating tips
1 TBS olive oil
1 cup diced onion
1 TBS minced garlic
½ cup raw cashews
2 cups water

Steam asparagus tips in small amount of water in saucepan just until fork-tender, set aside. In small skillet, sauté onion and garlic in olive oil until tender. Add stem pieces of asparagus to onions in skillet with ½ cup water. Cover and steam until tender. Pulverize cashews in food processor with remaining 1½ cups water. Remove cashew milk to bowl and set aside. Blend cooked asparagus stems in processor until smooth, add cashew milk. Return to saucepan and heat, adding water as needed. Add asparagus tips. Season with salt and pepper to taste.

Makes 4 servings.

Red Pepper and Squash Soup

GF, DF, LF, SYF, SF, VG, VGN

1 red bell pepper
1 medium squash (delicata or butternut), halved and seeded
1 TBS olive oil
1 tsp minced garlic
¼ cup diced onion
½ tsp salt
Pinch black pepper
1 tsp paprika
2 cups rice milk

Roast squash and red pepper in a pan of water In 400° oven until soft, 20 minutes. Meanwhile, heat oil in skillet. Add garlic and onion, sauté 5 minutes. Add salt, black pepper, and paprika. Stir to coat vegetables.

Transfer red pepper from oven to covered bowl to loosen skin. Scoop squash into food processor, add one cup of milk and blend. Pour into saucepan. Peel red pepper and put in processor with remaining milk. Blend until smooth. Pour into saucepan with squash. Heat over medium until heated through before serving.

Makes 2 servings.

Autumn Harvest Stew

GF, DF, LF, SYF, SF, VG, VGN

2 cups sweet potato, peeled and cubed
2 medium parsnips, peeled and cut into ½" pieces
2 small apples, cored and cut into ¼" slices
¼ cup diced onion
¾ tsp thyme
½ tsp rosemary
½ tsp salt
¼ tsp black pepper
2 cups water

In slow cooker, place potato, parsnip, apple, and onion in layers. Sprinkle with spices. Pour water over all. Cook on low 6 hours.

Makes 2 servings.

Roasted Carrot Soup

GF, DF, LF, SYF, VG, VGN

3 cups carrots, peeled and quartered
2 cups parsnips, peeled and quartered
½ cup diced onion
3 inch piece fresh ginger, coarsely chopped
1 TBS olive oil
3 TBS brown sugar
8 cups water
Pinch cayenne pepper powder

Combine carrots, parsnips, and ginger in baking pan. Drizzle with oil and stir to coat. Sprinkle with sugar. Bake in 350° oven 30 minutes, stirring often, until vegetables are fork-tender. Transfer to large saucepan, add water. Bring to boiling, reduce heat to medium and cook 10 minutes. Purée small amounts at a time in food processor. Return to saucepan to heat before serving. Season with cayenne.

Makes 6 servings.

Carrot and Parsnip Bisque

GF, DF, LF, SYF, SF, VG, VGN

1 TBS olive oil
½ cup diced onion
2 cups chopped carrots
1 cup chopped parsnips
1 cup cubed potato
1 tsp garlic, minced
5 cups water
Salt and pepper to taste

Heat oil in large skillet. Add onion, carrot, parsnip, potato, and garlic. Cover and cook 10 minutes, until soft. Add water, bring to boil. Reduce heat to low and simmer 20 minutes. In small batches, blend in food processor until smooth. Return to saucepan, season with salt and pepper, heat and serve.

Makes 4 servings.

Spaghetti Squash Soup
GF, DF, LF, SYF, SF, VG, VGN

2 TBS olive oil
1 cup cubed potato
1 cup diced carrot
½ cup diced onion
½ cup diced celery
2 tsp cumin
1 tsp thyme
2 cups cooked spaghetti squash
8 cups water

In large saucepan, sauté vegetables in oil until tender. Add spices, stir. Add water and squash. Bring to boil, reduce heat to simmer 30 minutes. Season with salt and pepper.

Makes 6 servings.

Vegetable Tortilla Soup
GF, DF, LF, SYF, SF, VG, VGN

6 (6-inch) corn tortillas, preferably a little old and dried out
1 TBS olive oil
½ cup chopped onion
½ cup each diced green pepper, and red pepper
1 TBS minced garlic, (2 cloves)
1 medium hot pepper or jalapeño chile, seeded, veins removed, chopped
4 cups tomato juice
1 cup diced tomatoes
1 TBS fresh lime juice

Place tortillas on a baking sheet and put them in the oven at 200° for 10-15 minutes to dry them. Cut tortillas in half; cut halves into ¼-inch strips. Set aside. Heat oil in saucepan over medium-high heat. Add onion and cook 2 minutes. Add garlic and peppers; cook 2 to 3 minutes, stirring frequently, until vegetables are crisp-tender. Stir in tomato juice and tomatoes. Heat to boiling. Reduce heat; add lime juice, cover and simmer 15 minutes. To serve, divide half of tortilla strips among 4 individual serving bowls; ladle in soup. Garnish with remaining tortilla strips.

Serves 4.

Sandwiches and Wraps

The Tunaburger story...

My brothers and I grew up eating this creation served on hamburger rolls and wrapped individually in aluminum foil for baking. My favorite thing was to peel the cheese from the foil and eat it. Oh, how I have changed! My mother, M. Elaine Webert-Kelly credits the invention to her sister, Gail Webert-Feathers.

Famous Kelly Tunaburger

GF (Rice Tortilla only), SYF, SF

2 cans tuna, no salt added, dolphin safe
4 oz extra-sharp cheddar cheese, cubed
½ cup diced celery
½ cup green olives, halved (optional but very yum!)
¾ cup Vegenaise (or other favorite mayonnaise)
6 tortillas

Drain and mash tuna in medium bowl. Add cheese, celery, and olives. Place scoop of mixture (½ cup) in center of each tortilla. Fold sides of tortilla over to make a "square", turn over so edges of tortilla are face down. Place in baking pan and cover with lid or cookie sheet. Bake in 350° oven for 15 minutes.

How *do* you use a rice tortilla?

*Steam tortilla on metal baking rack over boiling
water for 30 seconds on each side
OR cover in dampened paper towel
and microwave 20 seconds.
Use immediately.*

Tuna Salad Wrap

GF (Rice Tortilla only), DF, LF, SF

8-inch tortilla (multigrain or rice)
1 can dolphin-safe, tongol tuna, drained
½ cup diced celery
¾ cup Vegenaise

In small mixing bowl, flake tuna with fork. Add celery and Vegenaise. Mix well. Serve on warmed tortilla with fresh lettuce or greens.

Makes one serving.

Veggie Delite Wrap

GF (Rice Tortilla only), DF, LF, SF, VG, VGN

One tomato, thinly sliced
One cucumber, thinly sliced lengthwise
Lettuce leaf or handful of field mix
½ cup shredded carrot
Yellow (summer squash), thinly sliced lengthwise
Any other vegetable you like
Vegenaise or dressing of your choice
8-10" Tortilla of choice, warmed

Prepare vegetable slices. Warm tortilla on iron skillet for 2 minutes on each side. Spread Vegenaise on tortilla. Layer veggies in center of tortilla, fold edges of tortilla into center, and enjoy!

Note: May require a napkin.

Tortilla Pizza

GF (Rice Tortilla only), SYF, VG

8-inch tortilla (multigrain, rice, tomato-basil)
Marinara sauce
Veggies of choice, chopped (broccoli, shredded carrot, onion, spinach, green pepper, olives…go wild!)
Shredded mozzarella cheese OR vegan cheese substitute (optional)

Place tortilla of choice on baking sheet in 400° oven for 2 minutes. Flip tortilla over and bake 2 more minutes. Remove from oven. Spread sauce on tortilla. Sprinkle with cheese. Top with veggies. Return to oven for 5 minutes, until cheese is melted.

Serves one.

Let food be your medicine

Let medicine be your food

—Hippocrates

Entrées

Sloppy Lentil
GF, DF, LF, VG, VGN

"No Joe and just as hearty."

1 TBS olive oil
½ cup onion, diced
¼ cup green bell pepper, diced
1 TBS chili powder
3 cups water
2 TBS Braggs Liquid Aminos
1 ½ cup lentils, sorted and rinsed
1 TBS dry mustard powder
1 TBS brown sugar
Salt and pepper to taste
2 medium tomatoes, diced

Heat oil in medium saucepan, add onion and green pepper. Cook 5 minutes. Add chili powder, stir to coat. Add water, lentils, and Braggs. Bring to boiling. Combine brown sugar, mustard, salt and pepper. Stir into lentils with tomatoes. Cook on medium heat 4 hours, or until lentils are tender. Serve over steamed brown rice.

Makes 4 servings.

Spaghetti Squash Primavera

GF, DF, LF, SYF, SF, VG, VGN

"In the style of Spring" any vegetables you have on hand can be used.

1 spaghetti squash (about 3 lbs)
3 TBS olive oil
½ cup diced onion
1 TBS garlic, minced
1 cup diced carrots
3 medium tomatoes, cubed
½ teaspoon oregano and/or basil
10 ounces baby spinach, chopped
Salt and pepper
Grated Parmesan cheese, optional

Cut spaghetti squash in half, scoop out seeds. Place face down in baking pan. Add water to one inch level. Bake in 375° oven 30-45 minutes. Remove squash and turn over in pan. Let cool for 5 minutes. Using a fork, pull out the strands of "spaghetti."

While squash is baking, heat oil in skillet. Add onion and garlic. Sauté one minute. Add carrots and cook until fork-tender, about 5 minutes. Add tomatoes and oregano or basil, cook 10 minutes. Add spinach, cover and cook until spinach is just wilted. Remove from heat and stir. Season with salt and pepper. Serve over prepared spaghetti squash.

Serves 6.

Greens and Feta "Quiche"

GF, SYF, SF, VG

Filling:
½ bunch greens (chard, kale, and/or spinach), washed thoroughly and steamed
4 oz Vegenaise
4 oz plain, lowfat yogurt
¼ tsp fresh grated nutmeg
Dash hot pepper sauce
1 egg
1 TBS grated Romano cheese
1 TBS arrowroot powder

Crust:
¾ cup garbanzo flour
¾ cup rice flour
⅓ cup sunflower oil
3 TBS water

2 oz crumbled feta cheese
¼ cup diced onion

Combine first eight ingredients in food processor until smooth. In medium mixing bowl, stir together flours. Add oil and mix until evenly moistened. Add water, stir until mixture forms a ball. Press into 9 inch pie plate. Distribute feta and onions evenly over bottom of crust. Pour in filling-it will be full! Bake in 375° oven for 35 minutes.

Makes 6 servings.

Vegetable Pad Thai
GF, DF, LF, VG, VGN

Sauce:
¼ cup Braggs Liquid Aminos soy sauce
¼ cup fresh-squeezed lime juice
¼ cup water
¼ cup sugar
2 TBS peanut butter
1 green chile, minced

Main:
¼ package rice noodles, size small, approx 4 ounces
2 TBS sunflower oil
1 TBS sesame oil (optional)
½ cup onion, diced
1 clove garlic, minced
1 tsp grated ginger
3 carrots, sliced on thin diagonal
½ cup bean sprouts (optional)
1 cup snow peas

Whisk together soy sauce, lime juice, water, sugar, peanut butter and chile. Set aside.

Heat two quarts water to boiling. Remove from heat and drop in rice noodles.

Heat oil in skillet. Sauté onion, garlic, and ginger 2 minutes over medium heat. Add carrots and snow peas. Cover and cook over medium-low heat until fork-tender, about 2 minutes. Drain noodles. Add bean sprouts, noodles and sauce mixture to pan with vegetables. Stir well. Cook over medium-high heat until sauce is thickened and bubbly, about 3 minutes. Serve immediately.

Makes two servings.

Veggie Pot Pie

GF, DF, LF, SYF, SF, VG, VGN

1 TBS olive oil
1 cup carrots, diced
½ cup onion, diced
½ cup broccoli or yellow squash, chopped (optional)
1 cup potato, cubed
1 cup peas
1 tsp salt
1 tsp cumin
Pepper to taste
½ tsp sage
½ tsp marjoram
6 cups water

Sauté onion, carrot, and broccoli or yellow squash, in oil in large saucepan until tender, about 7 minutes. Add peas and spices. Sauté 5 minutes more. Add 3 cups water. Bring to boil, reduce to simmer 15 minutes.

In small saucepan, place potatoes in 2 cups water. Bring to boil and cook until fork-tender. Remove from heat and purée in food processor with cooking water, adding additional 1 cup water in small amounts while processing. Add puréed potato to vegetables and broth. Stir well. Reheat as needed. Serve over hot biscuits (recipe follows).

Makes 6 servings.

Baking Powder Biscuits

DF, LF, SYF, SF, VG, VGN

2 cups flour (1 ½ whole wheat pastry flour, ½ cup rice flour)
1 TBS baking powder
½ tsp cream of tartar
½ cup vegan buttery stick (1 stick)
1 cup (rice) milk

Stir together dry ingredients. Cut in buttery stick until mixture resembles coarse crumbs. Make well in center, add milk. Stir just enough for dough to cling together. Do not over-mix! Drop by spoonful onto baking sheet in six equal amounts. Bake in 450° oven for 10-12 minutes. Tops will be slightly browned and sound "hollow" when tapped with knife.

Spinach Fandango

GF, SYF, SF, VG

1 bunch spinach, washed thoroughly, chopped, and steamed
3 cups cooked brown rice
¾ cup yogurt
¼ cup Vegenaise
½ cup (2 ounces) shredded jack cheese
1 tsp basil

In bowl, combine all ingredients. Mix well. Pour in to casserole or loaf pan. Bake in 350° oven 25 minutes.

Makes 4 servings.

Vegetable Stir-Fry

GF, DF, LF, SYF, SF, VG, VGN

2 TBS olive oil
½ cup carrot, diced
½ cup broccoli, chopped
¼ cup onion, diced
Add other vegetables of choice: snow peas, yellow squash, pepper
½ cup cooked brown rice

Sauce:
1 cup water
1 TBS arrowroot powder
¼ tsp salt
1 TBS apple cider vinegar
1 TBS honey OR (VGN) agave nectar

In small bowl, combine sauce ingredients, set aside. Heat oil in skillet, sauté veggies 5-7 minutes, or until fork tender and still bright-colored. Add rice and sauce to veggies, heat over medium heat, stirring constantly until sauce becomes thick and clear.

Makes one serving.

Turkey Loaf Burgers

GF, DF, LF, SYF, SF

1 pound (Plainville Farms) ground turkey breast
½ cup chopped onions
8 grape tomatoes, halved or quartered, depending on size OR ½ cup diced tomato
1 tsp oregano

In medium mixing bowl, combine all ingredients. With hands, shape into four equal patties and place in baking dish. Bake in 350° oven for 30 minutes. Remove from oven and brown on cast iron grill pan, if desired. Serve on bed of salad greens, a favorite tortilla, or bread with Vegenaise.

Makes 4 burgers.

Note: Patties freeze well after baking. For a quick meal, defrost then heat in oven or 15 minutes.

Vegetable Lasagna
GF, SYF, VG

15 ounces prepared marinara sauce
3 medium yellow summer squash or zucchini, sliced in ¼" thick lengths
1 bunch leafy greens (spinach, kale, or swiss chard), washed and steamed
16 ounces cooked butternut squash
1 egg (optional)
¼ cup grated romano or parmesan cheese
1 TBS parsley
8 ounces mozzarella, shredded
½ cup shredded carrot

In medium mixing bowl, combine egg, butternut squash, parsley, romano, and 4 ounces shredded mozzarella cheese. Set aside. In bottom of 9x13 baking pan, spread one cup of marinara sauce. Line pan with single layer of sliced squash. Distribute steamed greens over squash. Spread butternut mixture over greens, top with shredded carrots. Place single layer of yellow squash on top of carrots. Cover with remaining marinara sauce. Top with remaining shredded mozzarella. Bake in 325° oven 35-45 minutes.

Makes 8 servings.

Vegetable Brown Rice

GF, DF, LF, SYF, SF, VG, VGN

¾ cup water
1 cup cooked brown rice
¼ cup onion, diced
½ cup carrots, diced
¼ cup celery, diced
½ tsp fresh grated ginger
½ tsp garlic, minced
Salt and pepper to taste

Put water in medium stainless sauté pan. Add all ingredients. Bring to boil, reduce heat to simmer. Cook 12 minutes, stirring often until water is absorbed and veggies are fork-tender.

Makes one serving.

Treats

Carob Krispies
DF, LF, SYF, SF, VG, VGN

1 package carob chips
1/3 cup raisins or chopped apricots
2 tsp sunflower oil
1 tsp maple syrup
1 cup brown rice cereal crisps

In heavy-bottom pan or double-boiler, stir oil, maple syrup, and carob ships until chips are well coated. Cook on low until chips are melted, stirring constantly. Stir in cereal and raisins. Remove from heat and drop by small teaspoon or melon-baller onto parchment-lined cookie sheet. Refrigerate until firm.

Makes two dozen 1-inch pieces.

Pumpkin Chocolate Chip Cookies
DF, LF, SYF, SF, VG, VGN

1 cup raw cane sugar
1 stick (½ cup) vegan buttery stick, softened
1 cup cooked pumpkin (or butternut squash)
1 tsp vanilla
1 egg OR Flax Mixture: 1 TBS ground flax + 3 TBS water
      (see instruction with Vegan Carrot Muffins)
2 ½ cups whole wheat pastry flour
1 tsp baking soda
1 tsp baking powder
1 tsp ground cloves
1 tsp allspice
1 tsp cinnamon
1 cup dairy-free chocolate chips

Cream together buttery stick and sugar. Add egg or flax mixture, mix well. Add pumpkin, stirring until smooth. In separate bowl, combine flour, baking soda, baking powder, and spices. Stir into pumpkin mixture. Fold in chocolate chips. Drop by tablespoon onto parchment-lined cookie sheet. Bake in 375° oven for 10-12 minutes.

Makes 2 dozen.

Vegan Carrot Muffins

DF, LF, SYF, VG, VGN

Flax mixture: 1 TBS ground flax seed + 3 TBS water
⅓ cup sunflower oil
⅓ cup brown rice syrup
1 ½ cup grated carrot
¼ tsp salt
½ tsp cinnamon
¼ cup brown sugar
1 ½ cup whole wheat pastry flour
¾ tsp baking soda
1 tsp baking powder
¼ cup raisins
¼ cup chopped walnuts

Grind flax seeds in coffee grinder or blender. Transfer to small bowl and add water, set aside until "gelatinous". In medium mixing bowl, combine oil, rice syrup, carrot, salt, cinnamon, and flax mixture. Stir well. Add brown sugar, stirring to dissolve any sugar lumps. Add flour, baking powder, and baking soda. Stir only until moistened. Fold in raisins and walnuts. Distribute batter evenly by spoonful into 12 muffin papers in muffin pan. Bake in 350° oven for 25 minutes. Enjoy plain or with Orange Cream Cheese Frosting (below).

Orange Cream Cheese Frosting

GF, DF, LF, SF, VG, VGN

1 cup Tofutti cream cheese, softened
2 TBS agave nectar or maple syrup
½ tsp vanilla
1 TBS orange zest

Stir all ingredients together until smooth. Spread on cupcakes. Garnish with walnut.

Ayurvedic Apple Chutney
GF, DF, LF, SYF, VG, VGN

All six Ayurvedic tastes

1 sweet apple
1 tart apple
½ tsp sunflower oil
1 tsp brown sugar
1 pinch cinnamon
1 pinch turmeric
⅛ tsp cumin powder
1 pinch black pepper
Salt to taste

Peel, core, and cube apples. Place in medium saucepan. Add oil, stir to coat apples. In small bowl, combine spices. Add to apples and mix well. Cover and cook over medium heat, stirring occasionally, until apples are tender, about 10 minutes.

Make it Raw:
Mix as directed, just skip the cooking!

Blueberry Muffins

DF, LF, SYF, VG

1 stick (½ cup) vegan buttery stick
1 cup sugar
1 egg
2 cups while wheat pastry flour
2 tsp baking powder
½ tsp salt
½ cup rice milk
1 tsp vanilla
1 ½ cups blueberries

In large bowl, cream buttery stick and sugar until light and fluffy. Add egg, beat in thoroughly. In separate bowl, combine flour, baking powder, and salt. Add flour mixture alternately to creamed mixture with milk and vanilla. Stir well between each addition. In small bowl, crush ½ cup berries and stir into batter. Fold in remaining berries and spoon into parchment baking cups in muffin pan. Sprinkle tops with sugar. Bake in 375° oven 30 minutes, until toothpick comes out clean.

Makes 12.

Snickerdoodles

GF, DF, LF, SYF, SF, VG

1 vegan buttery stick (½ cup), softened
¾ cup raw cane sugar
1 egg
½ tsp vanilla
1 cup gluten-free baking mix
¾ cup buckwheat, rice, or garbanzo flour
¼ tsp baking soda
¼ tsp cream of tartar

Soften and whip buttery stick. Add sugar, egg, and vanilla. Stir together. In separate bowl, combine baking mix, flour, baking soda, and cream of tartar. Add half dry ingredients to wet ingredients. Combine thoroughly. Mix in remaining dry ingredients. Chill one hour. Shape into 1" balls. Roll in: 2 TBS sugar + 1 tsp cinnamon mixture. Place on baking sheet. Bake in 375° oven for 7 minutes.

Makes 3 dozen.

Ginger Snaps

DF, LF, SYF, VG, VGN

1 ½ vegan buttery sticks (¾ cup), softened
1 cup sugar
1 egg
¼ cup molasses
2 cups whole wheat pastry flour
2 tsp ground ginger
1 tsp cinnamon
2 tsp baking soda
½ tsp salt
½ cup sugar

Beat together sugar and buttery stick until smooth. Add egg and molasses, beat until combined. In small bowl, stir together flour, ginger, cinnamon, baking soda, and salt. Slowly add flour mixture to wet ingredients. Stir until dough is smooth. Roll into 1" balls. Lightly dip tops in remaining ½ cup sugar. Arrange on parchment-lined baking sheet, sugar-side up 2 inches apart. Bake in 350° oven until fragrant and cracks appear on top, 9 minutes. Place on wire racks to cool.

Makes 3 dozen.

Using Arrowroot Powder

Mix desired amount of arrowroot powder in small amount of cold water before heating or adding to hot liquid. This prevents lumps and premature thickening.

Desserts

Parsnip Cake
DF, LF, SYF, SF, VG, VGN

1 ¼ cups parsnips, cooked and mashed
½ cup sunflower oil
½ cup honey or (VGN) agave nectar
¾ cup rice milk
2 tsp vanilla
2 ¼ cups whole wheat pastry flour
1 TBS baking powder
½ tsp baking soda
¼ tsp nutmeg

Combine parsnips with oil, honey, milk, and vanilla. In separate bowl, combine dry ingredients. Stir wet ingredients into dry ingredients. Pour into oiled 8x8 pan. Bake in 350° oven for 30 minutes.

Fruit Cobbler

DF, LF, SYF, VG

¼ cup sugar
1 TBS arrowroot powder
3 cups fresh fruit, prepared

Topping:
¾ cup whole wheat pastry flour
¼ cup gluten-free baking mix
¼ cup sugar
½ tsp cinnamon
1 egg, beaten
4 TBS rice milk
¼ cup chopped walnuts (optional)

Combine sugar and arrowroot in small saucepan. Add sliced or chopped fruit, stirring to coat. Bring to boil, stirring constantly one minute. Pour into 8x8 baking pan. In medium mixing bowl, combine flours, sugar, and cinnamon. In glass measure, whisk together milk and egg. Add to flour mixture. Stir until ball forms. Stir in nuts. Drop six spoonfuls onto hot fruit mixture. Bake in 400° oven for 20 minutes.

Makes 6 servings.

Make it Gluten-Free:
Substitute wheat flour with ¾ cup buckwheat or garbanzo flour.

Summer Blueberry Pie
GF (Rice Crust only), DF, LF, SYF, SF, VG, VGN

4 cups blueberries, washed and stemmed
¼ cup sugar
¼ tsp cinnamon
2 TBS arrowroot powder

Crust:
1 package of graham crackers
4 TBS vegan buttery stick, melted
1 TBS agave

For crust, grind graham crackers in food processor until fine, place in medium bowl. Stir in melted buttery stick and agave. Press mixture evenly into 9 inch pie plate. Bake in 350° oven for 6 minutes to set crust. Cool 15 minutes. In medium saucepan, combine 2 cups blueberries with sugar, cinnamon, and arrowroot. Cook over medium heat, stirring constantly until mixture thickens and becomes shiny. Remove from heat. Cool 15 minutes. Gently fold in remaining 2 cups blueberries. Spread into crust and refrigerate one hour before serving.

Makes 6 servings.

Gluten-Free Crust:

3 cups rice crisp cereal
4 TBS vegan buttery stick, melted
2 TBS agave nectar

In food processor, grind cereal until fine consistency. Remove to mixing bowl and add melted buttery stick and agave. Stir well. Press into 9 inch pie plate. Bake in 350° oven for 6 minutes.

Pear (or Peach) Crumble

GF, DF, LF, SYF, VG, VGN

6 pears or peaches, washed, peeled, cored, and quartered
1 TBS vanilla
1 TBS brown sugar
1 TBS arrowroot powder
½ tsp cinnamon
¼ tsp nutmeg
Topping:
½ stick (¼ cup) vegan buttery stick, at room temperature
½ cup brown sugar
¾ cup corn meal or gluten-free baking mix
½ cup chopped walnuts

Preheat oven to 350°. Place prepared fruit in large mixing bowl. Sprinkle vanilla over fruit, toss. In small bowl, combine brown sugar, arrowroot, cinnamon, and nutmeg. Sprinkle over fruit and toss to coat. Line fruit in 8x8 baking dish.

For topping, cut buttery stick into sugar and flour until coarse crumbs form. Add chopped nuts. Distribute mixture evenly over fruit. Bake in 350° oven until topping is slightly browned and crunchy and fruit is tender, 40 minutes.

Apple Crisp

GF, DF, LF, SYF, VG, VGN

6 cups apples, peeled, cored, and sliced
2 TBS sugar
½ tsp cinnamon
Topping:
1 cup gluten-free oats (Bob's Red Mill)
1 cup brown sugar
½ cup corn meal OR garbanzo flour
1 vegan buttery stick (½ cup)

Place prepared fruit in baking dish. Stir in sugar and cinnamon.

Topping: In mixing bowl, combine oats, sugar, and flour. Cut in buttery stick until mixture resembles coarse crumbs. Sprinkle over fruit. Bake in 350° oven on lower rack 35 minutes, until fruit is tender, topping is browned and "bubbling".

Strawberry-Rhubarb Crisp

GF, DF, LF, SYF, VG, VGN

1 quart strawberries, washed, stemmed, and quartered
4 stalks rhubarb, washed, and cut in ½ -inch pieces
3 TBS arrowroot powder
2 TBS orange juice
2 TBS balsamic or apple cider vinegar

Combine all ingredients in 8x8 baking dish. Top with crumb topping (see Apple Crisp). Bake in 350 oven for 35 minutes.

Vegan Chocolate Cake

DF, LF, SYF, VG, VGN

Stephanie's Favorite-with a little modification

2 ounces baby spinach
¼ cup water
1 cup sunflower oil
1 cup cold water
2 tsp vanilla
⅓ cup brown rice syrup

3 cups whole wheat pastry flour
⅓ cup cocoa
1 tsp baking soda
1 tsp baking powder
1 tsp salt
1 cup sugar
3 TBS apple cider vinegar

Oil and cocoa bottom of 9x13 pan. In small saucepan, steam spinach in water for 2 minutes, place in food processor. Add oil, water, vanilla, and rice syrup to processor , puree until smooth. In medium mixing bowl, combine flour, cocoa, baking soda, baking powder, salt, and sugar. Pour liquid mixture into dry ingredients and stir until smooth. Add vinegar and stir *briefly*. Baking soda will react with vinegar, making pale swirls in batter. Immediately pour batter into prepared pan. Bake in 375° oven for 30 minutes. Frost with Chocolate Peanut Butter Frosting or a dollop of Vegan Whip.

Chocolate Peanut Butter Frosting

GF, DF, LF, SYF, VG, VGN

½ cup cocoa powder
½ cup organic peanut butter
⅓ cup water
2 tsp vanilla
2 cups organic powdered sugar

Stir together cocoa, peanut butter, vanilla, and water until smooth. Add sugar, mixing until well blended. Adjust water to desired consistency. Spread on cake.

"Thou shouldst eat to live;
not live to eat."

— Socrates

Brunch Favorites

Spinach and Feta Frittata
GF, DF, SYF, SF, VG

2 TBS olive oil
¼ cup onion, diced OR four scallions, chopped
5 ounces spinach, washed and chopped
¾ tsp dried tarragon OR 1 TBS fresh tarragon, chopped
4 eggs
1 ½ ounces goat feta cheese, crumbled

Sauté onions in oil one minute. Add spinach and (dried) tarragon. Cook 3 minutes. Remove from pan. In small bowl, beat eggs and stir into spinach mixture (add fresh tarragon here). Heat broiler. Oil a 6" iron skillet. Heat skillet on medium for 1 minute. Pour in egg mixture. Sprinkle feta over top. Cook over medium heat on stove until bottom is golden brown and top is set, about 6 minutes. Broil in oven additional 3 minutes until center is completely set.

Makes two servings.

Breakfast Quinoa

GF, DF, LF, SYF, SF, VG, VGN

1 cup water
½ cup quinoa, rinsed and agitated
Maple syrup or agave
Nuts (optional)

Bring water to boil in small saucepan. Measure quinoa into fine mesh strainer. Shake vigorously in strainer while rinsing under cold water. Carefully pour quinoa into boiling water, cover and turn heat to low. Cook 20 minutes. Remove from heat, fluff with fork. Serve with sweetener and nuts, as desired.

Makes 2 servings.

Michael's Fiery Pear Compote

GF, DF, LF, SYF, VG, VGN

2 TBS oil
6 medium pears, peeled, halved, cut into ⅓″ slices
⅓ cup raisins or currants
¼ cup sugar
2 TBS vegan buttery stick
1 tsp vanilla
1 cup white cooking wine
⅓ cup brandy

Heat oil in heavy skillet. Add pears, sauté until tender and golden, about 15 minutes. Add raisins, sugar, buttery stick, and vanilla. Toss to coat. Add wine and cook until wine is mostly evaporated. Add brandy. Ignite brandy and allow flames to subside, shaking pan often. Serve hot over waffles or pancakes.

Makes 4 servings.

Gluten-Free Waffle or Pancake
GF, DF, LF, SYF, SF, VG, VGN

Using the Flax Mixture and Banana makes this a yummy, hearty version that's Vegan and Sugar-Free!

1 cup Gluten-Free All Purpose Baking Mix
1 egg OR Flax Mixture: 1 TBS ground flax + 3 TBS water
½ cup water
2 tsp sunflower oil
2 tsp agave OR ½ cup mashed banana
Vegan buttery spread (optional)
Maple syrup (optional)

Whisk wet ingredients together. Fold in dry ingredients. Mixture will be thick.

For Pancakes: Spoon onto hot greased griddle, cook about 2 minutes and flip when surface of pancake bubbles. Cook additional 2 minutes, until bottoms are lightly browned.

For Waffles: Spoon onto hot waffle iron, close lid and bake until steam subsides, 4 minutes.

Makes three (4-inch) pancakes or one waffle. Serve hot with maple syrup or Pear Compote.

Veggie Omelet
GF, DF, LF, SYF, SF, VG

2 large eggs, beaten with 1 TBS water
1 TBS each of favorite chopped vegetables: onion, green pepper, tomato, mushroom
½ cup baby spinach
1½ TBS sunflower oil

In small sauté pan, cook vegetables and spinach in 2 tsp sunflower oil. In separate non-stick (PFOA-free) omelet pan, heat 1 TBS sunflower oil. Add egg mixture. Cook over medium heat until edges are firm, tilting pan to cook all the egg. When surface of egg is no longer glossy, add sautéed veggies to one half. Carefully fold empty half of egg with spatula to cover vegetable half. Cook 3 minutes. Flip directly over on to serving plate.

Makes one serving.

Oatmeal

GF, DF, LF, SYF, SF, VG, VGN

1 cup water
½ cup gluten-free oats (Bob's Red Mill)

In small saucepan, combine water and oats and bring to a boil. Reduce heat to simmer and cook 7 minutes, stirring occasionally. Oats will be soft and creamy. Stir in fresh fruit, raisins, or nuts as desired.

Makes one serving.

Vegetarianism preserves life, health, peace, the ecology, creates a more equitable distribution of resources, helps to feed the hungry, encourages nonviolence for the animal and human members of the planet, and is a powerful aid for the spiritual transformation of the body, emotions, mind, and spirit.

—Gabriel Cousens, Conscious Eating

Glossary

Dairy-Free   No ingredients derived from cow's milk.

Gluten-Free   No wheat or gluten ingredients.

Lactose-Free   No lactose, casein, whey, cow's milk, or other animal milk ingredients.

Raw Food   No animal flesh. No cooked or processed ingredients. May be dehydrated or warmed to 150°.

Soy-Free   No soybeans or derivatives.

Sugar-Free   No refined sugar, cane sugar, or sweetener

Vegan   No animal ingredients, including animal byproducts like honey or eggs. Encompasses Dairy-Free, Lactose-Free, and Vegetarian

Vegetarian   No animal flesh. May include dairy, eggs, or honey.

Afterword

Speak Out for Healthier Food

In my twenty-eight years of experience as a professional registered nurse, I have silently watched people's health deteriorate at an accelerating rate. I have decided to speak out.

With ailments like diabetes, heart disease, obesity, celiac, and insurance premiums at an all-time high, it astounds me the number of patrons that continue to support "food" conglomerates on a daily basis. We do have a conscious choice here, folks! The temptation is high. Every corner has one, sometimes two, sugar-packed, grease-laden, caffeinated, carbohydrate-ridden, addiction-enhancer luring you in. You know their names. Are they acting in the best interest of consumer health? I don't think so. *Their* conscious choice is to push products known to be addictive and health-deteriorating just to make (a million) bucks.

Now here's a concept. Let's have these corporations pay insurance premiums for their customers. At the very least, have them offer community health education about the long-term effects of ingesting large amounts of carbohydrates, sugar, caffeine, preservatives, growth hormones, antibiotics, and pesticides inherent in most of the products served.

The one in charge of your health -and your children's health- is *you*. As Pollan states in his book "Food Rules", it's time to "vote with your fork." I propose responsible action includes voting with your fingers, spoon, and stir-stick as well.

The "local buzz" is that our community doesn't support healthier eating because of beliefs that it tastes bad (different), portions are small (not super-sized), and it's expensive (not 99¢). What price are you already paying for the convenience of disease-promoting products? The going rate for heart bypass surgery can be $100,000.00 when all is said and done.

Consumers drive product availability. It's time to demand health-promoting choices. Organic food ingredients are a start. More fruit, vegetables, whole grains, and beans are another. Less pastry, salt, sugar, and use/abuse of animals is a plus. The survival of healthier food restaurants is not dependent upon fanatical beliefs in veganism, vegetarianism, "raw-ism", or animal rights. It is about being passionate for healthier choices that encourage the body's innate ability to repair and heal itself, and that foster contentment with our bodies, ourselves, and our world.

For a society that boasts being a world "super-power", it is truly sad that we are one of the unhealthiest nations. We have the resources, the tools, and the conscious voice to say "no". Yet there are many who choose surgery and/or pharmaceuticals to repair the damages. Knock yourself out. Your insurance company, your tax-paying neighbor, or maybe even a corporation lawsuit will "cover it".

Green Chef Cathleen Kelly RN, BSN

Appendix

Herbal teas have been used for centuries for their medicinal properties. Speedy Green's favorites are listed here with a short description of each.

Serendipi~Teas
Great Tasting Teas that happen to have Healing Properties

Alfalfa
Contains all vitamins and minerals. Diuretic, lowers cholesterol, anti-inflammatory, detoxifies.

Blessed Thistle
Strengthens brain, lung, kidney, liver. Increases lactation, helps indigestion.

China Green
Antioxidant, lowers cholesterol, inhibits growth of cancer cells, antibacterial.

Cramp Bark
Female regulator. Prevents hemorrhages; diuretic. For cramps and spasms of all kinds.

Earl Grey
Black tea with bergamot flavor acts as antidepressant, antioxidant, reduces fever.

Eucalyptus
Decongestant, antiseptic. For nasal congestion, allergies, sinusitis, minor cuts, insect bites.

Gunpowder Green
Antioxidant, antibiotic, stimulant, increases energy. For asthma, high cholesterol.

Lady's Mantle

Anti-inflammatory, astringent, tranquilizer. For menstrual irregularity, wound healing, insomnia.

Lavender

Sedative, antispasmodic, digestive aid. For insomnia, nervousness, fatigue, yeast infection.

Lemongrass

Diuretic, antibacterial, detoxifier, antihypertensive. For jet lag, fatigue, insomnia, depression, acne.

Marshmallow Root

Relieves inflammation of mucus membranes. For wound healing, stomach ailments, cough, laryngitis, psoriasis.

Nettles

Source of vitamins and iron, calcium, and minerals. Astringent, expectorant, tonic, anti-inflammatory, diuretic.

Rooibos

Rich in antioxidants, minerals, vitamin C. Antiviral, antianxiety, antispasmodic. For allergies, insomnia, restless legs.

Uva-Ursi

Mild diuretic, anesthetic. For bladder and kidney infection, kidney stones, fluid retention, swelling.

White Willow Bark

Reduces inflammation. For fever, colds, headaches, minor aches and pains, toothache, arthritis.

Yerba Mate

Caffeinated, substitute for coffee. Improves digestion, regulates appetite. Detoxifies blood, antioxidant, diuretic.

Recommended Resources

Books

Batmananghelidi, F. (1992). *Your Body's Many Cries for Water.* Vienna, VA: Global Health Solutions, Inc.

Cousens, G. (2000). *Conscious Eating.* Berkeley, CA: North Atlantic Books.

D'Adamo, P. (1996). *Eat Right 4 Your Type.* New York: G.P. Putnam's Sons.

Pollan, M. (2009). *Food Rules.* New York: Penguin Books.

Pollan, M. (2009). *In Defense of Food: An Eater's Manifesto.* New York: Penguin Books.

Virtue, D. (2001). *Eating in the Light: Making the Switch to Vegetarianism on Your Spiritual Path.* Carlsbad, CA: Hay House.

Warren, C., Smith, L., & Ann, J. (1983). *Kripalu Kitchen: A Natural Foods Cookbook & Nutritiional Guide.* Kripalu Publications.

Weil, A. (2009). *Why Our Health Matters: A Vision of Medicine that Can Transform Our Future.* New York: Penguin Group.

Websites

http://www.bastis.org/greens.htm

http://lowcarbdiets.about.com/od/lowcarbsuperfoods/a/greensnutrition.htm

http://www.organicnutrition.co.uk/whyorganic/whyorganic.htm

http://www.liversupport.com/wordpress/2009/12/how-much-water-does-your-liver-need/

http://biomedx.com/microscopes/rrintro/rr1.html

http://www.balance-ph-diet.com/ph_scale.html

http://dinegreen.com/restaurants/standards.asp

http://www.grinningplanet.com/2004/11-09/chemicals-plastic-storage-containers-article.htm

Acknowledgements

To:

Jennifer and Jim Tom, the clients who started it all!

Dave Kelly for creating Dexter Rabbit and an amazing logo.

My mother, M. Elaine Webert-Kelly for her family recipes.

Stephanie Jones, the first amazing chef's apprentice.

Every challenging customer who helped stretch the boundaries and foster new creations!

My daughter, Jacquelyn Zehl, the "professionally-trained chef", for being my sounding board.

My daughter, Stephanie Zehl Venezia, for her encouragement and inspiration.

My beloved, Michael, for being there in *sooooo* many ways.

Thank you!

Notes

CPSIA information can be obtained at www.ICGtesting.com
262101BV00005B/1/P